AN INTERPRETATION OF EDMUND SPENSER'S *COLIN CLOUT*

by Sam Meyer

AN INTERPRETATION OF EDMUND SPENSER'S *COLIN CLOUT*

by

SAM MEYER

UNIVERSITY OF NOTRE DAME PRESS

First American Edition 1969
University of Notre Dame Press
Notre Dame, Indiana 46556

First Published 1969
Cork University Press
Cork, Ireland

Library of Congress Catalog Card Number: 79-78043

Printed in Ireland

TO SARAH

Curam ergo verborum, rerum volo esse sollicitudinem.
—Quintilian, *The Institutio Oratoria*

ACKNOWLEDGMENT

I wish to acknowledge with gratitude the part played in the writing of this study of Edmund Spenser's pastoral allegory, *Colin Clout,* by the trustees, former and present directors, and the staff of the Newberry Library of Chicago. The grant of a one-year Fellowship provided needed financial assistance. At all times the resources and facilities of this great institution were made freely available to me. To Rev. Edward Surtz, S.J., who read the manuscript in an earlier form and who offered sagacious advice for its improvement, I give my deep thanks. For Chapter II, the Editor of *Publications of the Modern Language Association of America* has kindly granted me permission to reprint, with minor changes, my article on the rhetorical figures which originally appeared in the issue of June, 1964. The dedication expresses inadequately my appreciation to my wife for her understanding and sustained encouragement during the period which I devoted to preparing this reading of Spenser.

SAM MEYER

Chicago, Illinois

CONTENTS

CHAPTER I

INTRODUCTION

The purpose of this study is to supply an interpretative reading of Edmund Spenser's pastoral allegory, "Colin Clouts Come Home Againe", bearing a Dedication under date of 27 December 1591 to his friend Sir Walter Raleigh[1] and published at London by William Ponsonby in 1595.

Fortunately, no special problem of bibliographical import arises to complicate unduly the task of interpretation. Although the interval of four years between dedication and publication suggests prior circulation in manuscript, the first certain appearance of the poem occurs in a volume named from it—a thin quarto of forty sheets, containing the Dedication (applicable to "Colin Clout" alone), the title pastoral, and seven elegies by various authors—including two by Spenser himself—on the death of Sir Philip Sidney (d. 17 Oct. 1586).[2] No organic connection exists, however,

1. My choice in spelling the name of this colorful and versatile Elizabethan as "Raleigh" is somewhat arbitrary. Contemporary documents spell the name in a variety of ways, as did the owner of the name himself. For example, the *Calendar of State Papers for Ireland, 1588-92,* has the name spelled as follows: Rawley, Raleigh, Ralegh, and Raleighe. Documents included in the *Calendar of the Carew Manuscripts, 1589-1600,* contain spellings of the name in these ways: Raleigh, Ralighe, Ralegh, Raleghe, Rawlie, Rawleighe, Rawley. According to Philip Edwards, *Sir Walter Raleigh,* Men and Books Series (London, 1953), p. vii, the knight himself used "Rauley" or "Rawleyghe" up to 1584, and after that, "Ralegh" only. The main justification for using the form "Raleigh" in this study is that the name is so spelled in all of Spenser's references to his fellow-poet and neighboring planter which occur in editions of Spenser's writings published during the author's lifetime. The name is spelled in this manner in the Dedicatory Letter, prefixed to *Colin Clout* and addressed to "Sir Walter Raleigh, Captaine of her Maiesties Guard", etc. The spelling is "Raleigh" in the two references contained in the 1590 edition of *The Faerie Queene*: the "Letter of the Authors" explaining the intention of the work; and the Dedicatory Sonnet addressed to the "sommers Nightingale". For additional information on the name, see appendix, "Raleigh's Name", to Willard M Wallace, *Sir Walter Raleigh* (Princeton, 1959).

2. For a complete bibliographic description of the volume, see Francis R. Johnson, *A Critical Bibliography of the Works of Edmund Spenser Printed Before 1700* (Baltimore, 1933), pp. 30-1.

between the title poem and the seven memorial pieces on Sidney bound with it. For reasons of his own the publisher never troubled to enter the *Colin Clout* volume in the Stationers' register, but no hint of impropriety is to be associated with this circumstance inasmuch as a large proportion—thirty or forty per cent, according to one reliable estimate—of all books published at London in the Elizabethan and Jacobean periods are absent from entry in the Clerk's Book at Stationers' Hall.

Likewise in common with so many contemporary books, *Colin Clout* underwent revisions while going through the press. As a consequence, the opening poem, which is our principal concern, exists in both a revised and an unrevised state. With one known exception the changes are confined to the four pages in the outer forme of sheet C. A comparison of the texts of the revised and unrevised sheets of the 1595 Quarto reveals that the thirty-four alterations of the late state are relatively minor, serving chiefly to emend the text and to improve punctuation. The text in the *Variorum Spenser,* the standard modern edition which I employ,[3] contains a number of departures from the revised Quarto, but these are too insignificant to have any material bearing on interpretation of the poem.[4]

The full-dress interpretation which I proffer in the succeeding pages has long been needed because no previous books, aside from editions, exist which concern themselves exclusively with *Colin Clout.* Brief studies may be found in articles and parts of books, but these offer only a limited view of the poem as a whole. Such cardinal literary aspects, moreover, as diction, imagery, tone and feeling, have hitherto received no consideration in the scholarship. Other central literary phases such as figures of rhetoric, versification in relation to diction, use of personal material, and unity are

3. *The Works of Edmund Spenser: A Variorum Edition,* eds. Edwin Greenlaw *et al.,* 10 vols. in 11 (Baltimore, 1932-57). Citation of this work will be in accordance with the system of reference established in the *Index* (p. 1), which covers the eight volumes of poetry only. References to the poetry and the editorial material thus disposed will be to *Works,* followed by the volume number. In this system, *Minor Poems,* Vol. I, becomes *Works* VII; *Minor Poems,* Vol. II, becomes *Works* VIII. The biography of Spenser by Alexander C. Judson will be cited as Judson, *Life.*

4. For a detailed study of the genesis and transmission of the text of the pastoral, together with some mention of the circumstances surrounding its publication, see my "*Colin Clout:* The Poem and the Book", *PBSA,* LVI (fourth quarter, 1962), 397-413.

the subject of only incidental mention in connection with the discussion of similar matters in other poems of Spenser. One possible exception to this last remark is the sensitive summary of the conceptual structure of *Colin Clout* which occurs in William Nelson's work centering on the intellectual content of Spenser's poetry. *Colin Clout* was not, however, selected as one of the shorter poems to receive special attention in this book. I do not mean to imply, however, that prior studies which touch upon separate aspects of *Colin Clout* or upon individual problems raised in the poem have not been helpful in varying degrees. Some of these studies furnish factual data; some, suggestions for expansion or further inquiry; and some, points of view with which I wish to register partial or total disagreement.

There exists in print, in addition to scattered pieces, a portion of one work which does, in a sense, constitute a prior general treatment of *Colin Clout*.[5] I am alluding to the Commentary in *Minor Poems,* Volume I (1943), the seventh volume of the Johns Hopkins *Variorum* edition of Spenser's *Complete Works.* No writer on *Colin Clout* can fairly disclaim indebtedness to this magisterial series. The Commentary on *Colin Clout* brings together, in excerpts from leading books and articles, the scholarship down to the year 1942, consisting almost entirely of sources and analogues, allusions, identifications of the poets and ladies at court. This background and topical material, however valuable in itself, does not automatically illuminate the poem. For *Colin Clout,* moreover, the editors did not include separate essays in the form of appendices as they did in the case of *The Shepheardes Calender,* the earlier pastoral included in the same volume. To offer a coherent general view of the pastoral was manifestly no part of the intention of the editors, nor would the characteristic method of variorum treatment followed—line-by-line notation—have lent itself to a unified interpretative approach.

5. For the sake of completeness, reference should be made also to an unpublished doctoral dissertation by Kathrine Koller, "Studies in Spenser's *Colin Clouts Come Home Again*" (Johns Hopkins University, 1932), which the present study in no wise parallels. The isolated elements of the poem treated by Miss Koller are *biographical*: Spenser and Raleigh, identification of personages, dating of poem with reference to time of publication of the *Daphnaïda;* and *literary*: versification, *Colin Clout* and the classical pastoral, relationship of themes in *Colin Clout* to those of court-of-love writings, and similarity of themes between *Colin Clout* and other poems of Spenser.

In conveying the inadequacy of previous scholarship as literary interpretation of *Colin Clout,* I have suggested indirectly the task before me. What I aim principally to offer is a reasonably comprehensive reading for its intrinsic merit of a poem which, despite the phenomenal increase in Spenserian scholarly criticism during the past half century, has received less than the share of belletristic attention commensurate with its length, much less with its importance. The main obstacle to a satisfying reading today is the unobtrusive changes in literary fashions which have taken place since the poem was composed. Accordingly, the real puzzles for the modern reader are often those which he is apt to fail to notice at all! For this reason, the present reading gives major attention to the conventions, attitudes, and understandings which appear to have been so influential in shaping production of imaginative writings during the Renaissance. My objective, in short, is to vitalize the "presentness" of the poem in part by restoring some of its true "pastness". At the same time, while attempting to read the poem primarily according to the literary canons of its own age, I have endeavored to retain awareness of it as an individual and unique composition—a self-inclusive product of literary art.

The method employed is mainly inductive, with the discussion proceeding from description and analysis to generalization. The order of presentation is that determined, insofar as practicable, by a progression from smaller to larger structural units. This order is reversed in the treatment of words (Chapter III) after that of rhetorical figures (Chapter II) in order to show the reciprocal effects of diction and versification upon one another. Because the inductive method largely prescribes the order of development, a knowledge of the design and meaning of the poem comes to the reader only gradually. The movement from particular to general ordinarily facilitates understanding on his part. There may be times, however, when the reader will find it expedient to turn to the early part of Chapter V for a statement regarding the division into three narrative episodes and five thematic parts, or when he will wish to turn to the final chapter for a synthesis of the pastoral allegory.

Discussing the poem mainly by literary elements according to an ascending order of generality may appear rather rigidly systematic. If so, this method has the compensating advantage of permitting a cross-check of findings. I hope that examining the poem from different vantage points and cumulating the findings under progressively larger perspectives will help reduce the occupational hazard of critics to see configurations which reflect their subjective fantasies. I am convinced that the poem has already suffered from such misreading in the past. If I have been able to correct some of these distortions, it is mainly because I enjoy the advantage of subjecting the poem for the first time to a thoroughgoing examination on its own terms.

It may not be amiss at this juncture to indicate in brief the kind of results which this long look at the poem has made possible. They consist in findings which frequently diverge rather sharply from views currently held. Confirmation of these findings must, of course, wait upon proofs to be advanced later. One of the fresh formulations, for example, is the cardinal role played by the abundant rhetorical figures in building up blocks of verse. Another is the intimate relationship existing between the distinctive vocabulary and the prosody. Still another new point of view is the drama-like quality of the poem and the emotional vibrancy underlying the utterances of the title character.

Focusing the gaze directly upon the poem as a work of literary art has made it possible, moreover, to fill some gaping holes in the criticism. A good example of this result is an explanation at long last of the Bregog-Mulla myth as an allegory illustrating what happens in the world of men when concord and love, divinely decreed by the "great Lord of Hierarchies", are breached. This myth, occupying 55 of the 955 lines in the poem, has been regarded as a pleasant "digression" by the few critics who concerned themselves about it at all.

Close attention directed to the text of the poem reveals how little the imagery is used to evoke sensuous responses, how much to objectify concepts and to symbolize values. The passages celebrating Queen-Cynthia and her retinue of aristocratic ladies have been much censured as being insincere or overly fulsome in their praise. The superlatives of these passages are supplied by figurative imagery. When the imagery is related to its contextual background and to its formulation by logic-taught modes, the descriptive sections which it interpenetrates take on a different coloration from the one commonly accorded them. The beauty and grace which the encomiums paint is not so much of the flesh as of the spirit. Far from being intended as realistic portraits of mortal women, the passages are seen in proper perspective to be praises of abstract and idealized beauty and virtue embodied in all womankind—

attributes which are here *exemplified* by the particular damsels alluded to. Concretely, Queen Elizabeth I, at the time of *Colin Clout's* publication a sexagenarian in manifestly poor health, is not made out by Spenser, as many have assumed, to be a latter-day Helen of Troy; nor is it likely that that well-tutored lady, who had her own personal copy of the first logic in the native language, would have thought so.

A fresh approach has also made one generally accepted notion regarding *Colin Clout* highly suspect, if not altogether untenable. That is the conception of the pastoral as primarily an autobiographical and historical account—a view held by generations of scholars and critics, including many of the present. A searching examination induces the beliefs that the poem is neither autobiography nor history, though it has elements of both; and that the most significant fidelity is not to the author's external affairs and relationships but to his imaginative life. In other words, artistic sincerity takes precedence over literal truths of time and circumstance, with the fundamental orientation being fictive, not factual.

One final example may suffice to give the reader an idea of the hitherto unperceived patterns the poem is seen to exhibit when brought under direct gaze. Over the centuries *Colin Clout* has received its fair share of commendation. But almost none of this critical approbation has been for its unity of design and theme. Yet the close look fixed upon the poem in this study has revealed both kinds of unity.

In setting forth the extent and nature of rhetorical patterning, the chapter to follow begins the "quest of inquirie" into the literary elements which combine to make this aulic poem an artistic entity.

CHAPTER II

THE FIGURES OF RHETORIC

Modern criticism has given increasing recognition to the functional, as distinguished from the decorative aspect, of rhetorical figures in the poetry of the English Renaissance.[1] The continuance of this emphasis is particularly appropriate to Spenser's later pastoral, where the relevance of the figures to the larger considerations of style—indeed, to the total discourse—is so cardinal. The importance of the figures is enhanced by the natural use of rhetorical arts by characters, set in a kind of *mise en scéne,* whose suasory speeches largely comprise the poem. Stress of the functional side of the rhetorical elements in the poem need not deny or denigrate the role of the figures in conferring upon the verse an aura of conspicuous beauty. The office of the figures in this respect is simply another manifestation of the same taste for elegance which reflected itself in Renaissance dress, manners, ceremonial processions, and décor. The beautifying characteristics of the numerous word orders, comprised of tropes and schemes, were recognized and frankly accepted by literati of the Tudor period. In their eyes, figures possessed value as ornament by reason of their constituting departures from everyday speech patterns. The idea is conventionally phrased by Abraham Fraunce, whom many believe to be the Corydon praised in lines 383-4 of the poem :[2] "A figure is a certeine decking of speach, whereby the vsual and simple fashion thereof

1. Rosemond Tuve, *Elizabethan and Metaphysical Imagery: Renaissance Poetic and Twentieth-Century Critics* (Chicago, 1947), maintains that all elements in figures of comparison assist in conveying meaning; and that classification of figures of any time would be clearer if similarities in logical nature (e.g., images of "quality" or "manner of doing") were observed. Herbert David Rix, *Rhetoric in Spenser's Poetry,* Pennsylvania State College Studies, No. 7 (State College, 1940), applies the teleological concept of the figures and other rhetorical formulae to the poetry of Spenser.

2. *Daphnaïda and Other Poems,* ed. W. L. Renwick, An Elizabethan Gallery, No. 4 (London, 1929), p. 186; Kathrine Koller, "Abraham Fraunce and Edmund Spenser", *ELH,* VII (1940), 108.

is altered and changed to that which is more elegant and conceipted".[3]

To belletrists of the Renaissance most assuredly—and it requires an effort for us to accept this—there was no discrepancy between the functional and embellishing aspects of figures. In that favored pamphlet of the era, the *Ars Poetica* of Horace, the aims of poetry are enunciated as being to teach (*prodesse*) or to delight (*delectare*), or to do both at once. To this dictum, which is rhetorical in its conception of the poetic art, the Renaissance conjoined Cicero's third aim of oratory—to persuade or sway—and applied it to the poet. To this humanistic formulation of moving as an object of eloquence in all forms, it required, in a Christian era, little extension on the part of critics and poets to make the direction of movement specifically ethical and moral.[4] Applied to poetry, the threefold aim of oratory meant that poetry teaches through its appeal to the intellect of the reader or listener by means of its content or *doctrina;* pleases through its appeal to the aesthetic sense by means of its style, elaborated largely through figures of speech; and moves to virtuous action by means of its appeal to emotion, acting through message and mode together. Thus, delight in poetry, whether achieved by means of pleasing fables or by means of patterned language, was not considered by discerning men of the period to exist for its own sake; and we may be reasonably certain that to mature critics like Sidney and George Puttenham, who were also practising poets, and to poetic craftsmen like Spenser, who was also a critic,[5] rhetorical figures would hardly be thought of as

3. *The Arcadian Rhetorike,* ed. Ethel Seaton, Luttrell Society Reprints, No. 9 (Oxford, 1950), p. 26.

4. See Bernard Weinberg, *A History of Literary Criticism in the Italian Renaissance* (Chicago, 1961), II, 721-4, for Daniello's view of the similarity between oratory and poetry in having for their object pleasurable teaching of exemplary morality; also pp. 737, 748, for emphasis on the same point by Minturno and Scalinger, whose *De Poeta* (1559) and *Poetices Libri Septem* (1561) respectively were prime sources for Sir Philip Sidney's *Apologie for Poetrie* (c. 1583, printed in 1595). G. Gregory Smith's notes to the *Apologie* in *Elizabethan Critical Essays* (Oxford, 1904), I, 382-403, reveal how closely Sidney, in numerous passages, echoes his Italian models.

5. The writer of the Argument to the *October* eclogue of *The Shepheardes Calender* refers to a book of the author's called the *English Poete,* which had just recently come into his hands. In *A Discourse of Englishe Poetrie* (1586), William Webbe expresses the wish that he might see the *English Poet,* which E.K., the author's friend, had promised to publish (*Eliz. Critical Essays,* I, 232).

elements superadded to poetry, even though they were often referred to as ornament.[6]

Of course, where taste is deficient and conception weak, abuses are inevitable. Renewed awareness of this gloomy truism doubtless prompted Henry Peacham to add a section entitled "Caution" to the discussion of each of his figures when he issued his revised edition of *The Garden of Eloquence* in 1593. Indeed, dutiful injunctions against abuse of the figures accompanied treatment of them in both ancient and Renaissance treatises. Classical authors of textbooks still used in the educational system of the sixteenth century warned, for instance, against inflated speech ("sufflata oratio"), outlandish metaphors ("verbis ... duriter aliunde translatis")[7] and excessive reliance upon the colors of rhetoric ("magis infucata vitia").[8] That those vices of overabundant and tasteless rhetoric which the anonymous author of the *Ad Herennium* and Cicero had inveighed against were by no means absent from the Elizabethan literary scene is made evident by Sidney himself in the famous passage about Matron Eloquence being at times "with figures and flowers, extreamelie winter-starued".[9]

Sidney's strictures here allude, one must not forget, to the *improper* employment of "figures and flowers". In their proper employment, formal patterns of words, phrases, and larger elements of discourse, together with locutions accorded special meanings,

6. Father Ong's reminder that the first meaning of *ornamentum* in Latin rhetorical terminology is "equipment or accoutrements, which the 'naked causes' of dialectic, like naked persons, would need rather more than pretty clothing to get along in this world", is pertinent here. He recalls that Miss Tuve (Ch. IV of *Elizabethan and Metaphysical Imagery*) and others have shown that the Renaissance notion of ornament "does not necessarily mean appliqué work in the way the English term ornament suggests today" (Rev. Walter J. Ong, S.J., *Ramus: Method, and the Decay of Dialogue* [Cambridge, Mass., 1958], p. 277).

7. *Rhetorica ad Herennium,* iv.10.15, Loeb Classical Library, trans. Harry Caplan (Cambridge, Mass., 1944), p. 264.

8. Cicero, *De Oratore,* iii.25.100, Loeb Classical Library, trans. H. Rackham (Cambridge, Mass., 1942), p. 80.

9. *Apologie for Poetrie,* in *Eliz. Critical Essays,* I, 201-2. Another less familiar but equally zestful contemporary diatribe against rhetorical affectation (which borrows its imagery directly from Cicero) is contained in a commencement oration delivered at Oxford University in 1572 by John Rainolds, a candidate for the M.A. (*Oratio in Laudem Artis Poeticae,* ed. William Ringler; trans. Walter Allen, Jr., Princeton University Studies in English, No. 20 [Princeton, 1940], p. 48).

could hardly exist as appliquéd ornament. On the contrary, conception and deployment of these rhetorical devices are linked on a general plane through content and through emotional appeal with the exacting disciplines of logic and rhetoric respectively—the heart and core of formal education during the period in which Spenser lived.[10] Inasmuch as many of the figures, particularly those which lend themselves to amplification of matter, derive from, or are identical to, the places of rhetorical or dialectical investigation, their connection with the basic compositional arts becomes integral rather than incidental.[11] The precise way in

10. For a selective list of references detailing the teaching of composition through the media of the trivium in English educational institutions of the Renaissance, see Wilbur Samuel Howell, *Logic and Rhetoric in England, 1500-1700* (Princeton, 1956), n. 1, p. 64. To this list should be added Donald Lemen Clark, *John Milton at St. Paul's School: A Study of Ancient Rhetoric in English Renaissance Education* (New York, 1948).

11. See William G. Crane, *Wit and Rhetoric in the Renaissance: The Formal Basis of Elizabethan Prose Style* (New York, 1937), p. 5, for a summary of the vital linkage between the figures and the places. Also see p. 55 for a brief statement on the effects of the Ramist reorganization of logic and rhetoric in relation to figures. For an expanded account of the whole movement for the reform of the Aristotelian and Ciceronian system of logic and rhetoric, see Howell, *Logic and Rhetoric in England,* Ch. IV. According to Howell, by the 1570s the struggle to keep Aristotle and Cicero supreme in logic and rhetoric respectively was beginning to be lost (p. 178). The supremacy of Cicero was challenged at Cambridge University as early as 1574, the year Spenser received his B.A. degree from Pembroke College. In this year Spenser's best friend, Gabriel Harvey (Hobbinol in the poem), as praelector in rhetoric at Cambridge, began preparation of the lectures delivered in 1575-76 and published in 1577 (pp. 247-8).

Whether Spenser came to adopt the Ramist reorganization is not known, although his acquaintance with the Cambridge and Sidney circles which advocated it would make his familiarity with the reformed disciplines virtually certain. Some details concerning Spenser's place in these circles is given in Miss Koller's article on "Edmund Spenser and Abraham Fraunce". *The Lawiers Logike* and *The Arcadian Rhetorike,* which Fraunce, a confirmed Ramist, published at London in 1588, are liberally interspersed with illustrative passages of poetry, including some one hundred from Spenser in the former and three in the latter work. These treatises of Fraunce serve to demonstrate not only the extent to which Ramist books in England point up places and figures with quotations from poetry but also to show how closely proponents of the reformed program of liberal arts continue to associate rhetoric and poetry. (See also Father Ong, *Ramus,* pp. 282-3, on Ramist conceptions of the relationship between poetry and rhetoric.) If Spenser can be counted among those who embraced the new approaches, his adoption in whole or in part of the revised system would not have required any basic readjustment of ingrained habit patterns as regards

which figures of rhetoric, especially those of comparison, are elaborated from the dialectical places is more than a matter of historical interest. This methodology and its relevance to meaning in *Colin Clout* is special and significant; but this aspect is reserved for Chapter IV, where it is more advantageously treated in connection with figurative images.

The specific aim of this chapter is to exhibit and discuss the figures of rhetoric found in a single Renaissance poem. But figurative elements in an age which deferred so much to tradition can hardly be studied profitably, or even intelligibly, without reference to literary positions which supply a context for their employment. In touching on relevant aspects of these positions, I strive, for the sake of brevity, to stick to the critical high roads. What I have said thus far has been intended to provide, in highly synoptic form, a frame of reference compatible with the canons of the age in which to examine figures in *Colin Clout*. These canons suggest that the contribution of the figures to the whole poem can be approached from two separate but related points of view: that of rhetoric, the open hand, which views figures in their overt aspect as patterns of a given variety, with specific textbook names; and that of logic, the closed fist, which views figures, more limited in number and type, as elaborations of ways to discover places and follow a method of inquiry. I shall confine myself in this chapter to the first and more inclusive of these approaches, with the reservation, in Howell's words, that to Englishmen of the sixteenth and seventeenth centuries "poetry was considered to be the third great form of communication, open and popular but not fully explained by rhetoric, concise and lean but not fully explained by logic".[12]

---

composition through logical and rhetorical modes. In Ch. XII of *Elizabethan and Metaphysical Imagery,* Miss Tuve treats, under the title "Ramist Logic: Certain General Conceptions Affecting Imagery", the possible effects of the redirection of peripatetic logic on the creation of poetic images during the latter part of the sixteenth and early part of the seventeenth centuries in England. She holds the influence of Ramus to have been inescapable on the part of writers of this era (p. 339). (This conclusion is strongly fortified by Father Ong in his recent book on Ramus.) However, Miss Tuve believes this influence, whether direct or indirect, to have resulted, not in images with new qualities, but in images with old qualities highlighted (p. 351). The change of emphasis fostered by the Ramists would, in her view, operate to produce images more notable for logical toughness and intellectual fineness (p. 353).

12. Howell, p. 4.

The real ubiquity of tropes and schemes in the poem is not evident to the reader who has merely noted Rix's incidental reference to the "profusion of tropes and schemes"[13] in *Colin Clout* or who has only read Miss Rubel's statement that, "as far as the rhetoric of *Colin Clout* is concerned, it is not so lavishly ornamental as that of the poetry which was intended to be more polite".[14] The Table which follows, identifying the figures for the last hundred lines, will give the reader a more adequate idea of their almost unbelievable multiplicity. Selection of the closing lines for the purpose of exhibiting the figures is a purely arbitrary choice; almost any section would show about the same relative frequency of figures. Counting only once alliteration (*paroemion*), which is well-nigh omnipresent, and reversals of normal syntactical order (*hyperbaton*), which occurs on the average of once in every six lines, I have found thirty-five figures in the last one hundred lines. On the same basis, I have counted thirty-one figures in the first one hundred lines. The average throughout the poem is approximately one figure for every three lines. Besides indicating the number and variety of figures, the Table, by presenting a consecutive listing of the figures in context, permits the reader to observe the complexity of rhetorical patterning—that is, the way in which the figures are interwoven within a passage. This interlacing is a conventional as well as integral part of the lore.

TABLE

THE FIGURES ILLUSTRATED FOR THE LAST ONE HUNDRED LINES OF *COLIN CLOUT*

Lines	*Quotation*	*Rhetorical Figure(s)*
851-54	So being former foes, they wexed friends, And gan by litle learne to loue each other: So being knit, they brought forth other kynds Out of the fruitfull wombe of their great mother.	compar antithesis
855-60	Then first gan heauen out of darkness dread For to appeare, and brought forth chearfull day: Next gan the earth to shew her naked head, Out of deep waters which her drownd alway. And shortly after euerie liuing wight, Crept forth like wormes out of her slimie nature.	distributio auxesis prosopopoeia

13. Rix, *Rhetoric in Spenser's Poetry,* p. 62.

14. Veré L. Rubel, *Poetic Diction in the English Renaissance from Skelton through Spenser,* The Modern Language Association of America, Revolving Fund Series, no. 12 (New York, 1941), p. 258.

863-64	Thenceforth they gan each one his like to loue, And like himselfe desire for to beget.	ploce
865-66	The Lyon chose his mate, the Turtle Doue Her deare, the Dolphin his own Dolphinet.	zeugma synonymia
871-74	For beautie is the bayt which with delight Doth man allure, for to enlarge his kynd, Beautie the burning lamp of heauens light, Darting her beames into each feeble mynd.	sententia ploce metaphora
883-86	So loue is Lord of all the world by right, And rules the creatures by his powrfull saw: All being made the vassalls of his might, Through secret sence which therto doth them draw.	sententia acclamatio
891-94	For their desire is base, and doth not merit, The name of loue, but of disloyall lust: Ne mongst true louers they shall place inherit, But as Exuls out of his court be thrust.	aetiologia synonymia antithesis comparatio
896-98	*Colin,* thou now full deeply hast divynd: Of loue and beautie and with wondrous skill, Hast *Cupid* selfe depainted in his kynd.	transitio
911-14	But who can tell what cause had that faire Mayd To vse him so that vsed her so well: Or who with blame can iustly her vpbrayd, For louing not? for who can loue compell?	pysma antanaclasis sententia
919-24	And well I wote, that oft I heard it spoken, How one that fairest *Helene* did reuile, Through iudgement of the Gods to been ywroken Lost both his eyes and so remaynd long while, Till he recanted had his wicked rimes, And made amends to her with treble praise.	periphrasis prothesis
925-26	Beware therefore, ye groomes, I read betimes, How rashly blame of *Rosalind* ye raise.	apostrophe
935-38	Not then to her that scorned things so base, But to my selfe the blame that lookt to hie: So hie her thoughts as she her selfe haue place, And loath each lowly thing with loftie eie.	anadiplosis antithesis
939-46	Yet so much grace let her vouchsafe to grant To simple swaine, sith her I may not loue: Yet that I may her honour paravant, And praise her worth, though far my wit aboue. Such grace shall be some guerdon for the griefe, And long affliction which I haue endured: Such grace sometimes shall giue me some reliefe, And ease of paine which cannot be recured.	ploce compar anaphora meiosis paroemion

947-50	And ye my fellow shepheardes which do see And heare the languours of my too long dying, Vnto the world for euer witnesse bee, That hers I die, nought to the world denying.	apostrophe polyptoton
952-55	So hauing ended, he from ground did rise, And after him vprose eke all the rest: All loth to part, but that the glooming skies Warnd them to draw their bleating flocks to rest.	hyperbaton chronographia

Among the numerous tropes, schemes of words, and schemes of thought and amplification,[15] Spenser employs, under Greek and Latin appellations, many standard compositional devices found in current writing, but his use of the figures differs most significantly from that in vogue today because, following typical Renaissance practice, he employs them to a degree heightened beyond that of the moderns to accomplish one or more of three distinct functions: (1) to constitute the framework and the substance of blocks of verse; (2) to control the stylistic level; and (3) to provide emotional fervor. The first of these ends has to do mainly with develop-

15. I assume as standard for the Elizabethan period the meanings ascribed to the figures by Rix, pp. 22-61. These meanings are made clear by definitions and specimens. The definitions quoted by Rix in this section are nearly all from Joannes Susenbrotus, *Epitome Troporum ac Schematum* (1563). The English translations of the Latin definitions are mostly from Henry Peacham, *The Garden of Eloquence* (1577). A great many of the specimens are from Alexander Gill, *Logonomia Anglica* (1619, rev. 1621). Gill devotes four chapters of his work to the various figures and illustrates many of them by quotations from *The Faerie Queene, The Ruines of Time,* and *The Shepheardes Calen*der. On pp. 19-20 of *Rhetoric in Spenser's Poetry,* Rix explains his division of the figures into tropes (words employed in other than their literal meanings, as in metaphor and metonymy) and schemes (words or longer units arranged or repeated according to a definite pattern, as in alliteration and simile). Rix refines the category of schemes by subdividing them into schemes of words and schemes of thought and amplification. His system of classification is an adaptation of one of the commonly accepted groupings in Spenser's period, although no two Renaissance sources agree *in toto* on precise classifications of different figures. In the ensuing discussion of the wide variety of stylistic devices which appear in *Colin Clout* and which are encompassed by the term *figures* in its Renaissance acceptation, I have found no need to maintain these distinctions in categories. I have profited much from the way in which Rix treats Spenser's use of rhetorical figures. For *Colin Clout,* however, Rix's coverage is negligible, since he includes only ten illustrative figures from the poem in his Table of Figures (pp. 21-61) and mentions in passing another figure (p. 71).

ment or amplification, which is subsumed within the two standard rhetorical divisions of *inventio* and *dispositio,* processes of discovering matter and arranging it. The latter two ends are aspects of tone and emotion.

With reference to the first end to which use of the figures is directed, the two famous passages evaluating contemporary poets and praising the ladies at court (ll. 377-449, 488-575) may serve to exemplify the efficacy of figures in providing both the form of the material and the material itself. These passages both employ *divisio* or *distributio,* by which figure, according to Peacham's rendering of Susenbrotus' Latin, "we dilate and spread abroade the generall kinde, by numbering and reckning vp the speciall kindes".[16] That is, the sections set forth concrete details to support a generality. They possess the character of a formal design, achieved to some extent in the section on the poets by the repetition of the transitional phrase "There is", and in the section on the ladies by the phrase "ne lesse praise worthie". That the second formula for transition was part of a common lore for the use of *distributio* or *merismus* is suggested by Puttenham's treatment and illustration in *The Arte of English Poesie* (1589), where he cites a passage in praise of the maiden Queen with the "*merismus* in the negatiue for the better grace".[17] *Distributio,* then, operates to create an orderly channel through which the poet can apply individualizing comments to persons in the two groups. The raw material, as it were, of the verse is constructed in the two passages largely out of another figure—*epitheton* or *appositum,* defined by Peacham as "when we ioyne adiectiues to those Substantiues, to whome they doe properly belong, and that eyther to prayse, disprayse, to amplify or extenuate".[18] With respect to *epitheton* or epithet, one might assume from the two illustrative lines cited by Rix out of *The Faerie Queene* that the figures might be limited, as in the modern conception, to adherent adjectives. The first of these illustrations, taken from the second edition of the elder Alexander Gill's *Logonomia Anglia* (1619), revised in 1621, is "But wise Speranza gave him comfort sweet". The second is "So false *Duessa,* but vile *Ate* thus". However, as King James VI of Scotland's *Ane Schort*

16. Rix, p. 48.
17. George Puttenham, *The Arte of English Poesie,* eds. Gladys Doidge Willcock and Alice Walker (Cambridge, Eng., 1936), p. 223.
18. Rix, p. 31.

Treatise (1584) and Puttenham's *Arte* clearly show,[19] the interchangeable terms *epitheton* or *appositum* could properly embrace not only pre-positional adjectives but post-positional adjectives and substantive phrases as well. Thus, in the passage on the poets one finds "good *Harpalus* now woxen aged,/In faithfull seruice of faire *Cynthis*" (ll. 380-1); "*Corydon* though meanly waged,/Yet hablest wit of most I know this day" (ll. 382-3); "sad *Alcyon* bent to mourne" (l. 384), etc.; and in the passage on the ladies one finds "*Vrania* sister vnto *Astrofell* (l. 487); "faire *Marian,* the *Muses* onely darling" (l. 505); *Mansilia,*/Best knowne by bearing vp great *Cynthiaes* traine" (ll. 508-9), etc. In short, two important sections of the poem are organized by one figure—*distributio,* and their content is derived largely from another—*epitheton.*

This use of figures to supply *copia* is so pervasive in *Colin Clout* that it will be profitable to observe the principle at work in more detail. For this purpose, we may select almost at random four additional examples. The first three show the process for separate figures. The fourth demonstrates the more complex technique of interweaving. The first example is the speech (ll. 22-31) of Hobbinol, in which all nature is represented as lamenting Colin's absence. Though this passage is in the main line of classical pastoral tradition by way of Ronsard's *Adonis,*[20] it is nevertheless built upon *prosopopoeia,* the personification of Nature in this case, which is the *raison d'être* of the unit. The second example is the *allegoria* of the ocean as Cynthia's pasture (ll. 240-51)—the "marine pastoral"[21] motif. The description is given a mythological coloring, but the chief element is the extended metaphor likening the sea to a meadow. Spenser's dispraise of the courtiers who pervert the sacred concept of love is the third example showing how he uses the figures to furnish the main substance of his units. The figure (ll. 786-92) through which Spenser has Colin ring the changes on the key words *serve* and *use* in their contrasting shades of meaning is *antanaclasis,* a play on words in their varying senses.

The final example of Spenser's use of figures to supply *copia* is Colin's blazon (ll. 464-79) in which he praises his mistress and

19. King James VI of Scotland, in *Eliz. Critical Essays,* I, 219; Puttenham, pp. 176-7.

20. Merritt Y. Hughes, "Spenser and the Greek Pastoral Triad", *SP,* XX (1923), 208-9, cited in *Works,* VII, 410.

21. Elkin Calhoun Wilson, *England's Eliza,* Harvard Studies in English, Vol. XX (Cambridge, Mass., 1939), p. 302.

protests devoted service and undying love. The passage is typical of the many in *Colin Clout* that employ an elaborate blending of figures to make up the block of verse, in this case, a lyric cry. It is one of two extended tributes by Colin to his mistress, Rosalind. The complaint opens with a mild *exclamatio,* followed by *aetiologia,* the reason that the speaker does not deserve ill of "gentle Mayds" (l. 465). The heart of the next six lines is *expolitio,* termed by Puttenham "the Gorgious", and said by him to be used to "polish our speech & as it were attire it with copious & pleasant amplifications and much varietie of sentences all running vpon one point & to one inte[*n*]t".[22] The entire speech is then rounded off with two lines of *acclamatio,* the summing up, and two lines of complicated word play, combining with epigrammatic neatness *antimetabole* and *antistrophe.*

While figures in *Colin Clout* perform the basic function of filling out details of a passage, they are also instrumental, along with diction generally, in achieving the second major objective of rhetorical patterning—that of adjusting the style to suit Renaissance notions of decorum respecting genre, subject, and persons, with genre being the most impelling determinant. The general relationship between the figures and the styles, as conceived by men of the period, is clear. Abundant use of figures is a distinguishing characteristic of the high style. The middle and low styles are marked by decreasing employment of the figures. The bald application of the principle governing decorum of the kinds would have resulted in *Colin Clout's* being written throughout in "the lowe kinde, when we vse no *Metaphores* nor translated words, not yet vse any amplifications but goe plainly to worke, and speake altogether in common wordes".[23] No poet of consequence, however, applies the theory undiscriminatingly. To do so would be to forgo the rich possibilities for registering fine discriminations in value—and consequent aesthetic effects—when changing from one subject or one person to another subject or another person.

In the Dedicatory Letter to Sir Walter Raleigh, when Spenser refers to *Colin Clout* as a "simple pastorall" and apologizes for the "meanesse of the style", which is "vnworthie of your higher conceipt", he is using in the first two quoted phrases terms familiar to

22. Page 247.
23. Thomas Wilson, *Wilson's Arte of Rhetorique,* 1560, ed. George Herbert Mair (Oxford, 1909), p. 169.

the critical discussions of the time. The conventional designation of pastoral was "simple" and, as Puttenham makes quite clear, the "low and base stile" was understood to be reserved for "all *Eglogues* and pastorall poemes".[24] In view of the multiplicity of figures in *Colin Clout,* hardly compatible with conventions governing the low style, one may feel that Spenser's statement in the Dedication is inconsistent with his practice, or that he is simply throwing the standard theory overboard. Actually, neither alternative reflects the true situation. His statement, when taken in a larger context, does not identify the poem unreservedly as written in unadorned style, nor would Sir Walter, in all likelihood, have construed the deprecatory phrases so to identify it. Perhaps the reasons for discounting Spenser's statement as an indication of his intention to eschew elevation should be specified. First, one has to make ample allowances for the convention of humility and disparagement in dedications to one's patron in the 1590s. Part of this engaging air of self-disparagement reflects also the courtly fashion of *sprezzatura,* the word Castiglione first uses in his influential *Il Libro del Cortegiano* (1528) to characterize the temper by which a gentleman conceals a purpose of high seriousness with a show of studied negligence.[25] Had not Spenser in his Dedicatory Sonnets disparaged even the high style of *The Faerie Queene* itself in such lines as the following to "The Right Honourable the Earle of Ormund and Ossory":

Receiue most noble Lord a simple taste
  Of the wilde fruit, which saluage soyle hath bred,
  Which being through long wars left almost waste,
  With brutish barbarisme is ouerspredd;[26]

or in such lines as the following to "The Most renowmed and valiant Lord, the Lord Grey of Wilton, knight of the Noble order of the Garter, &c"?—

Rude rymes, the which a rustick Muse did weaue
In sauadge soyle, far from Parnasso mount.[27]

24. Page 153.

25. *Il Libro del Cortegiano de Conte Baldesar Castiglione* (Venice, 1528), sig. biiii^r: "Et ciò è fuggir quanto piu si pò: & come un asperissimo, & pericoloso scoglio la affettatione, & per dir forse una noua parola, usar in ogni cosa una certa sprezzatura, che nasconda l'arte, & dimostri ciò che si fa, & dice uenir fatto senza fatica, & quasi senza pensarui."

26. *Works,* III, 192.

27. *Ibid.,* p. 194.

In alluding to the poem as "simple", Spenser was in little danger of creating for his immediate readers a misleading supposition as to its actual quality.

Second, Spenser may well have been using the word "meanesse" to accord with the conventional classification of style into three levels, "mean" being the term commonly employed to designate the intermediate level. Finally, even if, as is conceivable, Spenser meant "meanesse" to suggest a degree of baseness, the convention implied that *all* poetry was raised above common discourse[28] and that the lower flight merely restricted the kinds of figures and modes of using them, not the figures themselves. The copiousness of figures in an out-and-out pastoral like Spenser's *The Shepheardes Calender* indicates convincingly that the low style, at least in poetry, did not outlaw the figures. *Colin Clout,* moreover, being far from "pure pastoral" in genre, by reason of its containing matters "that concerns the Gods and diuine things" and the "noble gests and great fortunes of Princes",[29] would be pushed upward under the principle of decorum toward conventions of middle and high style.

Though all the figures inasmuch as they "passe the ordinary limits of common vtterance"[30] serve to raise the style, certain figures are more efficacious to this end than others. I shall confine myself to those figures in the poem which best examplify this function: *comparatio* and *allegoria; antonomasia* and *epitheton; periphrasis, sententia* and *acclamatio.* The first of these is quite plentiful. The main way in which *comparatio,* defined as "a comparing of thinges, persons, deedes, examples, contrairies, lyke, or vnlyke",[31] imparts elevation of style is in the drawing of its subject matter from biblical or mythological sources, with their rich store of associations for Christian humanists of the time. Cases involving the use of *comparatio* to call up biblical associations for the reader are the praise of Urania

> In whose braue mynd as in a golden cofer,
> All heauenly gifts and riches locked are :
> More rich than pearles of *Ynde* or gold of *Opher* (ll. 488-90)

and the figurative deification of Cynthia, whose

28. Puttenham, pp. 8-9.
29. *Ibid.,* p. 152.
30. *Ibid.,* p. 154.
31. Rix, p. 55.

thoughts are like the fume of Franckincence,
Which from a golden Censer forth doth rise.

. . . .

Emongst the seats of Angels heauenly wrought,
Much like an Angell in all forme and fashion. (ll. 608-9; 614-15)

An example of a comparison depending upon mythological lore for its effectiveness is the injunction by Colin to Daniel bidding that poet to "rouze thy feathers quickly" (l. 424) and "to what course thou please thy selfe aduance" (l. 425).[32] Thus the author of the sonnet-sequence *Delia* (which Spenser probably saw in manuscript)[33] is equated with, or considered to be under the inspiration of, the Muse of Poetry by way of Pegasus, the winged horse on which the Muses sometimes traveled. Similarly, the one clear example of *allegoria*—in Peacham's phrase, "a contynued Metaphor"[34]—derives its tone from the classical tradition. This is the ocean-meadow fancy (ll. 240-51) contained in "the shepheards" description of Cynthia's "Regiment" at sea. The marine divinities Triton and Proteus figure prominently in this description.

From one point of view, of course, *Colin Clout* is in its entirety an extended metaphor—an *allegoria,* in which a thin veil is thrown over all by the poet's casting the poem in the pastoral mode. Colin's life is placed in an atmosphere of shepherds and shepherdesses, bearing names appearing in prestigious classical works—the idylls of Theocritus and the eclogues of Virgil, for the most part. All locutions which arise from the pastoral mode were well understood by the convention to designate an order of things and beings different from such empirical things and beings as Ireland, Kilcolman, England, the English Court, Queen Elizabeth, Raleigh, Spenser, Harvey, Bryskett.

With reference to *epitheton* and *antonomasia,* the two succeeding figures in the above list of those serving to raise the style, both represent adaptations of utterances to reflect real or attributed differences in rank or dignity between the speaker, the shepherd Colin, and the person spoken about. *Epitheton* and *antonomasia,*

32. The comparison would now be called a metaphor, but Renaissance criticism normally has *metaphora* denote a single word "translated from the proper and natural signification, to another not proper, yet nie and/likely" (Peacham, in Rix, p. 22).

33. *Daphnaïda,* p. 187.

34. Rix, p. 24.

distinguished by Puttenham as "the Qualifier" and "the figure of attribution" respectively,[35] both serve to register the speaker's awareness of special deference owing to the subject persons. They create a kind of aesthetic distance between him and them. As pointed out in the discussion of the passages on poets and ladies as set pieces of conventional formalism, these two long passages (ll. 377-449; 485-575) are interpenetrated with epithets, each person, in fact, being honored by one or more appropriate "qualifiers". Among the poets, for instance, there is "*Alabaster* throughly taught,/ In all this skill, though knowen yet to few" (ll. 400-1); among the maids of honor, there are "Faire *Galathea* with bright shining beames" (l. 518), and Neaera, "the blosome of grace and curtesie" (l. 528). Interestingly enough, of the ten ladies lauded, only Stella has no epithet bestowed upon her. The reason for this, given by Colin himself, is that Sidney has already "prais'd [her] and rais'd [her] aboue each other starre" (l. 535).

There can be little question as to the efficacy of these qualifiers to enhance the dignity of the person to whom a description or qualifying word or phrase is attached, and at the same time to indicate the speaker's awareness of his comparative unworthiness. The value of *antonomasia* in creating a sense of aesthetic distance as between speaker and subject is even greater than that of the epithet. Puttenham terms *antonomasia* "the surnamer" and defines it as "the manner of naming of persons or things . . . by a conuenient difference, and such as is true or esteemed and likely to be true". His illustrations of the figure include reference to "the Westerne king" (King Philip II of Spain) and to "*The maiden Queene,* for that is her hiest peculiar among all the Queenes of the World".[36] In *Colin Clout,* too, *antonomasia* is used to register the speaker's humble position in relation to persons of high estate : the speaker's refusal to mention Queen Elizabeth's name outright and his referring to her instead as "*Cynthia* the Ladie of the sea" (l. 166), "that Goddesse grace" (l. 359), "dreaded Dread" (l. 406); and Colin's reference to Sir Walter Raleigh as "a straunge Shepheard" (l. 60) and as "the shepheard of the Ocean" (l. 358).

Of other figures calculated to raise the style, *periphrasis,* or circumlocution, is exceedingly rare in *Colin Clout,* being employed in only two instances. The first is the phraseology chosen by the

35. Pages 176-7.
36. Page 181.

speaker, Colin, to indicate that he had actually been in Elizabeth's presence: "since I saw that Angels blessed eie" (l. 40). In this case, the circumlocution permits Colin to avoid direct reference to a person greatly above him in rank and dignity. Thus, *periphrasis,* like *antonomasia,* is used to create aesthetic distance. The second instance is the *periphrasis* for Stesichorus:

> And well I wote that oft I heard it spoken,
> How one that fairest *Helene* did reuile,
> Through iudgement of the Gods to been ywroken
> Lost both his eyes and so remaynd long while. (ll. 919-22)

Here *periphrasis* acts to ennoble the language by bringing in an implied comparison between the shepherd and Stesichorus, a character connected with epic matter *par excellence*—that of Helen and of Troy.

Sententia, or the apothegmatic statement, is somewhat more common than *periphrasis,* though it must be conceded that the modern reader can easily overlook some aphorisms that Elizabethan readers recognized at once.[37] The gnomic figure is also more adaptable than *periphrasis* for the purpose of varying the stylistic level because it may be either learned or folkish in origin. Whatever the origin, however, *sententia* may be regarded as operating to elevate the tone. Something of this idea is contained in Erasmus' Preface to hs *Apophthegmata* (1531), where he says that "all these uniuersalle sorte of writyinges, as doe comprehende prouerbes, sage sentencies, and notable saiynges or actes, is moste fitte for Princes and noble menne".[38] The vogue of the commonplace books, which many compiled for themselves or had convenient access to in printed works like Erasmus' *Apophthegmata* or his earlier *Adagia,* testify to the value placed by men of Spenser's era on sententious materials as aids to wit.[39] Moreover, the tragedies of Seneca the Younger, abounding in quotable declarations, gave impressive classical sanction to the use of *sententiae* as an elevating

37. Cf. Morris Palmer Tilley, *A Dictionary of the Proverbs in England in the Sixteenth and Seventeenth Centuries* (Ann Arbor, 1940), p. v.

38. *The Apophthegmes of Erasmus,* trans. Nicolas Udall, from the edition of 1564, ed. Robert Roberts (Boston, 1877), p. xxii.

39. See William G. Crane, *Wit and Rhetoric in the Renaissance: The Formal Basis of Elizabethan Prose Style,* Columbia Univ. Studies in English and Comparative Literature, No. 129 (New York, 1937), Chs. II and III, for a discussion of commonplace books and the way in which they were utilized by men of the Renaissance as helps to composition.

device. In the *Apologie,* Sidney indirectly specifies the peculiar value Seneca possessed in the eyes of literary Londoners when he praises the English blood-and-thunder play *Gorboduc* for its "stately speeches and well sounding Phrases, clyming to the height of *Seneca* his stile, and as full of notable moralitie".[40] William Cornwallis' *Discourse upon Seneca the Tragedian* (1601) also reflects the strong interests of Elizabethan writers in the Stoic playwright's sententious line, which often took precedence over their interest in the tragedies themselves.[41]

In *Colin Clout,* gnomes with a vaguely bookish cast sometimes appear in the dialogue, as when Colin defends his reason for leaving the court to return "back to my sheep to tourne" (l. 672) rather than, "hauing learned repentance late, to mourne/Emongst those wretches which I there descryde" (ll. 674-5). The repentance reference is a slight turn of the proverb cited as "Repentance never comes too late" by Morris Palmer Tilley in *A Dictionary of the Proverbs in the Sixteenth and Seventeenth Centuries.*[42] Another example of proverbs appearing in the dialogue is the question by which Lucida seeks to excuse Rosalind's lack of reciprocity in love: "for who can loue compell?" (l. 914). This last truism receives more formal expression in the river myth passage earlier in the poem when Colin explains why Mulla refused to follow her father Mole's wish for her union with Allo: "For loue will not be drawne, but must be ledde" (l. 129). Tilley's entry for a series of quotations current in Spenser's time expressing the same idea is "Love cannot be compelled (forced).[43]

The foregoing examples of *sententiae* in the poem illustrate their customary office of raising the style. Owing to their currency in untutored language, proverbs were also available for the purpose of lowering the level of utterance. King James VI of Scotland, writing in *Ane Schort Treatise,* obviously has in mind the adaptability of proverbs for varying the style when, in a short section on "thrie speciall ornamentis to verse", he warns: "As for the *Prou-*

40. In *Eliz. Critical Essays,* I, 193-7.
41. *Discourses upon Seneca the Tragedian,* ed. Robert Hood Bowers (Gainesville, Fla., 1952), pp. iv-ix. For a full account of Seneca's influence on English letters, which, in opposition to Ciceronianism, was on the rise during the latter part of the sixteenth century, see Goerge Williamson, *The Senecan Amble* (Chicago, 1951).
42. Page 569, R80.
43. Page 395, L499.

erbis, they man be proper for the subiect". They must, he adds, be chosen on the same basis as comparisons. Of the latter, he had just specified that they ought to be "sa proper for the subiect that nather they be ouer bas, gif your subiect be heich, for then sould your subiect disgrace your *Comparisoun,* nather your *Comparisoun* be heich quhen your subiect is basse, for then sall your *Comparisoun* disgrace your subiect".[44] An outstanding example of the use of a proverb deliberately to debase the style occurs in the satirical passage in *Colin Clout* containing the most bitter denunciation of bad courtiers to be found in Spenser's poetry outside of *Mother Hubberds Tale* (1591):

> For each mans worth is measured by his weed,
> As harts by hornes, or asses by their eares. (ll. 711-12)

The proverbial nature of the "tailor-made man" concept is established by Tilley's numerous citations under the entry, "Apparel makes (Clothes make) the man".[45] While Tilley gives no proverb referring directly to horns as a distinguishing mark of the hart, he does cite the comparable byword of the Devil's being known by his horns.[46] There is no dearth of variations by sixteenth- and seventeenth-century writers on the theme that "An Ass is known by his ears".[47]

It remains true, nevertheless, that the customary effect of the *sententia* in *Colin Clout* is to confer dignity upon the places where it is used. Its contribution to this end is nowhere more clearly marked than in the miniature "Hymne in Honour of Love" near the end of the poem. Here the two lofty utterances of general truth combine *sententia* and another figure, *acclamatio,* the pithy restatement or summing up of preceding matter, to give added grandeur to the whole discourse:

> For beautie is the bayt which with delight
> Doth man allure,[48] for to enlarge his kynd.

44. Quotations from *Ane Schort Treatise,* in *Eliz. Critical Essays,* I, 219.
45. Page 16, A283.
46. Page 152, D252.
47. Page 20, A355.
48. Cf. Tilley, p. 28, B50, citations from Pettie, *A Petite Pallace of Pettie His Pleasure* (1576): "... he bit so greedily at the bait of her beauty, that he swallowed down the hook of hateful hurt"; also from Lyly, *Euphues, The Anatomy of Wit* (1578): "Beautie ... was a deceiptfull bayte with a deadly hooke".

. . . .

So loue is Lord of all the world by right
And rules the creatures by his powrfull saw.[49] (ll. 871-2; 883-4)

Acclamatio, without *sententia* but in combination with other figures, appears at intervals and elevates the style because of the stately and considered calm which it engenders. Note, for example, the following epitomizing declaration which Spenser has Colin make—a declaration of importance, moreover, since it helps clear away the apparent paradox in Colin's position : Why does a vicious element continue to exist in English court and society which otherwise are of such surpassing virtue and refinement? The answer is contained in the *acclamatio* :

For end, all good, all grace there freely growes,
Had people grace it gratefully to vse :
For God his gifts there plenteously bestowes,
But gracelesse men them greatly do abuse. (ll. 324-7)

The fact that Spenser's use of rhetorical figures in *Colin Clout* reflects on his part a conscious and deliberate control for clearly envisaged ends now seems evident. Spenser uses the figures to build up blocks of verse. This amplification, however, is not thereby necessarily mechanical or "unpoetic". Indeed, to let one example stand for many, one of the most admired passages of the entire poem, the charming river myth concerning the love of Mulla and Bregog (ll. 103-53) is a set piece embodying in the figure *topographia* the poet's imaginative conception. Spenser could have found numerous models in Boccaccio and in later Renaissance poets of Florence and Naples for the myth of locality.[50] Yet on this conventional pattern he has superimposed a story in which the actual physical environs of his Kilcolman estate, with meticulous accuracy of detail, are interwoven. This employment of the figures to fill out the matter of the poem is the first main use to which Spenser put rhetoric in *Colin Clout.* The second main use—to vary the style—has just been discussed. In general, Spenser

49. Cf. *ibid.,* p. 398, L527, citations from Wilmot *et al., Gismond* (1566-68): "Loue rules the world, Loue onely is the Lorde"; and from Wilmot, *Tancred and Gismond* (1591-92): "I . . . am that great God of Loue, who with high might ruleth the wast wide world, and liuing things".

50. Rudolph B. Gottfried, "Spenser and the Italian Myth of Locality", *SP,* XXXIV (1937), 111-14, 117-24.

applies the elevating power of rhetoric to maintain that studied level of tone and style which would not ascend too high for pastoral nor yet fall too low for the praise of noble persons and causes with which the poem is chiefly concerned.

I should like now to consider the most powerful of Spenser's three main overt uses of the figures—that of moving the affections or passions. The standard of the three styles is particularly relevant to a consideration of Spenser's reliance upon figures to "inueigle and appassionate the mind".[51] It is true that the doctrine of the styles was originally a concept applicable to oratory, but in an age like the Renaissance when men like Richard Stanyhurst could praise Virgil indifferently as a poet, an orator, or a philosopher,[52] the influence of rhetorical precept on poetic practice was bound to be immense. In the *Orator,* Cicero has a section describing the perfect orator and the highest eloquence. In it he comments that a poet deserves credit for seeking the virtues of the orator and that, despite the differences between the two arts of poetry and oratory, they are identical in the fact that both require discrimination in selection of subject matter and in choice of words. A large part of that discrimination, Cicero's subsequent discussion makes clear, lies in the ability of the man of eloquence to choose, control, and combine the three different styles, each of which has its particular forte. For each of the three aims—to prove, to please, and to sway—one style is most effective. The plain style is for proof, the middle style for pleasure, and the high style for persuasion. And of the three purposes, the last is the most important since, in the final analysis, the judge or deliberative body must be moved before it will accede to the pleas of the speaker.[53] Elsewhere in the same work Cicero relates the figures to stylistic levels by telling us that figures are used sparingly in the plain style, moderately in the middle style, and lavishly in the grand style.[54] Quintilian stresses, in the *Institutio Oratoria,* the efficacy of the intermediate and high styles for emotional persuasion. He distinguishes these styles from

51. Puttenham, p. 154. See Tuve, Ch. IX, for a valuable discussion concerning the way in which Renaissance notions of decorum and the styles affected the fashioning of figurative devices in poetic writing.

52. Dedication to *Thee First Foure Bookes of Virgil his Aeneis,* in *Eliz. Critical Essays,* I, 137.

53. Cicero, *Orator,* 67-70, Loeb Classical Library, trans. H. M. Hubbell, (Cambridge, Mass., 1939), pp. 354, 356.

54. *Ibid.,* 20-22, pp. 318, 320; 79-82, pp. 364, 366.

the low by their comparatively high proportion of ornamental devices. The pleader who uses the high style will, according to him, be able to call the dead to life, inspire anger or pity, and cause the listening judges to be swept impetuously from one emotion to another, as they weep and call upon the gods.[55]

The relevance of this kind of rhetorical teaching to which the Tudor scholar was almost continuously exposed in its application to poetry need hardly be labored. In connection with the three aims of eloquence, one should note in passing that they are considered complementary, not mutually exclusive. The Renaissance followed the classical writers in making no hard and fast distinction between feeling and intellect. Puttenham, for instance, emphasizes the inseparable nature of emotion and thought, in contradistinction to our modern dichotomy, in these words: 'For to say truely, what els is man but his minde? . . . He therefore that hath vanquished the minde of man, hath made the greatest and most glorious conquest. But the minde is not assailable vnlesse it be by sensible approches."[56] "Sensible", it need hardly be added, is employed in its usual sixteenth-century denotation of affecting the senses or passions.

As one might anticipate, the figures of principal import in helping achieve the aim of moving the passions are in the category of schemes of thought and amplification rather than of tropes—turns of a single word—or schemes of words only. Unlike similes, definitions, metaphors, and the like, these figures tend not to be definable by reference to common places or standard positions of argument. In Ramist manuals, therefore, most of them appear in the rhetorics rather than in the logics. This class of figures, which includes exclamations, moderations or revocations of exclamations (*epanorthosis*), apostrophe, and other fashionings largely in imitation of the spoken word, is called "figures of sentences" in *The Arcadian Rhetorike* of Abraham Fraunce. Fraunce recognizes the emotional force of this group in the paragraph introducing them: "now folow the figures in Sentences, which in the whole sente[*n*]ce expres some motion of the minde. These are more forcible & apt to perswade, than those of words, which be rather pleasant and fit to delight.

55. *The Institutio Oratoria of Quintilian,* xii,10.58-65, trans. H. E. Butler, Loeb ed. (London, 1922), IV, 482, 484, 486.

56. Page 197. See Tuve, pp. 166-75, 396-402, for a succinct discussion of Renaissance psychological theories, with particular reference to tropical language in poetry.

Generallie, as in tropes there is a certaine grace, in figures of words a kind of delicacie, so in these of sentences appeareth force and maiestie."[57] The schemes of thought and amplification that contribute so much to the emotive and dramatic effect of the poem are *exclamatio* or exclamation; *interrogatio* or rhetorical question; *pysma,* the extended form of *interrogatio; apostrophe* or direct address; and *synathroismus* or a "heaping up of many different things".[58] In stressing the emotive force of such figures as these, the Ramist rhetoricians were simply confirming what the older ones, following Cicero and Quintilian, had been saying all along. It is significant, for example, that the definitions of these figures from Susenbrotus, translated by Peacham, reflect the critics' awareness of the exclamatory quality of the particular figures, e.g., "Apostrophe, when we sodeinly forsake the former frame of our speach and goe to another";[59] "Pysma, when we aske often times together, and vse many questions in one place, whereby we do make the oration sharpe and vehement".[60] Collectively, these figures account in no small measure for the generally spirited tone of the entire poem, and as a result of their very frequent occurrence, constitute the leading means by which the emotions of friendship, love, and indignation are strongly imitated.

Though it is necessary to isolate the figures for the purpose of detailing their special office, it is not necessarily helpful to do so when one is attempting to show their cumulative force. Indeed, as the Table presented earlier shows, the figures seldom occur alone in Spenser; rather they frequently reinforce one another; and for key passages are often massed to make a triple assault, as it were, upon the reader or listener. This triple assault combines the possible effects envisaged by Puttenham in grouping all the figures into the three categories of auricular, "sensible", and sententious, that is, affecting the ear, mind, and all faculties respectively.[61] This massing is sometimes used to heighten the emotional quality even for passages of lesser importance. In the lines giving recognition to Alabaster, for instance, Spenser employs a combination of *exclamatio, interrogatio,* and *apostrophe* :

57. Page 63.
58. Rix, n., p. 52.
59. *Ibid.,* p. 41.
60. *Ibid.,* p. 39.
61. Pages 159-60.

Yet were he knowne to *Cynthia* as he ought,
His Eliseis would be redde anew.
Who liues that can match that heroick song,
Which he hath of that mightie Princesse made?
O dreaded Dread, do not thy selfe that wrong,
To let thy fame lie so in hidden shade:
But call it forth, O call him forth to thee,
To end thy glorie which he hath begun. (ll. 402-9)

There are three other cases of *apostrophe* in the same section on the poets. The figure, by reason of its purposeful abruptness, injects life into a passage which might otherwise lull the reader to sleep. Two of these invocations—those to Alcyon (ll. 388-91) and to Daniel (ll. 424-5)—are of lesser intensity. The third to Amyntas gains strength through being reinforced by *anaphora*, initial repetition, sometimes used, according to John Hoskins, to beat "upon one thing to cause the quicker feeling in the audience".[62]

Helpe, O ye shepheards helpe ye all in this.
Help *Amaryllis* this her losse to mourne. (ll. 436-7)

The poem closes, except for the completion of the narrative frame in the form of *chronographia* or description of the time of day, on the forceful and eloquent plea by Colin to his fellow-shepherds to witness his undying devotion to Rosalind:

And ye my fellow shepheardes which do see
And heare the languours of my too long dying,
Vnto the world for euer witnesse bee,
That hers I die, nought to the world denying,
This simple trophe of her great conquest. (ll. 947-51)

Interrogatio in the form of the rhetorical question is relatively abundant. At the conclusion of the first panegyric to Queen Elizabeth, Spenser has Colin exclaim:

Why then do I base shepheard bold and blind,
Presume the things so sacred to prophane? (ll. 348-9)

62. John Hoskins, *Directions for Speech and Style,* ed. Hoyt H. Hudson, Princeton Studies in English, No. 12 (Princeton, 1935), p. 13.

This figure has particularly incisive force in Colin's encomium to Love, where he poses the great crux: What is the secret force that attracts unlike elements to each other, causing them to unite and eventually to culminate in the creation of man?

> For how should else things so far from attone
> And so great enemies as of them bee,
> Be euer drawne together into one,
> And taught in such accordance to agree? (ll. 843-6)

With reference to the expanded form of *interrogatio,* there is only one passage employing *pysma,* a series of rhetorical questions. It is the comment by Lucida, one of the interlocutors, in response to Hobbinol's snide remark about how poorly women have requited Colin for stating the cause of love so well:

> But who can tell what cause had that faire Mayd
> To vse him so that vsed her so well:
> Or who with blame can iustly her vpbrayd,
> For louing not? for who can loue compell? (ll. 911-14)

The employment by Spenser of *synathroismus,* or congeries, aptly called the "heaping figure" by Puttenham,[63] to stimulate emotion can be well illustrated by the passage in which Colin characterizes England by contrasting it with Ireland. In England

> No wayling there nor wretchednesse is heard,
> No bloodie issues nor no leprosies,
> No griesly famine, nor no raging sweard,
> No nightly bodrags, nor no hue and cries;
> The shepheards there abroad may safely lie,
> On hills and downes, withouten dread or daunger:
> No rauenous wolues the good mans hope destroy,
> No outlawes fell affray the forest raunger. (ll. 312-19)

While some of the sense of excitement in this passage derives from the verbs, particularly the active participles, the repetitive insistence that in England no factors exist which are disruptive of peace and harmony compels attention and conviction. *Anaphora,* iteration of

63. Page 236.

the same sound at the beginning of successive lines, and *paroemion,* consonantal alliteration, help reinforce the sense. *Synathroismus* is also one important element of the rhetorically-rich passage in which Colin ecstatically expresses his chivalric devotion to his mistress:

> To her my thoughts I daily dedicate,
> To her my heart I nightly martyrize;
> To her my loue I lowly do prostrate,
> To her my life I wholly sacrifice:
> My thought, my heart, my loue, my life is shee. (ll. 472-6)

Here again, the insistent repetition, underscored by *anaphora* and alliteration and climaxed by *acclamatio,* takes on extraordinary passional force.

The foregoing account of the figures considers them as comprising all the linguistic patterns to which names are assigned in rhetorical manuals of the Renaissance. At the same time it takes cognizance of the fact that these patterns are by no means formulations distinctive to that period. The discussion attempts to set forth the main ways in which the figures are consciously used in one important poem of the high Renaissance in England for what we can be almost certain were ends predetermined by the poet. To recapitulate, the three main groupings of figures, conceived in terms of their special functions in *Colin Clout,* are: to furnish details of the matter, to give variety and elevation to the style, and to generate affective power at important junctures. To particularize the functional efficacy of the figures of rhetoric is not, again, to denigrate their aesthetic contribution. Poets of the Renaissance found it exhilarating to experiment with fashioning in the vernacular figurative formations which they had been taught to admire in Isocrates, Cicero, Virgil, Ovid, and Seneca. Readers of the time took frank delight in the figures as leading resources in providing the formal beauty of design which they deemed essential to a good poem. That delight was enhanced for those readers when the poet displayed logical aptness in turning up places and figures, which in many cases amounted to the same thing. This chapter reveals something of the part that internal pressure played in shaping outward expression—in producing a style nicely toned and modulated to changes in subject, person, and circumstances by the studied application of figures. It conveys how important the figures are to the texture and the architecture of *Colin Clout.* In this sense, they tend to exemplify the aesthetic principle enunciated elsewhere by Spenser in these lines:

> That Beautie is not, as fond men misdeeme,
> An outward shewe of things, that onely seeme;
>
> For of the soule the bodie forme doth take.[64]

64. *An Hymne in Honour of Beautie,* 11. 90-1, *Works,* VII, 206, and 1. 132, p. 207.

CHAPTER III

THE DICTION AND VERSIFICATION

Studies of the present century on Spenser's poetic diction tend to agree that Spenser's vocabulary, even in *The Shepheardes Calender,* which is avowedly experimental in language,[1] is considerably less anomalous than some of his contemporaries, notably Sidney[2] and Jonson,[3] indicate. These studies also concur in the judgment that the strictures of nineteenth century philologists on the supposedly unlawful liberties Spenser took with the mother tongue have to be greatly mitigated or completely withdrawn.[4] But when present-day scholars descend to particulars and attempt to classify words, phrases, and other linguistic elements as archaisms, dialect words, coinages, borrowings, variations, adoptions, and compounds, they frequently find themselves at variance. This lack of unanimity extends, to a lesser degree, to the explanation in a given case of such artificial elements in the vocabulary.

In his comprehensive study concerning two classes of Spenser's diction, archaisms and innovations, Bruce R. McElderry, Jr., suggests the difficulty of ascertaining with precision what words Spenser's readers would have regarded as "old" or "new" in light of the fact that the sixteenth century was a period of great linguistic change.[5] Other students of literary diction in the Renaissance in England similarly emphasize the unsettled state of vocabulary,

1. Dedicatory Epistle to the *Shepheardes Calender, Works,* VII, 7-9.
2. *An Apologie for Poetrie,* in *Eliz. Critical Essays,* I, 196.
3. *Timber, or Discoveries, Ben Jonson,* eds. C. H. Herford, Percy and Evelyn Simpson (Oxford, 1947), VIII, 618.
4. See Bruce Robert McElderry, Jr., "Archaism and Innovation in Spenser's Poetic Diction", *PMLA,* XLVII (1932), 144-5 and notes, for a summary of trends in critical thinking on Spenser's choice of words, together with references to specific studies on the subject. To McElderry's list of present-day scholars who share his view that there are definite limits to the degree of freedom that Spenser took with the language, should be added C. L. Wrenn, "On Re-reading Spenser's *Shepheardes Calender", Essays and Studies,* XXIX (1943), 43-4; and Veré L. Rubel, *Poetic Diction in the English Renaissance,* p. 271.
5. Page 145.

orthography, syntax, and grammar during the sixteenth century.[6] The absence of a fixed norm by which departures from a standard can be determined constitutes an omnipresent source of difficulty with respect to placing Spenser's words in categories. Even when sufficient reasons can be adduced for assigning a particular locution to a certain class of diction, the central problem for criticism of explaining the use of the given category remains to be dealt with. Nor is it satisfactory to assume, as some commentators seem to do, that generalizations found valid for any particular class in *The Shepheardes Calender* or *The Faerie Queene* will necessarily fit all the poems in which the category occurs.

As regards *Colin Clout,* the first difficulty—that of identifying particular locutions as belonging to definite categories, such as archaisms, dialect words, adoptions, and the like—can be overcome, to a reasonably large extent, by taking as raw data, subject, of course, to further inquiry, the locutions and constructions occurring in *Colin Clout* that are presented in a number of apposite modern studies. Assembling these data from the works of linguistic specialists who use them for widely different ends, and reducing them to a single frame of reference are considerable tasks, but they are an indispensable preliminary to overcoming the second main difficulty mentioned above—that of elucidating for *Colin Clout* alone Spenser's use of individual categories of specialized diction or construction. The numerous studies of the past half century dealing with linguistic aspects of Spenser's poetry are of little or no direct help in the accomplishment of this purpose, for at present there is extant no single book, chapter thereof, or article which has to do specifically with the language of *Colin Clout.* Nor is there any single source treating *per se* any major aspect of that diction for the poem. However, some of the more authoritative studies of a general nature can be of much indirect assistance, for they frequently contain basic material identifying and classifying elements of Spenser's diction which are common to many poems, including *Colin Clout.* In what follows, I have drawn freely upon this vein in order to make its ore yield a more commodious product—that is, in terms of elucidating the verbal art underlying the present poem. In adapting this material, to the extent practicable, to *Colin*

6. E.g., George Gordon, "Shakespeare's English", *S.P.E. Tract No. XXIX* (1928), pp. 257-9; Bernard Groom, "Some Kinds of Poetic Diction", *Essays and Studies,* XV (1929), 157-60; and Puttenham, *Arte of English Poesie,* eds. Willcock and Walker, pp. lxxxvi, xciii.

Clout, I essay, when circumstances warrant, to fill in lacunae and resolve contradictions in the earlier generalized coverage.

With the foregoing paragraphs sketching the approach to be used in this chapter to the problem of poetic language, it is now possible to proceed to examine the nature of specialized diction in *Colin Clout,* to explain the handling of the common stock of words and phrases, to probe the influence exerted on diction by the demands of the cross-rhymed iambic quatrain, and to explore the ways in which this reciprocal relationship carries over into details of the prosody and helps shape the character of the work.

In general, except for the abundance and multiformity of rhetorical figures—extremely important, as we have seen, in raising the level above that of ordinary discourse—*Colin Clout* is couched in language that is only moderately mannered. The poem does not hold to a uniform tenor of speaking, but contains a variety of styles. In this respect, Spenser had good classical sanction from no less an authority than Cicero. In a passage of the *Orator,* a treatise largely devoted to *elocutio,* Tully claims for oratory the same right to combine and vary the styles, even within a given selection, as he believes poetry freely exercises in the works of such masters of the epic as Homer and Ennius.[7] The choice of style in each case, according to Cicero's view, would depend upon the author's conception of the nature of the subject as being "parva", "modica", or "magna".[8] Puttenham, who like Spenser was thoroughly versed in classical literary theory, adopts the precepts of the ancients concerning oratory in arguing for the freedom of poets to vary the style in accordance with the topic under treatment. He expressly claims this privilege for pastoral, which was traditionally considered base in its "owne proper nature".[9] His understanding of the matter is expressed in these words : "for neither is all that may be written of Kings and Princes such as ought to keepe a high stile, nor all that may be written vpon a shepheard to keepe the low, but according to the matter reported, if that be of high or base nature".[10] A similar principle of appropriateness to the "matter reported" seems to have guided Spenser in casting *Colin Clout.* While the poem has no single homogeneous style, its predominant mode is that of the familiar, toned or raised, in conformity with the demands of con-

7. *Orator,* 100-9, trans. H. M. Hubbell, pp. 378-86.
8. *Ibid.,* 101, p. 378.
9. Page 150.
10. Page 151.

gruity, by a careful use of ordinary literary language and by the employment of a distinctive vocabulary.

One significant element of this distinctive vocabulary is the conscious use of archaisms to set the tone by giving the poem a slight flavor of rusticity. Archaic expressions are sprinkled throughout the poem. Even so, the archaic flavor is undoubtedly more pronounced for the modern reader than it was for the reader of the original printed version of 1595. As McElderry points out, speaking generally of Spenser's poetic output, many of the words which have a strongly archaic tinge for us were quite familiar and current among Spenser's first readers. Some of these words are *areed* (explain, deem, ll. 15, 565), *cleped* (call, l. 113), *mo* (more, ll. 261, 448, 576), *spill* (destroy, ll. 151, 814), and *wyte, wyten* (blame, ll. 747, 916).[11] McElderry also comments on the effect of archaism created by Spenser's general tendency to use inverted sentence order excessively. He instances one stanza of *The Faerie Queene* (IV.i.2) showing seven such inversions; all of these, McElderry feels, can hardly be explainable in a versifier as skillful as Spenser on grounds of metrical accommodation.[12] No previously published studies exist dealing with inversions in *Colin Clout.* In the first three hundred lines of this poem, I have found forty-six cases of inversion. Of these, all but eight are of the object-verb type; the eight are instances of the reversal of normal order of adjective followed by noun, subject followed by verb, and verb followed by object of the preposition. This relative frequency of inversions for the first three hundred lines is representative of the entire poem. Even though there are numerous short inversions, there are no extended involutions of the type Milton so frequently employs in *Paradise Lost.* One can safely conclude that the frequent shifts from prose order in *Colin Clout* occasioned no special notice on the part of the educated sixteenth-century reader. For the modern reader, less likely to be accustomed to the comparative flexibility of word order in highly inflected languages like Latin and Greek, the inversions in *Colin Clout* may make the language seem rather indirect and consequently quite archaic. But the pastoral setting itself probably suggests to today's reader the "far away and long ago" to a greater extent than it did to the reader of predominantly rural England and Ireland of the late Tudor period.

11. McElderry, pp. 146, 148, 157.
12. *Ibid.,* p. 158.

In considering the question of the nature and degree of archaism in the language of *Colin Clout,* one recalls the caveat enunciated by C. L. Wrenn when he gave attention to the same topic concerning *The Shepheardes Calender.* "It is," he asserts, "extremely difficult to be sure what was, and what was not, an archaism in Spenser's time in the absence of a complete Elizabethan *Thesaurus* which could be used beside the *O.E.D.*"[13] Because the matter is as important as it is delicate, and because the criticism is complicated by the lack of a clear-cut definition for the term *archaism,* a brief review of this scholarship, where it is applicable to *Colin Clout,* will help clarify part of the process which led me to the following conclusions about archaism in the poem : There exists in *Colin Clout* a sufficient number of words and usages that must have been non-current to the readers of the day to justify the assertion that Spenser intended the poem to have a slightly archaic quality. The archaisms were included, not to enrich the vocabulary, but to enhance the pastoral motif by reason of their connotative value. (That archaisms, along with other elements of specialized diction, fulfil an ancillary function in helping solve technical problems of verse composition will be made amply evident in the latter part of this chapter, which takes up versification.)

The earliest detailed study of the archaic content of Spenser's diction, that by Roscoe E. Parker, "Spenser's Language and the Pastoral Tradition",[14] compares the *February* eclogue (containing the moral fable about the Oak and the Briar) of *The Shepheardes Calender,* the first book of *The Faerie Queene,* and the first two hundred lines of *Colin Clout.* Parker finds the respective ratios of archaism as follows : one to thirty-one (3.19 per cent), one to about one hundred and twenty-three (.81 per cent), and one to ninety-one (1.1 per cent). Considering these three specimens as examples of early, middle, and late periods of Spenser's poetic writings, Parker concludes that "Spenser's pastoral poetry is purposely more archaic than his non-pastoral poetry".[15] Although Parker does not give the basis for assigning a word or form to the archaic category, he states in a footnote that in his lists he has"tried . . . to include all words which would appear archaic to an educated contemporary and to exclude such as would not".[16] Of the three archaic forms

13. "On Re-reading Spenser's *Shepheardes Calender*", p. 41.
14. *Language,* I (1925), 80-7.
15. *Ibid.,* p. 87.
16. *Ibid.,* p. 86.

and fourteen archaic words and meanings listed by Parker for the first two hundred lines of *Colin Clout,* only two, the archaism of the prefix *y-* retained in the participles *ycleepe* (call, l. 65) and *yshrilled* (sounded, rang out, l. 62) would be admitted to the category of archaisms set forth by Bruce R. McElderry in his essay, "Archaism and Innovation in Spenser's Poetic Diction". The criteria for archaisms are there stated as follows: "It seems reasonable to say that a word was not archaic to Spenser's contemporaries if *O.E.D.* gives, well scattered through this period [1500-1650], ten to fifteen quotations for it, some of them from well-known authors, and most of them in contexts where deliberate archaism would be unlikely".[17] Of Parker's "archaic words and meanings", McElderry, who, incidentally does not refer to the Parker study, calls *singulfs* (sobs, l. 168) and *aemuled* (emulated, l. 73) borrowings from other languages.[18] *Needments* (necessaries, l. 195) and *listfull* (attentive, l. 7) McElderry classifies as variant forms. Since these words have their first citation in the *Oxford English Dictionary* from Spenser, it is difficult to see how they could be classified by Parker as archaisms. Parker's *sith* (time, l. 19) [*sith* in l. 30 means "since", not "time", as Parker has it] and *sythe* (time, l. 23) would be eliminated under McElderry's criteria since the word occurs between 1500 and 1650 twenty-seven times.[19] Still another Parker archaism—*atweene* (in between, l. 81)—McElderry terms a dialect word.[20] The six remaining terms given by Parker are not referred to in McElderry's article, but since McElderry professes to list all the archaisms, presumably he would not admit them either.

The most recent work enumerating archaic terms and other specialized diction is Veré L. Rubel, *Poetic Diction in the English Renaissance,* Chapter XIII, "Spenser's Poetic Diction". With reference to *Colin Clout,* Miss Rubel states: "Much of the archaic effect is achieved rather from orthography and syntax than from the actual diction. For example, there are only five instances of the *y*-prefix in the poem—three of them, however, in markedly archaic words: *yshrilled* [l. 62], *ycleepe* [l. 65], *yrapt* [l. 623], *ybore* (pa. pple.) [l. 839], *ywroken* [l. 921]. The other conspicuous archaisms are *areed* [l. 15], *cleped* [l. 113], *fon* [l. 292], *wone* (dwell) [l. 307], *weet* [l. 927], *woxen* [l. 380], *wyte* [l. 747], and *to wyten* [l. 916], and the four variants *cond* [l. 74], *kend*

17. Page 147.
18. Page 162.
19. Page 148.
20. Page 150.

[l. 272], *kon* [l. 294], and *vnkend* [l. 294]."[21] Miss Rubel does not elaborate on her remark that much of the archaic effect is achieved from orthography and syntax rather than from actual diction, nor, like Parker, does she define her criteria for the inclusion of terms as archaisms. One might, however, infer from her fairly frequent references in the footnotes to Speght's edition of Chaucer (1598) that she accepts all words glossed by Speght as archaisms.

The *y-* formations are conceded by McElderry to be archaisms, although his comment on them (along with the inflectional *-en*, not found in *Colin Clout*) is significant: "It is very difficult to tell how far these forms were felt to be archaic by Spenser's first readers: certainly they did not much obscure his text".[22] Of the verbs mentioned by Miss Rubel, McElderry includes *wroke(n)*,[23] but specifically excludes *clepe*, grouping it with words that "we tend to read into them an archaism not there when Spenser used them".[24] The *Oxford English Dictionary* comments on the frequent occurrences of this verb during the sixteenth century. The three other verbs, surprisingly enough, are not included by McElderry in his lists of archaisms, though he states that he made a "pretty thorough check of the Concordance against *O.E.D.*",[25] for they conform to his test of having less than ten quotations in that dictionary during the period 1500-1650: *shrill* (sound shrilly), two quotations; *rapt* (deeply engaged in a feeling), two quotations; and *bore* (be born), none.

Of the group of "conspicuous archaisms" given by Miss Rubel, McElderry would not have allowed *areed* (explain, deem) and *cleped* (call),[26] *wyte* and *to wyten* (blame).[27] He would have admitted *fon* (fool)[28] and *wone* (dwell).[29] In his article McElderry does not allude to any of the four variants of the verb *ken* (know), but he does include the present tense form *con* as an

21. Pages 257-8.
22. Page 157.
23. Page 152.
24. Page 157.
25. Page 153.
26. Page 157.
27. Page 148.
28. Page 151.
29. Page 152.

archaism[30] and calls the infinitive form itself a dialect word.[31] For the two verbs not noted at all by McElderry—*weet* (know) and *woxen* (increased in years)—there are nine quotations in the *Oxford English Dictionary* for the former and only one for the latter. The *Dictionary* comments on *weet* as follows: "From the middle of the 16th c., if not earlier, the form *weet* seems to be obsolete in ordinary speech, but down to the second decade of the 17th c. it was frequent as a literary archaism (chiefly poet.) and is attributed in the drama to rustic speakers". *Woxen,* the past participle of the verb *wax* (grow), is the strong form of the verb which the *Oxford English Dictionary* says became weak in late Middle English. Accordingly, it should be considered archaic.

Using the term archaism to mean forms and meanings that were quaint to Spenser's readers and reconciling the disputed cases, one finds, then, among the archaisms in *Colin Clout,* first the *y-* prefix words: *y'bore* (born, l. 839), *ycleepe* (call, l. 65), *yrapt* (deeply engaged in a feeling, l. 623), *yshrilled* (sounded shrilly, l. 62), and *ywroken* (avenged, l. 921). Except for *ycleepe,* the words themselves were distinctly rare in Spenser's time. E.K., in his Gloss to *The Shepheardes Calender,* calls the *y-* "a poeticall addition".[32] Despite its well-established literary use,[33] the *y-* prefix construction did give the poem a rather unobtrusive touch of remoteness, which the rather unusual words enhanced. A similar charm of rustic remoteness was afforded by *fon* (fool, l. 292), applied by Colin to Cuddy as a term of affectionate rebuke, and *wone* (remain, live, l. 307). The form *woxen* (grown in years, l. 380), the strong form of which verb (*wax*) being already weak in late Middle English, as we have seen, must be considered archaic, as also must the use of the adjective *bright* as a noun in line 46.[34] Two other words—

30. Page 152.
31. Page 150.
32. *Works,* VII, 45.
33. In mentioning the writing of *ydone* for *done* in a series of common examples of poetic licence, George Gascoigne seems to imply that the *y-* formation with the past participle, though characteristic of the English language at an earlier stage, is not a true archaism if the verb itself is current (*Certayne Notes of Instruction* [1575], in *Eliz. Critical Essays,* I, 53-4). Gabriel Harvey comments in a marginal note following this passage in a Bodleian text of Gascoigne's treatise: "All theise in Spenser and manie like: but with discretion: & tolerably, though sumtime not greatly commendably" (*ibid.,* Notes, p. 361).
34. *Daphnaïda,* p. 183. Renwick calls the use "archaistic" and says it was commoner in old Scots poetry than in English.

hight[35] (to call oneself, be called, have or bear the name, ll. 15, 65, 81, 104, 108, 117, 118, 123, 173, 234, 456) and *ken* (know) with four variant forms, *cond* (l. 74), *kend* (l. 272), *kon* and *vnkend* (l. 294)—complete the list of archaisms.

Five of the eleven uses of *hight* occur in the tale of the Bregog and the Mulla (ll. 104-55), a set piece of *topographia* or topographical myth. *Kon* and its antonym *vnkend* in line 294 facilitate the rhetorical figure *polyptoton* or *traductio,* a play on a word obtained by repeating it in different forms.

When the archaisms of *Colin Clout* are taken as a whole, two conclusions about them emerge: they are so infrequent as to be no more than a coloration; and they are of such nature that they would not have interfered with the fluency and intelligibility of reading. Aside from the existence of kindred forms and meanings in current use during the late sixteenth century, the contexts in which the archaisms appear allow little possibility of their being misunderstood.

Closely related to archaisms in their function of affording a vaguely rustic or quaint element to the tone are dialect words. However, on the authority of McElderry, dialect is non-existent in *Colin Clout,* with the exception of *atweene* (between, l. 81),[36] but the deliberate use of the word as dialect is not very probable. Another scholar lists the words *betweene—atweene—atwixt—twixt* as variant forms at Spenser's disposal.[37]

Of a third class of specialized words in Spenser—coinages—there are no representatives in *Colin Clout.* The word-making faculty that gave to the language such striking neologisms as *Blatant* and *Braggadochio* was not brought into play for *Colin Clout.* It is true that one student of Spenserian linguistics considers as virtual coinages from foreign sources the words *gallantry, indignifie, paravant* and *singulfs,*[38] which McElderry, in his more rigid definition of coinages as "words known to *O.E.D.* first in Spenser which are unhistorical in development or uncertain in origin",[39]

35. The word is not glossed by E.K. in the *Shepheardes Calender,* where it occurs once (*December,* l. 3) in the sense of "was named", but is listed as archaic by McElderry (p. 160).

36. McElderry, p. 150.

37. Rubel, p. 234.

38. Frederick M. Padelford, "Aspects of Spenser's Vocabulary", *PQ,* XX (1941), 281.

39. Page 161.

calls borrowings or variations. McElderry makes a strong case for excluding these words as coinages in the statement: "In a century when language was changing as much as in the sixteenth century it seems unreasonable to apply the term *coinage* to words for which Spenser merely made a natural extension of meaning or adaptation of form".[40]

Colin Clout, not being experimental in language, has, as already noted, no real coinages, but it does contain a fairly large number of borrowings, variations, and adoptions. These are McElderry's terms. According to his definitions, borrowings are words of direct foreign origin, not found according to the *Oxford English Dictionary* earlier than Spenser. Variations are words slightly altered from current words in form and meaning. Variations are of two kinds: those words which the *Oxford English Dictionary* notes as first occurring in Spenser; and those words known to have been used once or twice within thirty years or so prior to Spenser's first use. This latter group McElderry calls adoptions.

The borrowed words in *Colin Clout* are *aemuling—aemuled* (imitating, imitated, ll. 72, 73), *paravant* (pre-eminently, l. 941), and *singulfs* (sobs, l. 168). Miss Rubel, like Padelford, lists *singulfs* and *aemuling—aemuled* as Spenser's own formations, that is, coinages. However, since they are neither "unhistorical in development or uncertain in origin", it is perhaps more accurate to adhere to McElderry's more logical classification. *Paravant,* according to the *Oxford English Dictionary,* is from Old French *paravant,* an adverb and a preposition meaning "before" in time and place. This *Dictionary* holds *singulfs* to be a misprint of "singults" from the Latin *singultus* (sob). However, as Miss Rubel points out, it was an "error" repeated three times in three other publications.[41] She concludes that the word is "either a misprint of a borrowing from the Latin *singultus* or Spenser's adaption of it".[42]

Variations, that is, variant forms of current words known first to be used by Spenser, are a numerous and important group in *Colin Clout.* With respect to form they are: *blandishment* (l. 671), *fleecie* (l. 606), *gallantry* (gallants collectively, l. 729), *indignifie* (dishonor, l. 583), *listfull* (attentive, l. 7), *needments* (l. 195), *rewardfull* (l. 187). With respect to meaning, variations are:

40. Page 161.
41. Page 227, n.
42. Page 258, n.

charming (playing a musical instrument, l. 5), *neighbor* (adj., nearby, l. 122),[43] *oaten* (ll. 5, 13, 194, 360, 441), *read* (see, ll. 279, 336), and *trophe* (memorial, l. 951). To these should be added a variant noted by Padelford, the word *insolence*[44] (l. 622), used in the sense of "exultation" rather than of "pride", the more usual sense.

The last general class of innovations to be considered are adoptions, that is, variations in current words not original with Spenser but known to have been used once or twice within thirty years or so prior to Spenser's time. In this class one finds the form *cooly* (adj., cool, l. 58) but not the *-y* adjective *soly* (l. 801). *Soly* is probably not included in McElderry's list of adoptions[45] because one can find nine quotations in the *Oxford English Dictionary* for it (with variant spellings) in the "test period", as contrasted with only two for *cooly*. Miss Rubel, on the other hand, mentions the two *-y* adjectives in connection with her discussion of archaisms in *Colin Clout.*[46] There are two additional adoptions—*bodrags* (raids, l. 315), and *direfull* (l. 202). *Bodrags* is held by the *Oxford English Dictionary* to be of Irish origin, and Renwick seems to confirm this finding by his statement that the word is common among the Irish State papers of the period.[47]

Speaking generally of the innovations found in *Colin Clout,* one can conclude that they comprise a relatively small part of the vocabulary, which is fairly conventional on the whole. The new words are in no sense freakish or licentious, but tend to fall into three groups, all of which are typical of other words being brought into the language at this time: imaginative derivations from classical or Romance languages, like *aemuled, paravant, indignifie, gallantry;* creations by additions of common suffixes, like *blandishment, needment, listfull, direfull;* or originations by extension of meaning, like *charming, trophe,* and *read.* Like the archaisms, the innovations are seldom obscure—only a little strange.

Unlike the archaisms, the new words are used, not to set the tone, but to enrich the language, to provide a word that will fill a felt need, whether that need be metrical accommodation, rhetorical

43. Originally glossed by E.K. in the *Shepheardes Calender, Works,* VII, 18.
44. Page 282.
45. Page 165.
46. Page 258.
47. *Daphnaïda,* p. 186.

force, or semantic precision. The innovations include words that would hardly be known to the shepherds who use them, but as Renwick emphasizes: "Spenser was not trying to write realistic poems either about or for shepherds . . . half the point of the business is just that these shepherds were not real shepherds, but poets and scholars and bishops, and even a queen was among them, so that learned words, though unsuitable to the supposed persons, were quite in keeping with the real, as they were with the subjects of the poems, with the kind, and with the audience to whom they were addressed".[48] Although Renwick makes these remarks about the language of *The Shepheardes Calender,* they apply equally well to *Colin Clout,* with the slight exception that none of the "shepheards" in *Colin Clout* were bishops.

Many of the innovations represent lengthening of words by means of prefixes and suffixes and the very sounds of the syllables *em-, -and, -full,* and *-ment* lend themselves to smooth rhythmical effects. In general, the innovations share with many words of conventional diction the function of adding rhythmic weight, rhetorical emphasis, and stylistic elevation to a fundamentally serious poem. *Bodrags* and *singulfs,* for example, though perhaps in their strangeness among the most exceptionable of the innovations, nevertheless contribute, with their gutturals, unmistakable force to the important passages in which they appear.

The compounds, another element of diction employed in *Colin Clout,* as elsewhere in Spenser, for a special artistic effect, furnish linguistic enrichment to the poem. In common with the innovations, the compounds impart vigor to the style and rhythmic weight to the sound. The rather small number of compounds employed as compared to certain other poems is another indication of the relatively unaffected diction of *Colin Clout.* According to the frequency table compiled by Padelford and Maxwell, the poem contains one compound to every eighty-seven lines, a small proportion in comparison with *Muiopotomos,* which has one compound word to every twenty-two lines, or with the *Hymnes,* which average one to every forty-two lines.[49]

The article by Padelford and Maxwell lists for *Colin Clout* the following compounds which the poet either coined outright or

48. W. L. Renwick, *Edmund Spenser: An Essay on Renaissance Poetry* (London, 1925), p. 77. This work will henceforth be cited as *Essay.*

49. Frederick M. Padelford and William C. Maxwell, "The Compound Words in Spenser's Poetry", *JEGP,* XXV (1926), 506.

"employed for a conscious poetic effect" : verbal adjectives—*bright shining* beams (l. 518), *deawy dropping* beard (l. 250), *high aspiring* thought (l. 612), *life giuing* light (l. 861), *well deemed* name (l. 695), and *well tuned* song (l. 418); nouns—*fellow shepheardes* (l. 947) and *self-regarde* (l. 682).[50] Compounds excluded by the authors from the main list on the ground that they are commonly used are all nouns : *landheards* (l. 277), *shepheard swaines* (l. 6), *Turtle Doue* (l. 865), *water course* (l. 109), and *water-courses* (l. 151).[51]

With respect to Spenser's compounds in general, Padelford and Maxwell hold : "Judged by the severe standards of certain later poets, such as Keats, Tennyson, and Rossetti, the greater part of them seem rather tame and colorless".[52] Padelford and Maxwell feel, nevertheless, that "to the sixteenth-century reader, less accustomed to such diction and freshly conscious of a renaissance of word-building, they must have seemed much more precious".[53] Bernard Groom, however, in "The Formation and Use of Compound Epithets in English Poetry from 1579", contends that "to stimulate the reader's pictorial imagination is not the usual or typical effect of Spenser's compound epithets".[54] With reference particularly to *The Faerie Queene,* Groom concludes that Spenser "seems, on the contrary, to use them with two main intentions of a different kind—to heighten the emotion or fervency of a passage, and to 'swell out' a line with resonant polysyllables".[55] This intention is equally applicable to Spenser's use of compounds in *Colin Clout,* particularly with reference to the verbal adjectives, although graphic power can hardly be denied to "deawy dropping beard". The epithets "high aspiring thought", coming at the conclusion of the rich passage in praise of Cynthia, and "life giuing light", referring to the personified sun's creative power in the glorification of Love passage, are good examples of compounds that help raise the pitch of certain sections to their desired intensity. On the other hand, the substantival compounds like "self-regard" and "shepheard swaine" have no special significance beyond enriching the

50. *Ibid.,* pp. 499-503.
51. *Ibid.,* pp. 503-4.
52. *Ibid.,* p. 509.
53. *Ibid.*
54. *S.P.E. Tract No. XLIX* (1937), p. 299.
55. *Ibid.*

vocabulary, which, according to Groom, was considered at the time to have suffered from an excess of monosyllables.[56]

The specialized diction in *Colin Clout* has been given detailed attention because it represents collectively a significant part of the poem's total vocabulary and because its close study opens an avenue to an understanding of the poem. Examination of this diction, moreover, reveals the degree to which Spenser, a disciplined literary craftsman, drew upon for the purposes of this poem a great variety of legitimate resources, native and foreign, in order to have available a vocabulary of adequate richness, breadth, and flexibility.

But the deep concern which scholars and critics have justly manifested in uniquely Spenserian diction ought not to cause us to neglect the choice and use of words which Spenser shared with his fellow writers. That choice in *Colin Clout,* along with versification, has resulted in a poem notable for a combination of popular and learned phrases into a style which is fluent, direct and clear.

It is remarked in the preceding chapter that Spenser's apology for the poem's "meanesse of stile" must be taken with reservation and in a relative sense only to indicate that the decorum of the pastoral disguise necessitated some words of homely use. Actually, the greater part of the vocabulary is, in Renwick's phrase, "courtly Southern English"[57]—for the most part, elevated and polysyllabic.

The introductory speech of Hobbinol, while not especially rustic, nevertheless stands apart from the rest of the poem in being largely monosyllabic. The paucity of light syllables, plus the preponder-

56. *Ibid.* George Gascoigne, however, is among those older contemporaries of Spenser who felt that the abundance of monosyllables in English is an asset. His recommendation for their copious use in poetry is based on two highly questionable propositions: one, that "the most auncient English wordes are of one sillable, so that the more monasyllables that you vse the truer Englishman you shall seeme"; and, two, that "wordes of many syllables do cloye a verse and make it vnpleasant, whereas woordes of one syllable will more easily fall to be shorte [i.e., accented] or long [unaccented] as occasion requireth, or wilbe adapted to become circumflexe or of an indifferent sounde" (*Certayne Notes of Instruction,* in *Eliz. Critical Essays,* I, 51). Judging by his practice in *Colin Clout,* one can be reasonably certain that Spenser would have been inclined to agree, not with Gascoigne, but with the anonymous annotator who wrote the following comment alongside the above-quoted passage from *Certayne Notes* in the Bodleian copy of the text: "*Non placet.* A greater grace and maiesty in longer wordes, so they be current Inglish" (*ibid.,* Notes, p. 360).

57. *Essay,* p. 84.

ance of long vowels in accented positions, noticeably slows down the tempo, which elsewhere in the poem is moderately rapid. The appropriateness of the diction to the sadness of the emotion represented hardly requires comment.

The remarkable lucidity of the poem is to some extent due to the simplicity of the syntax. One critic summarizes the stylistic differences between Spenser and Shakespeare as follows : "But in general we may say that Spenser exemplifies the direct, logical statement of the narrative tradition going back to Chaucer and enriched by Ariosto and Tasso; Shakespeare the oblique statement, the double or triple meaning, the elliptical phrase of drama".[58] The contribution made to clarity by a singularly apt choice of words from those in common currency has not been remarked upon. Aside from two rather minor instances (ll. 322 and 659),[59] there is no place in the poem where Spenser's phraseology gives rise to obscurity. Particularly noteworthy in *Colin Clout* is Spenser's practice of choosing judiciously words of vivid particularity and those of expansive abstractness. This practice makes both for clarity and interest sustained by variety. The passages which are especially concrete and circumstantial in their language are the myth of Mulla and Bregog (ll. 92-155), the narrative of the voyage (ll. 196-289), the indirect description of Ireland in terms of evils not present in England (ll. 312-19), and the account of the abuses at court (ll. 660-794). The contrasting passages are the long section of tribute to the poets and ladies at court (ll. 485-583), the paeans to the Queen (ll. 332-52, 590-615, 620-47), and the passage on Venus and Cupid (ll. 783-822). These units of strongly emotive connotation abound in abstract words and phrases, often from the learned vocabulary of courtly love. So extravagant is the middle passage in laudation of the Queen that even Cuddy is represented as noticing the change in language :

> *Colin* (said *Cuddy* then) thou hast forgot
> Thy selfe, me seemes, too much, to mount so hie :
> Such loftie flight, base shepheard seemeth not,
> From flocks and fields, to Angels and to skie. (ll. 617-19)

The climactic section on the power and nature of Love (ll. 835-94) seems to blend the two styles with felicitous congruence. All in

58. W. B. C. Watkins, *Shakespeare and Spenser* (Princeton, 1950), p. 267.
59. See *Daphnaïda,* pp. 186, 189.

all, the technical skill, the inventive daring, and the taste which Spenser manifests in fashioning the diction of *Colin Clout* to the demands of his respective topics can hardly command anything but admiration from the reader.[60]

Brief references have been made earlier in the chapter to the frequency of syntactical inversions, particularly of the object-verb type, to innovations which facilitate the meter and the rhyme, and to prefix and suffix additions which play a part in creating smooth rhythmical effects. These suggest the virtually inseparable nature of diction and versification. The tendency on the part of modern scholarship dealing with Spenser's diction to minimize or neglect altogether this reciprocal relationship is rather surprising in view of the emphasis it receives in the critical writings of Spenser's contemporaries, notably George Gascoigne, George Puttenham, and Ben Jonson. These authorities do not always agree on specific points of technique, but having themselves struggled long and hard to meet the exigencies of rhyme and meter they clearly recognize the problems of the relationship. For example, Gascoigne asserts that unless a poet guard against the danger, his inability at first to find a rhyming word may cause him to distort the originally intended meaning. Gascoigne's general advice to the verse practitioner is, therefore: "But do you alwayes hold your first determined Inuention, and do rather searche the bottome of your braynes for apte wordes than chaunge good reason for rumbling rime".[61] He goes on to say that if the search is unsuccessful, then it is permissable for the maker to alter the last word of his earlier line, although he should not willingly "alter the meanying of your Inuention".[62] Puttenham puts himself on record as being particularly unyielding in the matter of "licentiousness" on the part of the poets in their efforts to accommodate words to rhyme. For instance, he condemns one of the "common rimers of the day" [George Turberville] for rhyming with *joy* the word *Roy* [king], "which word was neuer

60. This judgment is partly contradictory to W. B. C. Watkin's unsupported comment on the style of *Colin Clout*: "*Colin Clout* is at best superior in style to *Mother Hubberds Tale,* varying from passages of exquisite delicacy to savage invective. But its style is less of a piece, is occasionally marred by verbal horseplay and by seemingly aimless experimentation. None the less, it is the peer of the *Epistle to Dr. Arbuthnot* and deserves an equal hearing" (p. 274, n.).

61. *Certayne Notes of Instruction,* in *Eliz. Critical Essays,* I, 52.

62. *Ibid.*

yet receiued in our la[*n*]guage for an English word".[63] With reference to another aspect of rhyme, the distance at which "concords" might properly be placed, Puttenham deems alternate rhymes (which *Colin Clout* employs) satisfactory.[64] Jonson, on the other hand, told Drummond of Hawthornden in 1619 that he opposed cross-rhyming on the ground that it is dangerously apt to force the sense to fit the pattern.[65]

But irrespective of the view advanced regarding a given aspect of technique by theorists, poetic form imposes adaptation. This is apparent from Spenser's use of inversions, among other practices. Gascoigne wishes his apprentice poet to "frame all sentences in their mother phrase and proper Idióma",[66] and censures as Latinisms inversions involving the placement of adjectives after substantives. Yet there can be no real doubt that in *Colin Clout,* Spenser's indulgence in inversions of a syntactical nature is occasioned largely by the demands of rhyme or meter, or both, as in line 438, where the proper noun is placed before the predicate: "Her losse is yours, your losse *Amyntas* is". Generally the shift to complete the rhyme results in the placement of a word at the end of a line which in normal order would not be there. Typical of the many object-verb inversions for this purpose is line 457: "Shepheard, enough of shepheardes thou hast told". Yet the reversal is often appropriate, as here, on the grounds of rhetorical emphasis.

Even the antique *y-* formation for the past participle offers a slight metrical help in supplying the unaccented syllable: "And how he hight, himselfe he did ycleepe" (l. 65); "I feel my selfe like one yrapt in spright" (l. 623). And it can hardly be coincidental that of the eleven uses of the obsolescent *hight,* five occur at line ends to begin or complete an alternate rhyme. Not a little of the freedom in vernacular enrichment results in prosodic accommodation. Of the Spenserianisms noted, *blandishment, direfull, indignifie, insolence, read, rewardfull* and *y'bore* fall in rhyming positions, while *listfull, needments* and *trophe* facilitate scansion. The preceding instances in which Spenser has caused the demands of diction and of versification to coincide should in no wise be

63. Page 82.

64. Page 86.

65. *Ben Jonson's Conversations with William Drummond of Hawthornden, Ben Jonson,* eds. C. H. Herford and Percy Simpson (Oxford, 1925), I, 132.

66. *Certayne Notes of Instruction,* in *Eliz. Critical Essays,* I, 53.

construed to imply that the versification of *Colin Clout* is strained or awkward. As a case in point, the inversions, whose frequency has been noted earlier, never give rise to other than a minor degree of indirectness, and the reader is hardly aware of them unless his attention is invited to them. Indeed, the versification harmonizes with the diction in being flowing, easy, flexible, and dignified.

The references above to the use by poets of alterations in the usual order of phrasing a thought to help out the meter or the rhyme may recall to the reader from the previous chapter that this artificial device has a special name as a rhetorical figure—*hyperbaton.* It may also remind him of the intimate connection between choice of words and rhetorical figures. This connection was, of course, a commonplace to classical rhetoricians and to those of the Renaissance who followed in their footings. Rhetoricians of both periods regularly treated the figures as a major topic under the subject of style. Quintilian adverts matter of factly to this overlapping of rhetoric and diction in the eighth book of the *Institutio Oratoria,* when he states that rhetorical ornaments, like clearness, may inhere either in individual words or in groups of words.[67] He is referring here to the commonly recognized broad categories of tropes and schemes respectively, the one customarily embracing changes in a single word; the other, comprising special treatments of phrases and sentences. At the beginning of the ninth Book, he concedes that one cannot, nor indeed need not, differentiate between them since both involve alterations to language and hence both have been given the name *motus* (which men of the Renaissance often render "translations"). Moreover, he continues, both tropes and schemes have the same function of adding force and charm to the subject. He instances *hyperbaton* and *onomatopoeia* specifically as cases of "motions" which he treats as tropes, whereas other distinguished authors have classified them as figures of speech or schemes rather than as tropes.[68]

The student of Renaissance language also comes to see that the influence of *elocutio,* with its concern with figures of speech, is pervasive both as to diction and versification and quite frequently, in fact, affects both at the same time. In this area of tropes and schemes, such student quickly discovers without surprise that many of the elaborate classifications in the handbooks of Spenser's time

67. *Institutio Oratoria,* viii.3.15, III, 218.
68. *Ibid.,* ix.1.2-3, p. 348.

are as intimately concerned with producing sound effects, melody or discord, as with governing the choice of locution. The most important of these rhetorical kinds are alliteration (*paroemion*)—Puttenham's "figure of like letter"[69]—and the more extended figures of repetition—*anaphora* and *ploce*. These devices are most prevalent in passages of rather exalted nature. When Spenser wishes to be most moving and emphatic, using figures is his normal mode of expression, and the particular figures, in their very nature, exert a controlling force upon the choice of words. In the following climactic passage, in which Colin speaks of the essential irreligion of the court, the reader may observe clearly how turning the three interlaced figures of *anaphora, paroemion*, and *ploce* depends almost entirely upon the poet's finding exactly the right words:

> For end, all good, all grace there freely growes,
> Had people grace it gratefully to vse:
> For God his gifts there plenteously bestowes,
> But gracelesse men them greatly do abuse. (ll. 324-7)

In this passage the reader may see also a perfect exemplification of the *soave* or sweet style described by Emma F. Pope as consisting "first, in the elegance and fecundity of slow, resounding words, next, in a conjunction of words which admits no harshness, no break, no rough breathing, no long digression; rather the words must be adapted to the spirit, be like and equal, and so selected from opposites, that numbers may respond to numbers, and like to like".[70] The alliteration, both initial and medial, echoes the sense and aids strophic cohesion. The pace is slowed for emphasis by the assonance of the long *o*'s and *a*'s and by the varied caesuras, but the smooth flow is facilitated by the abundance of sibilants and liquids. Similarly, the section praising "great Cynthiaes goodnesse and high grace" is filled with highly alliterative lines, like

> For euerie gift and euerie goodly meed,
> Which she on me bestowd, demaunds a day;
> And eurie day, in which she did a deed,
> Demaunds a yeare it duly to display. (ll. 592-5)

69. Page 174.
70. "Renaissance Criticism and the Diction of *The Faerie Queene*", *PMLA*, XLI (1926), 590.

Or the alliteration may take the form of *onomatopoeia,* rare in this poem but striking in line 199: "Horrible, hideous, roaring with hoarse crie", which gives through rough breathing an effect of harshness and stridency to suggest the turbulence of the waves and their clamor. Another highly onomatopoetic line is 636: "The speaking woods and murmuring waters fall".

In the memorable passage which contains this line, *anaphora* and *ploce* contribute greatly to the smoothness and "sweet consent"[71] of the stanzas interlocked by the figures. The passage, deserving to be quoted in full, is the rodomontade of Colin's passionate promise to immortalize Cynthia's name:

> Her name recorded I will leaue for euer.
> Her name in euery tree I will endosse,
> That as the trees do grow, her name may grow:
> And in the ground each where will it engrosse,
> And fill with stones, that all men may it know.
> The speaking woods and murmuring waters fall,
> Her name Ile teach in knowen termes to frame:
> And eke my lambs when for their dame they call,
> Ile teach to call for *Cynthia* by name. (ll. 631-9)

Here the *anaphora* of "her name" in the opening lines starts an insistent repetition which echoes melodically through the rest of the speech. That the reader may not miss the fervency of the avowal the narrator records that

> Much was the whole assembly of those heards,
> Moov'd at his speech, so feelingly he spake. (ll. 648-9)

The influence of rhetorical modes goes beyond prescribing the selection of words to help create such melodic patterns as those mentioned and illustrated above. The influence extends as well into the organization of lines, thus giving rise to still another nexus between diction and prosody. The function of rhetorical figures as structural timber of discourse in *Colin Clout* has already been set forth at some length in the previous chapter. Now it becomes appropriate to invite attention to a refinement of this function as an important factor in stanzaic formation. Since the poem is in

71. *Epith.* (l. 83), *Works,* VIII, 243.

dialogue except for the narrative frame, we should expect, and actually do find, that it is composed in speech units—for the most part, Colin's speeches, interrupted in a kind of rhetorical punctuation by the other interlocutors, Colin's "fellow-shepheardes". These speeches usually contain a series of continuous quatrains which, according to one authority, "assume a strophic character".[72] Davis instances lines 308-27, Colin's contrast of England with Ireland and his explanation for the downfall of a state; lines 464-79, the Petrarchan avowal by Colin of praise for, and devotion to, his mistress; and lines 596-615, Colin's encomium of Cynthia. Since these passages, as shown in the last chapter, are the very ones which display the most elaborate massing of major rhetorical figures, it becomes accurate to say that in *Colin Clout* Spenser composes largely by schemes of rhetoric. Other cohesive "strophes" could be added at will to Davis' examples—passage after passage which has as its base at least one major scheme of thought and amplification. A few typical cases in point are the *icon* or comparison of Cynthia to the "crowne of lillies", the "circlet of a Turtle true", and "faire Phebes garlond", a sequence structured by *carmen correlativum* (ll. 337-43); the "salute" to the contemporary poets composed of *epitheton* and arranged by *distributio* (ll. 377-449); and the last of the three bravuras on Cynthia or Elizabeth, a passage beginning with *meiosis*, regulated by *carmen correlativum*, followed by *expolitio*, and reinforced throughout by *ploce*, *comparatio*, and *prosopopoeia* (ll. 624-39).

Consideration of the rhetorical modes of expression as defining elements in strophic grouping prompts a direct glance at the actual stanza form of *Colin Clout*. Both in the original edition of 1595 and in subsequent editions up to the present the poem is properly printed with no spaces to set off stanzas. For this reason the fact that the verse is predominantly what is now known as the elegiac stanza may escape immediate notice. Possibly the same observation holds true for the first readers of Thomas Gray's *Elegy Written in a Country Churchyard*, whose fame following its publication gave the distinctive appellation to the decasyllabic quatrain with interlaced rhyme. The reader may recall that through his friend, Horace Walpole, Gray imparted specific instructions for the Elegy to be printed without any intervals between the stanzas for the

72. B. E. C. Davis, *Edmund Spenser: A Critical Study* (Cambridge, Eng., 1933), p. 201.

reason that the sense was in some instances continued beyond them.[73] The reader of the original quarto of 1751 could, however, distinguish the separate stanzas fairly easily if he were at all observant. The printer, R. Dodsley, while following Gray's prescription in printing the poem without breaks, circumvented the author's intention by indenting the first lines of the successive quatrains by an em space of about three-eights of an inch.[74]

The matter of Spenser's precedence in the use of the stanza which Gray made renowned needs clarification to counter the view that Spenser chose it for other than artistic reasons. The belief expressed in the last century by Edmund Gosse that Spenser intended to compliment Sir Walter Raleigh by adopting for *Colin Clout* "the very stanza in which the *Cynthia* was written"[75]—an opinion seconded in substance more recently by Kathrine Koller[76] —does not now seem tenable. The poem by Raleigh to which Gosse refers is *The XIth and Last Book of the Ocean to Cynthia,* the main fragment, in 522 lines, of MS Hatfield, Cecil Papers 144. This poem, written mainly in heroic quatrains, is at present held on convincing evidence to have been composed in 1592 or shortly thereafter,[77] thus having a date of origin later than that of *Colin Clout,* which was dedicated to Raleigh at the end of 1591. References to Raleigh's *Cynthia* made prior to 1592, such as the one in lines 163-75 of *Colin Clout,* are held by Oakeshott to be to the series of Raleigh's occasional verses to Queen Elizabeth. Of these, there are three short pieces ascribed by Oakeshott to Raleigh which were printed prior to 1592 and which employ the elegaic quatrain, but with the addition of a concluding couplet. These are Oakeshott's Nos. IV ("Praised be Diana's fair and harmless light"), IX ("See those sweet eyes, those more than sweetest eyes"), and XVIII ("Feed still thyself, thou foundling, with belief"). Nos. IV and XVIII, containing four and five quatrains respectively, were printed in *The Phoenix Nest* (1593). No. IX, comprising two quatrains, appeared in William Byrd's *Songs of Sundrie Nature* (1589).

73. *Correspondence of Thomas Gray,* eds. Paget Toynbee and Leonard Whibley (Oxford, 1935), I, 341-2.

74. *An Elegy Written in a Country Church Yard,* ed. Francis Griffin Stokes (Oxford, 1929), p. 19.

75. "Sir Walter Ralegh's *Cynthia*", *Athenaeum* (9 Jan. 1886), p. 66.

76. "Spenser and Ralegh", *ELH,* I (1934), 44-5.

77. *The Poems of Sir Walter Ralegh,* ed. Agnes M. C. Latham (London, 1929), p. 179; Walter Oakeshott, *The Queen and the Poet* (London, 1960), pp. 136, 138.

Since all three of these lyrics were printed without attribution of authorship and since none of them employs the pastoral motif, one can be virtually positive that Spenser did not intend to recall them to his readers as models for the stanzaic form of *Colin Clout,* nor to pay in this covert manner a compliment to their putative author, Sir Walter Raleigh.

With further reference to the "uniform four-line stanza" employed in *Colin Clout,* Gosse stated in 1886 that the only example, important or unimportant, of this stave before 1589 that he knew of was the "Eclogue of Melicertus" in Robert Green's *Menaphon* (1587).[78] Actually, the stanzaic form, with or without the coda of two rhymed lines, had been used for a variety of poetic kinds well before 1589. It had, for example, been used by the Earl of Surrey for complaint in the comparatively long lyric, "Prisoned in Windsor, he recounteth his pleasure there passed" (Tottel's *Songs and Sonnets,* 1557), and by Thomas Howell for another plaintive poem, "When he thought himself contemned" (*The Arbor of Amity,* 1568); by Barnabe Googe for an obsequy, "An epitaph of the death of Nicholas Grimald" (*Eclogues, Epitaphs,* and *Sonnets,* 1563); for a verse dedication, "The Earl of Oxford to the reader of Beddingfield's Cardanus", a translation of Cardanus's *Comfort* (1576); and by Thomas Procter for a reflective lyric, "Respice finem" (*Gorgeous Gallery of Gallant Inventions,* 1578).[79] However, Spenser himself seems to have been the first to use the stanza for pastoral poetry in the *November* and *April* eclogues of *The Shepheardes Calender.* In that poem, it is true, the quatrains are linked by rhymes. The links start with the third quatrain in *November,* and are intermittent in *April.* But even in *Colin Clout* the regular scheme of continuous heroic quatrains is varied slightly at the beginning and end of the poem. By assuming the insertion of a tercet in the opening passage (ll. 5, 6, and 7), with line 6 linking in rhyme with lines 2 and 4, one can, however, avoid the complicated theory proposed by one investigator[80] that Spenser's

78. "Sir Walter Ralegh's *Cynthia*", p. 66.

79. The poems by the Earl of Surrey, Thomas Howell, Barnabe Googe, and Thomas Proctor may be conveniently found in *Poetry of the English Renaissance, 1509-1600,* ed. J. William Hebel and Hoyt H. Hudson (New York, 1947), pp. 32, 79, 74, 192, respectively. The poem by the Earl of Oxford may be found in *Miscellanies of the Fuller Worthies' Library,* ed. Alexander B. Grosart (privately printed, 1872-76), IV, 422-3.

80. Roland B. Botting, "A New Spenserian Rhyme Scheme?", *JEGP,* XXXVI (1937), 384-6.

unit is not a closed quatrain, but an open one linked with its predecessor by a common rhyme—a scheme which, in any event, breaks down at line 32. Here the units of sense and the closed quatrain settle into persistent coincidence. Near the end of the poem, the last quatrain (completing the frame), though standing as an independent unit rhythmically and syntactically, is connected by the "quest" rhyme to the preceding section (body of the poem).

I have described briefly the metrical form of the poem as a whole and noted the availability to Spenser of a variety of early models of the particular stanza which he eventually chose. I shall attempt now to indicate the artistic motivation for this choice through a detailed examination of a comparatively short passage. The concluding lines of the dialogue, which complete the poem except for the narrative frame, have been selected for this purpose. Besides revealing Spenser's easy mastery of numbers in *Colin Clout,* the analysis, carried out in terms readily apprehensible to critics and readers of Spenser's period, will perhaps serve more specifically to demonstrate the variety and flexibility of its versification, and to suggest the artful way in which Spenser reconciles the metrical pattern to the demands of speech rhythm and phrasing.

/ / x x x / x x x /
Such grace || shall be | some guer|don for | the griefe, 943

x / x / x x x / x /
And long | afflic|tion || which | I haue | endured: 944

/ / x / x / x / x /
Such grace || sometimes | shall giue | me some | reliefe, 945

x / x / x / x x x /
And ease | of paine || which can|not be | recured. 946

x / x / x / x x x /
And ye | my fel|low shep|heards || which | do see 947

x / x / x x x / / /x
And heare || the lan|guours of | my too | long dy|ing, 948

/ x x / x / x / x /
Vnto | the world || for eu|er wit|ness bee, 949

x / x / / x x / x /x
That hers | I die, || nought to | the world | deny|ing, 950

x / x / x x x / x /
This sim|ple trop|he of | her great | conquest. 951

One finds some interesting variations in Colin's final speech. First, as to caesuras, the masculine caesura comes after the second stress of the second foot in lines 946, 949, and 950, and after the first accented syllable in line 948, which succeeds a run-on verse. It comes after the second beat of the first spondaic foot in the parallel lines 943 and 945. The feminine caesura in the other two lines occurs after the first unstressed syllable of the third foot in line 944 and between the syllables of the pyrrhic foot in line 947. For the concluding line of the speech, no pause is required by the phrases, which can be uttered in a single expulsion of breath, and none is wanted for the effectuation of a smooth finish. The placing of the pause exhibits skillful variation within a fairly set pattern.

Even in this short excerpt we find one example of enjambment, although ordinarily the lines are end-stopped. Fifty-two of the 955 lines are run-on.[81] However, the stops differ considerably in their length, and Elizabethan punctuation is not always a reliable guide. Some lines, for instance, do not conclude with punctuation but nevertheless call for pauses as long as many that do. In the former category are lines 188, 279, 430, 521, 534, 678, 683, 751, 815, 821, 843, 849, 853, 865, and 921. Also, the preponderance of end-stopped lines is not an indication of line-by-line composition. Rather, it is an adaptation of speech phrasing to the rhyme and meter. As has been stated, neither lines nor quatrains are the basic composition units: the basic composition units are speeches, and within them, rhetorical schemes.

With respect to rhyme,[82] aside from slight interlinking referred to before but not illustrated in this passage, the above specimen exhibits one case of feminine rhyme (ll. 948, 950), relatively frequent in *Colin Clout*. The significance of the abundance of feminine rhyme in *Colin Clout* is probably the same as that ascribed by one scholar to Spenser's tendency to use double rhyme liberally

81. See Robert Ellrodt, *Neoplatonism in the Poetry of Spenser* (Geneva, 1960), pp. 221-2, for figures giving ratios of enjambment for lines in the five sections into which he divides the poem. Ellrodt presents his ratios under headings which reflect three modes of calculation. My findings of an overall enjambment ratio of one run-over line to every twenty agree roughly with proportion figures listed under his second heading of "compulsory", based on a conservative allocation of lines to the run-on category.

82. Renwick calls attention to line 693, which is unrhymed. He conjectures a possible missing line between 694 and 695, but concedes the possibility that the omitted rhyme may represent an oversight on Spenser's part (*Daphnaïda*, p. 189).

(163 times) in the last three books of *The Faerie Queene* as compared with their almost complete absence (one occurrence) in the first three books: to make the movement natural and free.[83]

The rhymes in *Colin Clout* are, for the most part, of the conventional one-syllable, perfect type. There are, however, a number of anomalous rhymes, which show that Spenser did not intend to be more unduly restricted by the demands of conventional rhyme than he did by the demands of conventional diction. It is worthy of note, though, that in the passage under consideration, Colin's concluding address, Spenser allows no anomalous rhymes of the type banned by the textbooks which he permits himself elsewhere; e.g., identical rhymes—*lament-merriment* (ll. 28, 30), *crew-accrew* (ll. 653, 655); unstressed rhymes—*jeopardie-crueltie* (ll. 273, 275), *chastitie-modestie* (ll. 469, 471); impure rhymes—*leprosies-cries* (ll. 313, 315), *applie-worthylie* (ll. 373, 375).[84]

With reference to the accentual pattern of lines in this passage, the principle of purposeful variety, carried out within a circumscribed range, is quite manifest. None of the lines is perfect iambic pentameter. The variation is alike in lines 944 and 951, where the third is a pyrrhic foot; and in lines 946 and 947, where the fourth is a pyrrhic foot. In line 943, an initial spondee is compensated for by a pyrrhic foot following it. Line 945 paralleling line 943 also has an initial spondee. The irregular line 948 is a particularly good example of how the poet has secured an onomatopoetic effect by lengthening the line by an extra syllable; by making the last foot a spondee instead of an iambus; by including a long *e* sound and two velar stops (g), both of which slow up the line and suggest travail; and by ending on a falling rather than a rising syllable. Line 949 has a trochee in place of an iambus in the opening foot. The beat on the first syllable of the line calls for a rise in vocal pitch appropriate to the peroration. In the third foot of line 950, the substitution of a trochee for an iambus is also particularly

83. Floyd Stovall, "Feminine Rimes in the *Faerie Queene*", *JEGP*, XXVI (1927), 91-5.

84. Many pairs in *Colin Clout* which do not rhyme according to today's pronunciation were perfectly good rhymes in Spenser's period. Most of these can be ascertained from Henry Cecil Wyld, *Studies in English Rhymes from Surrey to Pope* (London, 1923). Among these are types like *beare-appeare* (ll. 93, 95), or *eares-beares* (ll. 712, 714) (Wyld, p. 66); like *preferre-farre* (ll. 121, 123) (Wyld, pp. 83-4); like *was-has* (ll. 280, 282) (Wyld, pp. 68-70); and like *nature-feature* (ll. 860, 862 (Wyld, p. 53).

effective in that it gives the negative "nought" the highly emphatic position after the caesura which the sense calls for.

The plasticity of the verse is chiefly what gives Colin's final plea the effect of natural speech, heightened, of course, in deference to its lofty subject matter and fervent emotion. The rhythms of speech are accommodated within the fairly regular pattern by occasional substitution of a pyrrhic or trochee for an iambus, by the shifting of the caesura within the respective lines, and by the fact that some of the lines tend to have three, rather than five strong beats, and these are usually on the long vowel sounds; e.g., l. 945: gr*a*ce, somet*i*mes, rel*ie*fe; l. 946: *ea*se, p*ai*ne, rec*u*red; l. 948: h*ea*re, l*a*nguours, d*y*ing; l. 950: D*ie,* n*ou*ght, den*y*ing. B. E. C. Davis calls attention to this feature of three strong beats to a line, which he believes helps adjust the verse to speech rhythm, "the counterpoint of this polysyllabic phrasing against an iambic norm".[85]

In this chapter I have tried to demonstrate that there is a consistency in the poem achieved through careful and imaginative employment of language and prosody. The result is a construct which satisfies quite well those two complementary demands of good poetry spoken of by Puttenham in his *Arte of English Poesie*—*enargia,* "to satisfie & delight th'eare onely by a goodly outward shew set vpon the matter with wordes, and speaches smothly and tunably running"; and *energia,* "by certain intendments or sense of such wordes & speaches inwardly working a stirre to the mynde".[86]

85. Page 195.
86. Pages 142-3.

CHAPTER IV

THE IMAGERY

The discussion in the preceding two chapters is concerned with rhetorical modes and devices, and with vocabulary and verse patterns; it furnishes a view of the constituent features of *Colin Clout* from the outside, so to speak. In their presentational aspects, the linguistic and prosodic elements thus far dealt with tend to appear as independent units, oriented for the most part to matters lying beyond the poem and therefore seeming to operate in a manner somewhat centrifugal to it. This autonomy, as it were, of these individual elements is both real and justifiable. Existing in a totality which seeks to exhibit itself as an aesthetic object, these patterns must not only function as parts of the whole, but must themselves be whole and perfect, able by themselves to gratify the artistic tastes of the discerning reader. Certainly, belletrists of the Renaissance who by precept and proclivity were constantly searching out delightful figures would have found no fault except that of incompleteness with Coleridge's definition of poetry as "the production of a highly pleasurable whole, of which each part shall also communicate for itself a distinct and conscious pleasure".[1] In order for the discussion to move to a view of the poem from the inside, however, the concept of the individual structural units as provisionally self-existent entities must be replaced by a concept of these units as potentially component parts of a putative total organization of consciousness, which is the poem entire. Such a deliberate shift in emphasis proves fruitful at the outset because the enlarged outlook which it fosters enables one to discern quite clearly a strong centripetal tendency, hitherto only indistinctly apprehended, in many of the configurations of language and metrics already closely examined from a different perspective. I wish now to explore in some detail these configurations of language, assisted by metrics, which portend this total organization and which are comprised under the name of images.

1. *Coleridge's Shakespearean Criticism,* ed. Thomas Middleton Raysor (Cambridge, Mass., 1930), I, 164.

More specifically, I shall regard images as linguistic and rhetorical foci which, with varying degrees of obliqueness, mediate experience—that is, "imitate" sensation, thought, and emotion. Such foci of sensibility I shall discuss under three groupings. The reason for considering images in the respective categories will best appear as the discussion proceeds, but a synopsis of the groups now should help to clarify the detailed treatment to follow. Images in the first category, based on appeal to the physical senses, are largely descriptive details. Though these are sensory images psychologically, their impact upon the senses is weak because they lack vividness or because they patently imitate a conventional matter or mode. Images in the second category, based on appeal to conceptual associations assumed as resident in the minds of Spenser's first readers, are concretions of character, setting, action, and thought. These concretions are latently allegorical because they call up their full range of meaning—including emotional overtones—only when they are taken in the pastoral context created by the poet as the imaginative universe of the poem. In such a context, these concretions designate an order of things and beings different from empirical things and beings. In the third category are images which are distinguishable by their nature as figurative formations. These are mainly rhetorical figures of comparison containing, in I. A. Richards' well-nigh universally accepted terms, a tenor and a vehicle, with the relationship between the two expressed by his statement that the tenor is "the underlying idea or principal subject which the vehicle or figure means".[2] In Richards' view, the co-presence of these components results in a meaning which is unattainable without their interplay, and the relative importance of the contributions of vehicle and tenor to the resultant meaning may vary considerably.[3] In *Colin Clout* the relationship between the two parts of the whole figure is typically that of object-idea (tenor) and definition-illustration-amplification (vehicle). Mention of such a relationship

2. I. A. Richards, *The Philosophy of Rhetoric* (New York, 1936), p. 97. Scholars of the Renaissance sometimes used the terms *proposition* and *reddition* for the respective two parts of a comparison. See, e.g., Abraham Fraunce, *The Lawiers Logike* (London, 1588), fol. 72r. Elder Olson has proposed new terms which would substitute *referent* for *tenor, analogue* for *vehicle,* and add a third term *continuum* to express the "ground of likeness, whether in fact or thought, which permits the analogy" ("William Empson, Contemporary Criticism, and Poetic Diction", in R. S. Crane, ed. *Critics and Criticism: Ancient and Modern* [Chicago, 1952], p. 81).

3. *Philosophy of Rhetoric,* p. 100.

brings to mind the close connection existing in Renaissance times between poetry and the twin communicative arts of logic and rhetoric. The processes central to these arts as ways of "judging" and "inventing" matter—inquiring into the true nature of things, dividing the whole into its parts, distinguishing substance from accident, and drawing a subject through the various "places"—inevitably give rise to images. Exploring the implications of the probable genesis of figures in the poem from modes taught in the disciplines of logic-rhetoric will constitute the focus of my treatment concerning this third category of images. In the process of this exploration, I shall examine at some length the particular topics contained in the vehicles, together with the relationship of such topics to the subject of the tenor. The result of both these lines of inquiry will be to indicate how the logical bases of these images operate to control the meaning of the images and to give them a predominantly conceptual and valuative function.

While I believe that it is critically fruitful to treat images under three separate heads, the sophisticated reader will be aware that maintaining such a division in practice is difficult because the three kinds work together and sometimes even interpenetrate one another. Nevertheless, certain points about these groups, which emerge from the foregoing brief descriptions, may be discerned. The first- and last-named categories are somewhat more localized than the middle one. The last-named category differs from the two preceding ones in that it places as much emphasis upon form as upon content. For this reason, it may include images in the first category where descriptive passages contain explicit metaphorical structures. Also, this final category overlaps the second one when the ideas or themes of illustration or amplification fall, as they ordinarily do, within the specific background area of pastoralism or of areas which pastoral poetry from classical to Tudor times had assimilated.

A single typical image taken at random from the poem will help show why the categories, to be critically valuable, cannot be self-inclusive. One of the maids of the court, Charillis, according to Colin, is "like a goodly beacon high addrest" [situated] (l. 562). Is the reference to "beacon" primarily intended to evoke a sensory response in the modality of vision? Why, precisely, is Charillis characterized in terms of luminosity? Does the poet perhaps assume a special knowledge on the part of his audience which will enable them to connect "a goodly beacon" to an allusive context larger than that of the immediate passage? What is the function of the simile as such? The first three questions above mainly concern content; the last one, mainly form. One can hardly answer all the questions from the same frame of reference, even though they all pertain to a single image. And until one has answered all the questions he can scarcely "take in" the image as an instantaneous perception of thought, emotion, and sensation. Hence, the possible consideration of a particular figurative image—and figurative images are superabundant—under three separate but reciprocally enlightening categories.

Turning now to examine directly the images which are conformable to the first-named category—those based on descriptive appeal primarily to the bodily senses—one finds a considerable amount of imagery that is visual, some that is kinesthetic and auditory, a small amount that is olfactory and gustatory, and none that is tactile.[4] He finds, moreover, that a given descriptive passage will ordinarily contain an appeal to more than a single physical sense. It is possible, however, for the sake of illustration, to designate somewhat subjectively a passage as appealing mainly to a single sense and then to note incidentally the subsidiary appeals.

One may properly begin with visual imagery, the most prevalent type. The greatest amount of visual imagery occurs in what is roughly the first third of the poem, ending with line 327. This distribution is what one would expect when he recalls that the first part locates Colin and his auditors in a bucolic setting, narrates a myth concerned with topographical detail, and describes a ship and an ocean voyage, whereas the last two-thirds of the poem is, generally speaking, persuasive in nature.

Perusing the descriptions, one is struck by the fact that they ordinarily lack both sharp particularity and a high degree of sensory vividness. An exception to this general observation, with respect to graphic vividness, may occur in the case of set descriptive pieces

4. I. A. Richards first used these terms (and others like them which have since become part of the received critical vocabulary) in *Principles of Literary Criticism,* originally published in 1924. Richards speaks of images as "fugitive elusive copies of sensation" (*Principles,* 5th ed. [New York, 1934], p. 106). He warns against placing too much emphasis on the purely sensory quality of images because, in his view, "what gives an image efficacy is less its vividness as an image than its character as a mental event peculiarly connected with sensation (p. 119). Thus, to him, an image is not so much a copy or revival of sensory experience as it is a "relict" or "representative" of sensation (pp. 119-20).

going under the rule-book name of *descriptio*,[5] such as those grouped together by Puttenham as *prosopopeia* (personification), *topographia* (description of a place), or *pragmatographia* (description of an action).[6] Another exception, with reference to sensuous force, may be found when special types of rhetorical figures, like *onomatopoeia*, are used. Still a third exception to the general paucity of representational detail may occur when the description is an imitation of a well-known passage from an earlier writer. The purely sensuous effect of descriptions within any of these exceptions is necessarily weakened for the reader who is conscious of the conventionalized nature of such images. There is ample evidence that the Renaissance poet, when he consciously employs imitation of another's manner or matter, intends to let the reader's recognition of the imitation lessen the sensuous effect.

Typical of many descriptions is the one in the introductory frame of the poem—a vignette which pictures the group gathered around the returned traveler, Colin:

> Who all the while with greedie listfull eares,
> Did stand astonisht at his curious skill,
> Like hartlesse deare, dismayd with thunders sound. (ll. 7-9)

This passage calls up a scene to the reader's mind and thus can be said to appeal mainly to the visual imagination. Yet the description is hardly circumstantial enough in detail to enable the reader to form a really vivid mental picture. Besides, there are the allusions to "listfull eares" and to "thunders sound", expressions which tend to evoke an auditory sensation. The same scene is reproduced later in non-figurative terms:

> With that they all gan throng about him neare,
> With hungrie eares to heare his harmonie:
> The whiles their flocks deuoyd of dangers feare,
> Did round about them feed at libertie. (ll. 52-5)

This passage, like the earlier one depicting the herdsmen gathered around Colin, also evinces a lack of specificity. Again, the appeal of the passage seems predominantly visual, but the strong action

5. Quintilian, *Institutio Oratoria,* IV.3.12, II, 126.
6. *Arte of English Poesie,* p. 239.

verbs "throng" and "feed" produce in the reader a sensation of motion and thus justify calling that image at least in part kinesthetic. The phrase "with hungrie eares to heare his harmonie" reinforces the auditory impression of the first passage.

In the myth of Bregog and Mulla, the course of the Mulla through the ancient city of Kilnemullah is sketched with a few broad strokes:

> The Nimph, which of that water course has charge,
> That springing out of *Mole,* doth rune downe right
> To *Butteuant,* where spreading forth at large, ... (ll. 109-11)

These lines convey a somewhat vague impression of the river in terms of features distinguishable by the power of sight. From this point of view the image can properly be termed visual. Yet the observation places emphasis on *movement.* From this second point of view, the image can also be considered kinesthetic.

Descriptions in terms which seem more evocative of emotion than those cited above occur in connection with Colin's first glimpse of the sea as

> A world of waters heaped vp on hie,
> Rolling like mountaines in wide wildernesse,
> Horrible, hideous, roaring with hoarse crie, (ll. 197-9)

wherein

> Thousand wyld beasts with deep mouthes gaping direfull
> Therin stil wait poore passengers to teare. (ll. 202-3).

In these two passages, the description arises from impressions obtainable through both the sense of sight and the sense of sound. The emphasis on violent motion in both excerpts is evident in the phrases "heaped vpon hie", "rolling like mountaines", "mouthes gaping", and "wait poore passengers to teare". The depiction of the sea in such striking terms is appropriate to the naïve shepherd, but for the knowing sixteenth-century reader, bred on the classics, the effectiveness of the passage with its markedly onomatopoeic line 199 probably owed as much to his appreciation of a skilfully-done echo of Ovid[7] as to any vicarious thrill which the lines might arouse.

The section following the one just discussed has considerable vivid detail which blends the modalities of sight and motion—"Dauncing vpon the waters back to lond" (l. 214), "Yet had it armes and wings, and head and taile/And life to moue it selfe vpon the water" (ll. 218-19)—but the elaboration only *appears* to be for the purpose of realism; a closer look reveals that it is directed to turn the rhetorical figure—*prosopopoeia.* The passage, like the one previously cited, has a classical model in Cicero's *De Natura Deorum,* which contains a similar description of a ship as seen by another nonnautical rustic observer.[8]

Perhaps the most graphic line in the poem is "With hoary head and deawy dropping beard", a descriptive phrase applied to Proteus and containing the compound epithet alluded to in the preceding chapter. The quatrain in which this line occurs, itself a part of the encompassing sea-pastoral metaphor, is a hardy perennial of rhetorical practice—*pragmatographia* or *rei descriptio.*[9] No classical parallel has been noted for this "description of a thing", but both its subject and tone suggest classical origin.

Outside the first part of the poem, one of the encomiums—the first of three sustained ones by Colin on Cynthia—contains a purple passage of visual imagery:

> I would her lyken to a crowne of lillies,
> Vpon a virgin brydes adorned head,

7. *Daphnaïda,* p. 185. *Tristia,* i.2, which Renwick cites as an analogue to the passage, contains both the "world of water" (montes aquarum) image and an expression similar to line 227, "And nought but sea and heauen to vs appeare". The apposite passage in Ovid is as follows:

> What boysterous billowes now (O wretch) amids thy waues we spye,
> As I forthwith should haue bene heu'de to touch the Azure skye.
> What vacant vallies be there set, in swallowing Seas so wrought,
> As presently thou lookes I should, to drery hell be brought.
> I lookt about: saue Seas and sky, nought subiect was to sight,
> With swelling surges one, with cloudes the other threatned spight.

(*The Three First Bookes of Ovid de Tristibus,* trans. Thomas Churchyarde [London, 1580], fol. 2v).

8. John Jortin, *Remarks on Spenser's Poems* (London, 1734), pp. 137-8, cited in *Works,* VII, 460.

9. See Rix, *Rhetoric in Spenser's Poetry,* p. 59, for a definition of this figure by Susenbrotus.

With Roses dight and Goolds and Daffadillies;
Or like the circlet of a Turtle true,
In which all colours of the rainbow bee;
Or like faire *Phebes* garlond shining new,
In which all pure perfection one may see. (ll. 337-43)

Here the vivid flowers and the dove's neck conjure up an impression of variegated color, but one can hardly relate this impression to the physical appearance of the Queen. Moreover, the potentially sensuous implications of the flowers, the dove, the rainbow, and the moon ring are almost totally repressed by being sublimated into metaphor.

Common to all the foregoing passages, taken mostly from the first third of the poem, is visual imagery. Imagery of this sort appearing in the present sampling seems to be devoted to a minor extent only to a realistic representation of the actual world of sight.

Although kinesthetic imagery is present, as noted, in a number of passages already cited, it may be instructive now to glance directly at two new passages which embody kinesthetic images. One such passage, occurring within the topographic myth, describes the action of Father Mole in punishing Bregog for trickery practiced in the latter's courting of daughter Mulla. According to Colin's version, Father Mole

Who wondrous wroth for that so foule despight,
In great auenge did roll downe from his hill
Huge mightie stones, the which encomber might
His passage, and his water-courses spill. (ll. 148-51)

Here the rapid falling cadence of "roll downe from his hill" and the positioning of "His passage" to force a reading pause, paralleling the semantic sense, simulate the effect of opposed forces meeting: that of Mole exerted in carrying out the punitive deed; that of Bregog in unsuccessfully attempting to circumvent the boulders. From this point of view, the imagery serves a conceptual purpose—to support the idea of Mole's indignation and that of Bregog's relative helplessness.

Another passage of kinesthetic imagery, which suggests motion or forceful action, stands in the section of court satire. Attributing to wit a life-like quality, Colin says the Court has no need for it unless it can make itself the instrument of flattery—

> Vnlesse to please, it selfe it can applie :
> But shouldred is, or out of doore quite shit. (ll. 708-9)

It should be observed that although the image exhibits an undoubted sensory quality, it has for its primary effect the strengthening of the idea that the possessor of wit will be given short shrift at court unless he is willing to use his verbal gift for sycophancy.

Auditory imagery is not an outstanding feature of *Colin Clout,* but the poem does, in a somewhat limited way, exhibit Spenser's well-known facility in suiting sound to sense. The last chapter instances two highly onomatopoeic lines, 199 and 636. Some of the more subtle effects of verse harmony are touched upon in the ensuing chapter on "Tone and Feeling".

Rare gustatory and olfactory images appear in a passage of singularly fervent glorification of Queen-Cynthia spoken by Colin :

> Her deeds were like great clusters of ripe grapes,
> Which load the bunches of the fruitfull vine :
> Offring to fall into each mouth that gapes,
> And fill the same with store of timely wine.
> . . . .
> Her thoughts are like the fume of Franckincence,
> Which from a golden Censer forth doth rise :
> And throwing forth sweet odours mounts fro thence
> In rolling globes vp to the vauted skies. (ll. 600-3; 608-11)

The first simile employs natural phenomena of grapes to appeal directly to the gustatory faculty; the second employs the religious connotation of incense to appeal to the olfactory sense. The fact that the images are embodied in similes suggests that the tempting grapes and the sweet odors are not there purely or even mainly to gratify the sensory imagination. Indeed, the rich religious symbolism behind both images would have been quickly grasped by Spenser's first public. The grape-cluster, in particular, was a commonplace of Christian and ecclesiastical typology from the eleventh or twelfth century until well into the seventeenth. It symbolizes the blessings conveyed upon mankind by self-immolating love. Here the image conveys the unselfish devotion of the Queen to her subjects.[10]

The consideration of the physical senses reveals the presence of all but one main type—that appealing to the sense of touch—and thus affords an idea of the author's imaginative span in the poem. It is to be observed that sense imagery frequently occurs in association with figures or with conscious imitations. This fact tends to reduce its ability to convey the sensuous side of experience. If this conclusion is warranted, the glimpse just taken of sensory images has served to indicate that conveying sensational events or rendering perceptual experiences in the realm of the senses very likely does not loom large as a poetic purpose in *Colin Clout*. But this is a negative result. The reader of the poem still remains unaware of the significance of the experience imitated by the poet in a given image; moreover, he is still unable to see what a single such image may mean in a context larger than that of its immediate surroundings. In short, the consideration of images under the first-named category offers limited help in getting inside the poem. For a more promising approach in this regard, one is therefore quite willing to proceed to a consideration of imagery under the second basis of classification.

This second system of classification, the reader will recall, views images in terms of their appeal to associations already resident in

10. In *A Reading of George Herbert* (Chicago, 1952), pp. 112-37, Rosemond Tuve treats in detail the uses to which George Herbert puts the set of conceits associated with the ancient symbol of Christ as the miraculous grape-bunch. She alludes to the series of woodcut vignettes which depict scenes from that tradition in the editions of "Queen Elizabeth's Prayerbook" (STC 6428 ff., 1569, '78, '81, '90, 1608). The edition of 1590, *A Book of Christian Prayers,* revised from the original of his father's by Richard Day, portrays on the left and lower margins of folios 6^{v} and 25^{v} two men carrying a huge cluster of grapes on a pole between them. The other scenes and accompanying biblical texts on these pages make the equation between the symbols of the Israelites crossing the Red Sea, the finding of the grapes as the first fruit of the Promised Land, and Christ's baptism. The only known surviving copy of the original edition compiled by John Day (now at Lambeth Palace) is a personalized one which belonged to the Queen herself. In this edition, the series from Scriptures containing the grape-bunch complex is repeated six times. All Renaissance editions contain as the frontispiece a full-page portrait of Queen Elizabeth kneeling in devotion (Rev. William K. Clay, ed. *Private Prayers Pur Forth by Authority During the Reign of Queen Elizabeth* [Cambridge, Eng., 1851], pp. xvi-xxi; David Ramage, comp. *A Finding-List of English Books to 1640 in Libraries of the British Islea* [Durham, Eng., 1958]).

the reader's mind. The method is largely an outgrowth of pioneering studies by Caroline F. E. Spurgeon. The results of these studies were first publicized in a lecture given before the Shakespeare Association in 1930, and brought into greater prominence by the subsequent publication of a work dealing with all of the imagery.[11] In the opening chapter of this latter work, *Shakespeare's Imagery and What It Tells Us,* Miss Spurgeon stresses her concern with the content rather than the form of images. Images themselves she defines comprehensively as "connoting any and every imaginative picture or other experience, drawn in every kind of way, which have come to the poet, not only through any of his senses, but through his mind and emotions as well".[12] Images work through emotions and associations aroused in the reader by the "something else" with which a description or an idea is overtly or latently compared.[13] Miss Spurgeon's concept of the term image is broad enough to admit at its furthest range an entire scene from a play by Shakespeare, such as, for instance, the one near the middle of *Richard II* (III.4), in which England, after the horrors and long-continued neglect occasioned by the civil wars, is spoken of in terms of a vast untended garden.[14] In her subsequent discussion of this particular image, Miss Spurgeon describes it as a "leading theme" gathered up in the scene as a "kind of allegory".[15]

The expanded type of image to which Miss Spurgeon refers here suggests the pastoral allegory of *Colin Clout*. Richard H. Fogle has given the term "complex image" to such a figurative amalgam, in which the ordinary distinctions of tenor and vehicle tend to become submerged. "A complex image," he tells us, "may be a fusion of simple images, a poem, a scene from a play, or even the play itself; it may be a recurring theme with a symbolic significance, like a Wagnerian leitmotiv."[16] As instances of such complex images, Fogle gives, among others, the ulcer-image in *Hamlet* and the blood-image in *Macbeth*.[17] Fogle adds that an image embody-

11. *Leading Motives in the Imagery of Shakespeare's Tragedies* (Oxford, 1930); and *Shakespeare's Imagery and What It Tells Us* (Cambridge, Eng., 1935).

12. *Shakespeare's Imagery and What It Tells Us,* p. 5

13. *Ibid.,* p. 9.

14. *Ibid.,* pp. 5, 220-3.

15. *Ibid.,* p. 222.

16. *The Imagery of Keats and Shelley: A Comparative Study* (Chapel Hill, 1949), p. 22.

17. *Ibid.,* p. 21.

ing a recurrent motif "tends toward the unification of concept, emotion, and sensation within a single form or object".[18]

The way in which pastoral representation supplies a recurrent motif in *Colin Clout* was glanced at in Chapter II. There it was noted that the poem is throughout an extended metaphor—an allegory,[19] in which the life of the phenomenal world is reflected and refracted through the epiphenomenal speculum of pastoral. Thus, all locutions which arise from the pastoral allegory are individual images designating an order or category of things and beings different from empirical things and beings. Collectively, these images, which serve to adumbrate Spenser, his friends, Ireland, Spenser's estate of Kilcolman in Munster, Queen Elizabeth, lords and maids of the court, etc., comprise the complex pastoral image coterminous with the poem. In accordance with this imaginative projection, Colin's life is placed in a milieu of shepherds and shepherdesses. The setting is rural both in Ireland and at court. The seasons mourn in the stock pastoral fashion (ll. 22-31). Colin is bodied forth as "the shepheards boy" (l. 1); Raleigh as "the shepheard of the Ocean" (l. 66); and Queen Elizabeth as "so great a shepheardesse" (l. 369). The very ocean waves are "the hills . . . the surges hie,/On which faire *Cynthia* her heards doth feed" (ll. 240-1). The poets at court are likewise shepherds who "blow/ Their pipes aloud" (ll. 378-9). Colin's own inamorata is distinguished from the others in that she "is not like as the other crew/ Of shepheards daughters which emongst you bee" (ll. 931-2). Many additional locutions occurring at intervals in the poem take their origin from the received pastoral vocabulary. Such, for instance, are the natural phenomena pictured as mourning in the opening speech of Hobbinol—woods, birds, fields, running water, fish. Such are the manifold allusions sprinkled throughout to pipes, sheep, lambs, folds, and the like.

In *Colin Clout,* the pastoral image—or succession of interlaced images—does not seem so clear-cut in its implication as Miss Spurgeon apparently conceives her garden image to be, or Fogle his complex images which utilize motifs of ulcers and of blood.

18. *Ibid.,* p. 22.

19. Puttenham, p. 187, states the usual Renaissance acceptation of allegory as follows: "and because such inuersion of sence in one single worde is by the figure *Metaphore* . . . and this manner of inuersion extending to whole and large speaches, it maketh the figure *allegorie* to be called a long and perpetuall Metaphore".

One reason which quickly suggests itself for this difference is that pastoral is a literary genre, a conventionalized mode of expression, whereas ulcers and blood are corporeal entities which can readily be equated with disease and with physical violence. As a genre, pastoral cannot be readily equated with any set theme or philosophy. For poets of the Renaissance during the last quarter of the sixteenth century, pastoralism was not just "a point of view", as one critic remarks apropos of *Colin Clout;*[20] it was potentially many points of view; and it was just this versatility that made the mode ideal for Spenser. Pastoralism was in vogue.[21] It permitted freedom within a form. It afforded aesthetic distance for the decorous delineation of persons far above the title character in station and rank. It possessed built-in tensions which, given the requisite skill on the part of the poet, could be exploited with brilliant results. The conventions which had accrued to pastoral poetry during the long period of its development from classical to Renaissance times furnished both a justification for, and a method

20. *The Complete Poetical Works of Spenser,* ed. R. E. Neil Dodge, Cambridge ed. (Cambridge, Mass., 1908), p. 686.

21. E.g., *England's Helicon,* published only five years after *Colin Clout,* was designed as an anthology of pastoral poems. Many of the pieces in this magnificent collection were converted from other modes into pastoral expressly for the miscellany, although the changes are often quite superficial. For alterations of this kind made by the editor of the miscellany, see *England's Helicon,* ed. Hyder Edward Rollins (Cambridge, Mass., 1935), II, 63-6. For a complete history of English pastoral poetry, see W. W. Greg, *Pastoral Poetry and Pastoral Drama* (London, 1906), the standard history which continues to be eminently useful. For a good selective bibliography of the subject to date, see the one at the end of the anthology, *English Pastoral Poetry: From the Beginnings to Marvell,* ed. Frank Kermode (New York, 1952). In *Theories of Pastoral Poetry in England, 1684-1798* (Gainesville, Fla., 1952), Chs. I and II, J. E. Congleton presents the continental and English backgrounds for the theory of pastoral prior to 1684. S. K. Heninger, Jr., "The Renaissance Perversion of Pastoral", *JHI,* XXII (1961), 254-61, develops the thesis that pastoral in the Renaissance suffered by reason of its assumption of new roles as satire, moral allegory, and sentiment; and by reason of its assumption of new forms of prose, drama and verse. *Colin Clout* is not mentioned by name in the article by Heninger, but the poem would presumably be included in the blanket indictment because of its sizeable admixture of moral and satirical elements. Hallett Smith, *Elizabethan Poetry: A Study in Conventions, Meaning, and Expression* (Cambridge, Mass., 1952), has in the first chapter, "Pastoral Poetry", an extended and illuminating treatment of the Elizabethan pastoral, which includes a suggestive discussion of *Colin Clout* (pp. 54-7).

of ordering, the varied matters in the poem, many of which were originally identified with more restricted genres.

By 1579, when he published *The Shepheardes Calender,* Spenser had already assimilated to pastoral poetry more of these later elements than had any of his continental or insular predecessors.[22] In *Colin Clout* these newer elements by means of which Spenser vitalizes the older tradition come to comprise means and matter gleaned from such varied genres and sub-genres as the following: pastoral romance; Platonic and Neo-Platonic dialogues; court-of-love poems; Petrarchan sonnets and *canzoni,* which combine Plato, Dante, and the Provençal troubadours in one blended strain; classical philosophical poems, like those of Empedocles and Lucretius; Ovidian and Virgilian mythological poems; Hebraic biblical history and Song of Solomon marriage poems. These annexed modes and their related content areas become equally with the traditions of "pure" pastoral like the singing match and the complaints of love part of the larger contextual setting of the poem. This larger contextual setting, to which all the subject areas can be related, necessarily conditions the meaning of descriptive details, concretions, and figures. The figures, in particular, utilize almost exclusively as their second terms topics drawn from these ingested genres. The detailed treatment of these topics, will, therefore, be most illuminating when undertaken in direct connection with their occurrence as vehicles of particular images, where they are subjected to a special kind of control by reason of their being embodied in metaphoric structures. The last section of this chapter deals with images under the third category of figurative expressions. Now it is in order to sketch the contextual setting of the poem in the large by showing how Spenser has interwoven many of the relatively novel ingredients from the annexed genres with conventions from the older tradition.

One of these conventions, the assembly of shepherds, makes possible the gathering of a group to hear the recital of Colin's recent adventures. It is true that the early tradition which Spenser himself adheres to in the *Calender* calls for two or three participants, but now borrowing from the contemporary romances which also exploited pastoral, Spenser enlarges the group to ten. The convention of the singing match permits Colin and the Shepherd of the Ocean to engage in a friendly contest of "improvised" lays.

22. *Shepheards Calender,* ed. C. H. Herford (London, 1895), p. xxvii.

Frequently the subject of these lays, as in Theocritus, Virgil, and Mantuan, is myths narrating familiar stories of deities, most of whom are, of course, personified natural phenomena. By having Colin recite the ill-starred love of Bregog for Mulla, Spenser utilizes the convention. The material of Spenser's myth is new, but the form is old. Similar topographical myths are found in non-pastoral poems of Ovid and Pausanias as well as in the poems of Italian humanists.

In the ancestry of the pastoral, the subject of the contestants' songs is lovers' complaints. The tradition thus allows the Shepherd of the Ocean to voice the wrongs done him, the "faultlesse" (l. 167) shepherd, by his "loues queene, and goddesse" (l. 170). The same pastoral element of love praise or complaint permits Colin later in the poem to make his avowal of vassalage in fourteen impassioned lines to "one, whom all my dayes I serue" (l. 467). It also gives sanction to conclude his dialogue with an eloquent plea to Rosalind for grace after the long affliction he has endured. But these sophisticated effusions of Colin's are a far cry from the relatively simple mingling of praise and recrimination voiced by Colin's classical prototypes, by the "desperate lover" in Theocritus' third idyll, for example, or by Corydon in Virgil's second eclogue. The vocabulary of courtly love poems and Petrarchan sonnets—vassal, love's martyrdom, beauty's beam, guerdon for grief, grace to recur pain—these terms of Colin's declarations of eternal devotion to his beloved amply attest the overlay of more complicated motifs upon the simpler themes of the earlier love songs.

There was also ample precedent in the living pastoral tradition for the panegyric vein so prominent in the poem : panegyrics upon a monarch (ll. 187-91, 333-51, 592-615, 624-47); praise of fellow poets (ll. 376-451); and glorification of influential ladies (ll. 486-577). Theocritus had started the laudatory tradition in pastoral with his sixteenth Idyll,[23] a more or less general plea for patronage. To support the plea, he instances a number of persons who owe their fame to poetic commentators. Virgil and Calpurnius enlarged upon the eulogistic precedent.[24] Both panegyric and allegory play a larger part in the poetry of Clément Marot, "Spenser's most immediate predecessor, both in form and treatment".[25] Marot's

23. *The Shepherd's Calendar,* ed. W. L. Renwick, An Elizabethan Gallery, No. 5 (London, 1930), p. 190.

24. Greg, *Pastoral Poetry and Pastoral Drama,* p. 16.

25. *Shepheards Calender,* ed. Herford, p. xxxiii.

Éclogue au Roi, addressing Francis I under the name of Pan, was available as a model to Spenser, particularly in the "justness of sentiment ... which saves the verse from degenerating into mere sycophancy".[26] Though panegyric is one of the well-established elements in pastoral verse, the superabundance of this vein in *Colin Clout* connects the poem with demonstrative oratory as well, one of the three standard divisions of the art in Ciceronian rhetoric. The purpose and devices of demonstrative oratory are elaborated upon in Quintilian's *Institutio Oratoria,*[27] prescribed by the Statues of the Realm for textbook use at Cambridge during Spenser's stay there. In the Gloss to *April,* an elaborate panegyric on the "Queene of Shepheardes all",[28] E. K. calls attention to what follows line 73 as "a sensible Narration, and present view of the thing mentioned".[29] The "narration" would be only too familiar to the Renaissance reader as the second of the "seuen partes in euery Oration"[30]—the statement of the case.

Following the praise of the ladies is a long section of court satire (ll. 680-730, 749-70, 775-882). As a mode of discourse, dispraise was studied from classical times forward in connection with the demonstrative speech.[31] Since demonstrative oratory was still a flourishing form in the last quarter of the sixteenth century,[32] one cannot be certain as to whether the dispraise should be derived from the tradition of epideictic oratory or from pastoral ancestry for which it also had long-standing warrant. In view of the fact that poetry was everywhere thought of as closely akin to oratory in its persuasive functions, the two influences very likely reinforced each other. Renaissance pastoral had gotten an effective start in the satiric vein with Petrarch's pastorals denouncing ecclesiastical corruption,[33] and with those of Mantuan satirizing sharply both the abuses at Rome and the foibles of women.[34] The diatribe in *Colin Clout* against characteristic evils at court—ostentation, slander, licentious love—utilizes more coarse words than any other

26. Greg, p. 62.
27. III.7.1-28, I, 464-78.
28. *S.C., Works,* VII, 37.
29. *Ibid.,* p. 43.
30. *Wilson's Arte of Rhetorique, 1560,* ed. Mair, p. 7.
31. This can be observed from the *Arte of Rhetorique* (p. 11), an English version of classical theory.
32. Howell, *Logic and Rhetoric in England,* p. 107.
33. Greg, p. 22.
34. *Ibid.,* pp. 26-7.

section of the poem. Some figures from this section, as noted in Chapter II, are drawn from vulgar proverbs. Much of its imagery, as will be shown later, depends for its effect on a reversal of Platonic terms of essence, light, virtue, and beauty. One passage, lines 692-702, picturing the rivalries, the chicanery, the ambitious striving which prevail at court, strongly suggests the jargon of sorcery or witchcraft, especially in such phrases as "subtill shifts", "finest sleights deuise", "creeping close into his secrecie", and "guilefull hollow hart". The connotation is highly effective for the purpose, contrasting by implication the guileless simplicity of country life with the dark doings in the city. This contrast is another firmly entrenched tradition of pastoral, exemplified at the very start of recorded pastoral writings by the twentieth idyll of Theocritus.[35] In this selection a shepherd recounts how his advances elicit scorn from Eunice, a city-bred girl.

Corylas interrupts Colin's strictures on court life to ask about love there, since he thought that love was "our God alone:/And only woond in fields and forests here" (ll. 773-4). The interruption ushers in Colin's lengthy disquisition on love (ll. 799-886). This speech presents, largely in philosophic terms, the birth of Love in the garden of Adonis and Love's power to unite the four basic elements. This union, according to Colin's account, set the stage for creation and later, procreation. The phraseology in these eighty-eight lines carries strong overtones of the disparate borrowings which go to make up the passage: Plato's *Symposium* and Ficino's *Commentarium,* Ovid's *Metamorphoses,* Lucretius' *De Rerum Natura,* and Genesis.

Though the general literary backgrounds of this section have long been recognized (but its precise sources have not been entirely agreed upon), the relation of its material to pastoral has not been so clear. One scholar states that the philosophical discussion on love does not belong to the pastoral tradition at all.[36] There are, however, a number of nexus which make the admissibility of this material to pastoral quite understandable and appropriate. The religious element in Theocritus is one such link to the central line of the passage—the deification of love and the religion of love—even though, to be sure, the worship of Pan, alluded to in the first

35. Kermode, *English Pastoral Poetry,* p. 20. See pp. 37-42 for the relevance of this ancient contrast to pastoral literature in Elizabethan London.
36. Koller, "Studies in Spenser's *Colin Clout*", p. 126.

idyll, is not a prominent feature of Theocritus. As mentioned, songs which the shepherds sang in pastoral poems often deal with allegorized natural phenomena. One such pastoral song is Bion's famous "Lament for Adonis". Primitive religion embodied in the myth conceives the short-lived sun (Adonis) as slain by darkness (the boar) and mourned by twilight or the dawn (Venus), which cannot exist without the light. Several of the idylls of Theocritus deal with the "matter of Troy", in which gods of the sea and sky figure prominently. One of the idylls—the twenty-seventh—opens with an allusion to the neatherd who ravished Helen. The central imaginative concept of the Trojan story pertains to that same shepherd lad, Paris, who is called upon to make a judgment as to the rival claims of Juno (wealth, power), Pallas Athene (wisdom, fame), and Venus (love). *Colin Clout* contains a slight reference to the judgment of Paris in the little *exemplum* of Helen's revenge upon Stesichorus, who in his rhymes had dared to slander her divine beauty.

The third and most important nexus connecting the detailing of the birth, nature, and power of love to pastoral is the cosmology with which the section ends (ll. 841-86). In the opening lines of Virgil's famous fourth eclogue, foretelling the advent of a new era on earth, Virgil invokes the Sicilian muse of Theocritus to permit a raising of pastoral matter away from the humble tamarisk and the vintage grove. In his less well-known sixth eclogue, Virgil represents Silenus, the satyr, as singing the song of creation to Chromis and Mnasylus.[37] Virgil's cosmogony, which includes the combining of the four elements, the separation of the sea from the

37. Silenus also sings a number of myths. In one of these, Gallus, a friend of Virgil's who is both a soldier and a poet, is introduced upon Parnassus to Apollo and to the Muses. There he is presented with the pipe of Hesiod. *Colin Clout* brings Spenser's friend, Sir Walter Raleigh, also a soldier and a poet, rather prominently into the narrative. In *Colin Clout,* however, it is the narrator rather than the narrator's friend who is presented by the latter upon the new Parnassus of the English court, and there granted by the foremost patron, not the pipe of Hesiod, but a more substantial reward in the form of a pension of £50 per year. While one need not make too much of the matter, nevertheless it is not likely that the parallel and the contrast were lost upon the favored Elizabethan reader, who, if he did not know the Latin original, had access to several recently published translations into English. One of 1591 was by Abraham Fraunce, a member of the Pembroke circle. (For Renaissance translations of Virgil's *Eclogae,* see R. R. Bolgar, *The Classical Heritage and Its Beneficiaries* [Cambridge, Eng., 1954], p. 538.)

land, and the taking of form by living creatures, had become a commonplace of Spenser's day.[38] Though, as one literary historian remarks, "this mixture of obsolescent theology with Epicurean philosophy probably possessed little reality for Vergil himself",[39] once introduced, the cosmology became a firm part of the tradition, imitated first by Calpurnius and then by others.[40]

The above sketch of the literary backgrounds with which pastoral imagery is associated shows that in *Colin Clout* Spenser confines himself to the modes and subject areas already sanctioned by a long succession of pastoral writers. The only elements common to pastoral which he faintly suggests but does not include are those of the dirge proper and of Arcadia. The connotative value of the rich store of familiar accretive matter was high for the Renaissance reader. Lacking familiarity with this lore, the reader would indeed miss the echoes, the overtones, and the points of view—the built-in tensions—which are such a large element of the meaning.

This synopsis of modes and themes in *Colin Clout* recalls to the reader the material he needs to associate with the images—concretions, descriptive details, and figures—if he is to register them against a larger contextual setting. The synopsis even accounts, to some extent, for the presence of the content elements which often seem to the modern reader so "diversified in tone and subject".[41] The résumé fails, however, to indicate that the imagery embedded in the pastoral matrix has more than a generally connotative function. It tends to give the impression that all that is required for the reader to respond to the imagery is free mental association. It also tends by inference to attribute to the Renaissance poet a comparative looseness of thought which is hard to reconcile with the

38. Cf. R. Ellrodt, *Neoplatonism in the Poetry of Spenser,* p. 101, with explicit reference to *Colin Clout*: "Spenser's cosmogony . . . was woven out of mediaeval or Renaissance commonplaces. None of his notions therefore can be securely traced to any single author". Even so, almost immediately following this statement, Ellrodt invites attention to the remarkably close parallels between Spenser's account of the creation of the World and material contained in the Epilogue to the first book of *Le Sympose de Platon, de l'Amour et de Beauté* (1558) by the French humanist Loys (or Louis) Le Roy. This work is a commentary on the *Symposium* and an epitome of earlier classical and Renaissance discourses on love.

39. Greg, p. 15.

40. *Ibid.,* p. 16.

41. Waldo F. McNeir, "Spenser's 'Pleasing Alcon' ", *Études Anglaises,* IX (1956), 138.

recognized preoccupation in school and college of sixteenth-century England with the trivium, which the reader will recall as consisting of grammar, rhetoric, and logic—the very tools of the precisionist in language. It is perhaps this assumption of deficiency in firm control of materials which leads one critic to declare that the long insertion about love is not appropriate,[42] and another to characterize the author in respect to this poem as "untied by argument or ulterior object", rejoicing in "pure irresponsible self-expression".[43]

These critics clearly imply that *Colin Clout* evinces a lack of decisive control on the part of the author. If one is content to view imagery almost exclusively in terms of associative meanings, he finds it hard to meet this fairly common criticism. Fortunately, there is a way to consider imagery which will show how it functions to help control meaning. This is the way which places great weight upon the close analysis of logical relationships between the parts of images, viewed, according to my third category, as metaphorical structures. This emphasis is predicated upon a belief in the shared understanding which is deemed to have existed between Renaissance writer and reader largely as an outcome of their common education, grounded in the three liberal disciplines of grammar, rhetoric, and logic. Training received in these basic arts of communication must have made educated people of the period, especially writers, acutely conscious of the structure of images and of their logical nature. This awareness on their part seems credible because, as will appear shortly, images arose naturally—almost inevitably—out of techniques and practices inculcated over the years of learning as essentials of these arts. I am, of course, referring to the processes encompassed in great measure by the related terms "judgment" and "invention".[44]

42. Adolphus Alfred Jack, *A Commentary on the Poetry of Chaucer and Spenser* (Glasgow, 1920), p. 247.

43. Davis, *Edmund Spenser,* p. 47.

44. See Rev. Walter Ong, S.J., *Ramus,* pp. 276-7, for a statement regarding the placement of these studies in the educational curriculum of Spenser's time. The important position occupied by the study of logic and rhetoric in Renaissance education, as well as the influence of these subjects upon all educated persons of the time, is summarized by Miss Tuve in *Elizabethan and Metaphysical Imagery,* pp. 281-4. On p. 281 she cites the more important works of modern scholarship regarding the Renaissance veneration of logic in particular. To these references should be added Howell, *Logic and Rhetoric in England, 1500-1700.* See above, n. 10, Ch. II, for Howell's list of works dealing specifically with the trivium as an organon for the teaching of composition in Spenser's period.

In the remainder of the chapter I shall adhere for convenience to the present-day practice of referring to these procedures as "logical" in their orientation, although, to be sure, Renaissance theory, Ramus and his partisans excepted, regarded them as integral parts belonging both to rhetoric and to logic. In this theory, which followed Aristotle and Cicero, the machinery of analysis and synthesis for purposes of initiating and continuing discourse was duplicated in the two disciplines, existing there as substitute forms available for use on two levels of application—one for the popular and one for the learned audience. In the Ramist system which flourished in England and elsewhere during the last quarter of the sixteenth century, the reader will recall that judgment and invention were assigned exclusively to logic, and style and delivery to rhetoric. The integration of the two disciplines for purposes of communication was still maintained, however, since the Ramist system required the writer or speaker to go to logic for thought and form and to rhetoric for presentation.

One authority has suggested that the Ramist appropriation of all the loci by logic or dialectic reinforced the hold of logic on the poetry of the period, with especial reference to the creation of images.[45] At any rate, writers of Ramist persuasion seem to be highly conscious of the logical elements in tropes. These they customarily treated under four headings—metonymy, irony, metaphor, and synecdoche—all reducible in the matured theory to metaphor, taken in the modern sense.[46] For example, in *La Rhetorique Francoise* (1555), a French version of Talaeus's *Rhetorica* (fifth ed., 1552), the author, Antoine Foclin, arranges his tropes in the exact same order that Ramus in his *Dialectique* enumerates the ten places of argument, with cause first, effect second, subject third, and so on.[47] In England, the works of Abraham Fraunce, a younger satellite of the Sidney galaxy to which Spenser and Harvey belonged in the late 1570s, furnish clear evidence of the keen awareness on the part of Ramists of the close connection between logical processes and invention of matter, of which creation of images was an important part. In *The Arcadian Rhetorike* (1588), a translation of Talaeus, Fraunce, like Foclin, takes up each species of trope

45. See above, n. 11, Ch. II.
46. Cf. Ong, *Ramus,* p. 274.
47. Howell, pp. 168-9.

coming under one of the four main kinds on the basis of its derivation from one of the places of invention and in accordance with the order of that place in Ramus's basic list. Thus, for metonymy, we find metonymy of the cause (efficient and material), of the thing caused (that is, of the effect), of the subject, and finally of the adjunct.[48] Fraunce's explanations in the *Rhetorike* of the individual tropes which precede the illustrative passages reflect a conception of logical analysis as helping form a bridge between writer and reader. This view, which Fraunce shared with his coevals, whether or not of Ramist persuasion, is made very explicit from a passage in *The Lawiers Logike,* the counterpart of the *Rhetorike* and published the same year with it. The passage, occurring near the end of the first book of Invention, functions both as a general summary of the first book and as an introduction to the concluding illustration, in which Fraunce takes the words *Nobilitas* and *Amicitia* through the places: "If we shall for exercise sake vse to draw any one woord through these generale places of inuention, it will breede a great plentie and varietie of new arguments, while wee marke what be the causes, effects, parts, whole, generall, speciall, subiectes, adiunctes thereof, and so forth in all the rest: *and this either in making and enditing our selues, or els in resoluing, and as it were dismembring that which others have doone*".[49]

Fraunce finds it possible to illustrate virtually all the terms of logic—places, axioms, syllogisms, method—by means of some one hundred quotations from *The Shepheardes Calender,* which shares, along with Virgil's *Aeneid* and Sidney's *Arcadia,* favored place as a source of logical exemplification. Of particular interest to our study is the prominence Fraunce gives to comparatives. Departing somewhat from his master Ramus's doctrine, he groups "likes" and "unlikes" together under the single term "comparisons", whereas in strict Ramist grouping there would be two places, opposites and comparatives. Moreover, he removes comparatives from their regular order in Ramus's list of places and puts them in a separate section of four chapters at the end of the first book.[50] He also enhances their importance by making them one of two basic divisions of arguments, simple and compared.[51] In this section of

48. *Arcadian Rhetorike,* ed. Seaton, pp. 7-10.
49. *Lawiers Logike,* fol. 81^{v}. Italics mine.
50. Fols. 72^{r}-81^{r}.

comparatives, chapters XX-XXIV, there are twelve passages from the *Calender* illustrating *similitudes* and *dissimilitudes.* "Comparison," Fraunce tells us, "is eyther in qualitie or quantitie."[52] These concepts of quality and quantity, one recalls, are distinct places in scholastic logic. An image of quality, where there is no "note" (that is, sign of the comparison), is illustrated by Thenot's speech in *February*:

> For youth is a buble blowne vp with breath,
> Whose wit is weakenesse, whose wage is death,
> Whose way is wildernesse, whose Inne penance,
> And stoope-gallant age the host of greeuance.[53]

Fraunce's understanding of the function of images as being aids to clarity and supports to argument is standard for his age.[54] This view is reflected in the logical analysis of Virgil's second eclogue. This analysis Fraunce took over from John Thomas Freigius, a professor at Basle. It is the first of two analyses which bring the *Logike* to an end. The analysis divides the entire eclogue into two parts, of which the second is the complaint and lamentation of Corydon, the lover, speaking to his beloved, one Alexis. Corydon accuses his lover of cruelty, which is argued by a series of comparisons, as quoted below from the analysis:

51. Fol. 72r.
52. Fol. 72r.
53. Fol. 72v.
54. Cf. Sidney and Puttenham, for example, on the similitude. Sidney speaks of the function of the similitude in these terms: "for the force of a similitude not being to prooue anything to a contrary Disputer but onely to explane to a willing hearer, when that is done, the rest is a most tedious pratling" (*Apologie for Poetrie,* in *Eliz. Critical Essays,* I, 203). Puttenham, a non-Ramist, pays tribute to the eloquence of the similitude by saying that "no one thing more preuaileth with all ordinary iudgements than perswasion by similitude" (*Arte of English Poesie,* p. 240). Puttenham, incidentally, seems to have acted upon this conviction in using a particularly ingenious similitude as the motto for the woodcut portrait of Queen Elizabeth which prefixes the *Arte* and which serves as a Dedication. The motto reads: "Che se stessa rassomiglia & non altrue"—i.e., To that lady who resembles herself and none other. (The woodcut and motto are reproduced opposite the facsimile of the original title page of the *Arte* in the edition by Willcock and Walker.)

> First by comparison of the vnlikes, the proposition consisteth of three vnlikes, the beastes, Lysardes, and reapers seeke shade : the reddition is, but yet I burne with loue.
> 2. By the lesse Amaryllis and Menalcas are too cruell, but thou more cruel then they.
> 3. By the cause of his pride, whiche was his beautie, and yt [that] is extenuated by a simile. As white primprint fales, but blacke Violets bee gathered, so beautie decayes, and blacknes remaines.[55]

Corydon, after indulging in accusations, attempts to entice Alexis to come to his house. Corydon tries to persuade the shepherd by heaping praise upon himself through reference to his own adjuncts. He is rich, he is skillful in singing, he is fair, and he is frank and free. All these attributes are "proved" in some way or other. The most common way is by comparisons—metaphorical structures. For example, Corydon proves that he is skillful in singing "By a comparison of the equall, in that hee is equall to Amphion : and heere an obiection is preuented by a comparison also of the equall : neither thinke it a shame to play on a pype, for Amyntas thought well of it".[56]

All this seems unbelievably cumbersome to modern minds and raises the question of the degree to which Renaissance writers relied in actual composition on inventional modes studied assiduously in logic. Unfortunately, the question can never be subjectively resolved now.[57] In any event, the validity of an approach to the study of Renaissance images which leans heavily on the easy familiarity of writer and reader with these processes does not depend upon establishing such methodology as a self-conscious, highly deliberative act on the part of either. The validity of the approach can properly be gauged only by its help in illuminating the images and through them the poem itself.

55. Fol. 123r.

56. Fol. 123v.

57. See Tuve, *Elizabethan and Metaphysical Imagery,* pp. 290-1, 284-7, 295, and 311-12, on this point. Her general conclusion is stated on p. 284, as follows: "I think that Renaissance poets were more conscious than we of the exact nature of the logical processes they utilized in their poems. However, the specific relation with images is chiefly a matter of the transference of habitual modes of thought which had been engrained by years of familiarity, of practice, of analysis."

Somewhat analogous to the question above in its relevance to a study of images in one of Spenser's poems is that of Spenser's own training in, or predilection for, either the orthodox logic and rhetoric or the reformed system of Ramus and his associate Talaeus. The answer to the question is uncertain at present,[58] and it is rather surprising that Miss Seaton, in her edition of *The Arcadian Rhetorike,* appears to base her contention that Spenser "can be counted among the faithful" on E. K.'s Glosses to the *Calender* and on Fraunce's quotations from it in the *Logike.*[59] But the resolution of this problem, if it should prove possible to resolve decisively, would not importantly effect the usefulness of the approach to images via logical bases. This is true because both the older and newer system of compositional disciplines counted heavily on fundamentally the same processes of invention, which were designated and arranged rather differently in each.

I shall attempt, in the ensuing final section, to show how the presence of the generic relationship between images and processes of logical invention helped prevent the readers of *Colin Clout* from being thrown upon their own resources in responding to images, or, more specifically, from construing the connoted second terms of a metaphor (using the word in its present wide sense) in a completely fanciful way. As this statement suggests, the center of focus in the subsequent canvas of images will be rhetorical figures, now looked at from a somewhat different point of view than in the second chapter on "The Figures of Rhetoric". Giving metaphors and their extensions (like personification and myth) the most emphatic position and most expanded treatment of the three categories under which images are treated in the present chapter is fully warranted not only by the variety and multiplicity of such images in *Colin Clout* but also by the high regard generally with which Renaissance theorists and practitioners of poetry regarded the *similitude* as a device of rhetorical and poetic efficacy. This regard they shared with Aristotle, who, it will be recalled, expressed the opinion that it is a sign of poetic genius to be a master of metaphor, "since a good metaphor implies an intuitive perception of the similarity in dissimilars".[60]

58. See above, n. 11, Ch. II.
59. Page xii.
60. *Poetics,* 22, 1459a, trans. Ingram Bywater, Vol. XI of *The Works of Aristotle* (1924), ed. W. D. Ross, 12 vols. (Oxford, 1908-52).

It may be helpful at this juncture to draw together the considerations which give promise to an investigation of images, as they are employed in a particular context, which relates figures to inventive techniques. For the sake of clarity, these considerations may be stated positively, although, as has been noted, allowance must be made for different degrees of emphasis to be accorded the various points. While logical applications are by no means confined to figures, nevertheless, the fact that figures, whether metaphors or similitudes, express a relationship between one thing and another conduces to their formulation by logic-taught modes. In the metaphor and similitude, a thing is illuminated, limited, or defined by being compared with something else (that "something else" being, of course, implied in the case of a metaphor) in terms of cause, adjuncts, quality, quantity, etc. The incessant practice given Renaissance scholars in "inventing" matter by "going through" the places and predicaments made these standard routines virtually indispensable processes when these same students turned to composing poetry. Is it any wonder that images struck off like sparks from flint when students were drilled over a period of many years in a set "method" applicable to all compositions? Thomas Wilson defines the method as "the maner of handling a single question, and the readie way how to teach and set forth anything plainly, and in order, as it should be".[61] The method called upon students to initiate composition by habitually asking the following questions :

1. Whether it be or no.
2. What it is.
3. What the partes are.
4. What the causes are.
5. What are the effects or proper working.
6. What are the next adioyning, what are like, what happen thereby.
7. What doe disagree, or what contrarie.
8. What exa[*m*]ple there is to proue it.[62]

It is important to notice that images which resulted from such a process were in response to questions already stated in terms of

61. *The Rule of Reason* (London, 1567), fol. 16ᵛ.

62. *Ibid.*, fol. 17ᵛ. (The word *proue* in No. 8, misprinted in the 1567 edition, has been corrected from the first edition, *The Rule of Reason* [London, 1551], sig. E6ʳ.)

intended logical functions. Although, to be sure, images can be and are formed without reference to such an ingrained method, the Renaissance poet, by reason of thorough training in logic and rhetoric, could scarcely help growing highly aware of the precise office the images were to accomplish when he employed them. The relevance of this method and the allied procedures of logic to the formation and control of figurative images will be made clear as the various images are studied.

The first such image—a similitude—is considered as a visual image in the part of this chapter surveying images on the basis of their appeal to the physical senses. There attention is invited to the comparative generality of the picture drawn—the lack of sensuous impact. Since the image is short, it can conveniently be repeated here. It occurs in the introductory frame describing, in the familiar mode of classical pastoral, the "shepheard" playing upon his oaten pipe for the entertainment of his fellows,

> Who all the while with greedie listfull eares,
> Did stand astonisht at his curious skill,
> Like hartlesse deare, dismayd with thunders sound. (ll. 7-9)

This image is formed in response to the question of the "method" —"what are like". The comparison between the attitude of the shepherds listening to Colin with that of deer frozen into immobility by the sound of thunder is intended to suggest to the reader of the poem the impression that the skill of the musician made upon his auditors—that they were "astonished" (literally, "turned into stone"). The comparison is also intended to convey empathically to the reader the attitude that he himself should adopt towards Colin's words, in somewhat the same way that the chorus in a Greek play conveys the response appropriate to the audience. It is significant to observe that in this, the first figurative image of the poem, Colin's listeners are being likened to deer in one main respect—their common pose of motionlessness, inspired by awe. Though one may freely concede that the scene evoked is pleasant to the visual imagination, the *primary* purpose of the image is not to "picture" either the audience or the deer. The main function is to emphasize the posture of attention and anticipation on the part of the group. This being the case, there is no need for details which might enhance the value of the image as sensuous stimulation but which would tend to obscure the conceptual function.

Examining the structure of the image in the light of formal logic,[63] one quickly finds that it is composed of the topic or place *similitude* or "Things like", as Wilson calls it,[64] with respect to the predicament *substance*[65] (deer)[66] and the predicament *man-*

63. It has seemed desirable for the sake of clarity and consistency to follow, in the main, Miss Tuve's phrasing of logical terms and methods from Ch. XI of *Elizabethan and Metaphysical Imagery*. They are based, for the most part, on two successful handbooks of the time: Thomas Wilson, *The Rule of Reason,* the first English logic, originally published in 1551, with five subsequent editions, including the last of 1580; and Thomas Blundeville, *The Arte of Logicke,* a treatise for Englishmen who knew no Latin, first published in 1599, but according to Howell (p. 285) probably written around 1575. Howell devotes the first part of Ch. II of *Logic and Rhetoric in England* to the *Rule of Reason,* and has his main treatment of the *Arte of Logicke* on pp. 285-91. I have consulted the 1567 edition of Wilson and the 1617 edition of Blundeville. Reference to the two manuals will be to these editions. I have profited greatly from the exposition in Miss Tuve's important work. She nowhere treats the present poem, however, nor does she employ portions of it for illustrative purposes.

64. Wilson's explanation in the *Rule of Reason* of the way "places", or standpoints of thought, were used for "working up" matter is particularly instructive. He says a "place" is the "resting corner of an argument, or else a marke, which giueth warning to our memorie, what wee may speake probably, either in the one part or the other, vpon all causes that fall in question" (fol. 37r). On the same page he compares the finding of matter for discourse through a process of "going through" the places (he allows twenty-four places in all) to a hunter's search for a fox. "For," he continues, "these places bee nothing els, but couerts or boroughes, wherein if any one search diligently, he may find game at pleasure." Elsewhere in the same work Wilson compares the process of inventing by means of the places to searching for gold in the veins of the earth and bringing the treasure to light for man's exclusive use (fol. 36v).

65. The predicaments, originally set forth in Aristotle's *Topica,* on which Wilson's treatment of the places is ultimately based, were categories to which a disciplined logical thinker like Spenser could refer or apply all things to discover their true nature. In Wilson's view, a representative one for his age, "A Predicament is nothing else in English, but a shewing or rehearsing what wordes may be truely ioyned together, or els a setting forth of the nature of eury thing, and also shewing what may bee truely spoken, and what not" (fol. 7v). Wilson divides the predicaments into two main categories: the substance and the accident (fol. 7v). The concept of the substance is the concept of the inseparable nature of anything, without which it could not be what it is. The concept of the accident is the concept of a thing as having something customarily related to or associated with it but not absolutely essential to it. There are ten predicaments in typical peripatetic logic, nine of which are concepts of accident and one of substance. Blunderville's manual agrees substantially with that of Wilson.

ner of suffering—two modes of operation in logic very familiar to learned readers and to a larger class of not-so-well-educated perusers of sixteenth-century handbooks of logic. In this first image, the observer can witness the practical use to which Spenser, in common with his fellow writers, puts his long years of training in the Aristotelian system of "inventing" and "disposing" subject matter. In the light of this typical employment of places and predicaments in logic to aid in defining or characterizing the nature of something, the reader is placed on his guard at the outset not to over-read the images.

Yet it would be equally unfortunate to underread the images by failing to give proper emphasis to the logical elements as controls. One may, in fact, be tempted at first to regard images embodied in two additional passages early in the poem simply as parts of the stock machinery of a faded tradition. The first of these, the all-nature-mourns speech of Hobbinol (ll. 22-30) is discussed in the chapter on rhetorical figures as an example of Spenser's use of the figures (in this case, *prosopopoeia* or personification) to build up blocks of verse. The second, Colin's song of the romance of Bregog (ll. 104-55), is mentioned as an example of how a rhetorical scheme (in this case, *topographia* or topographical myth) could function both as a set piece and as exposition of Kilcolman environmental features. Yet these mythopoeic passages regarded now as images which have a logical purpose yield a richer vein of meaning than when considered as rhetorical figures only. The speech of Hobbinol, opening the dialogue, cites the hyperbolically imagined *effect* of Colin's prolonged absence. The fact that woods, fields, and running brooks are personified to express the general grief occasioned by the absence acts to reflect strong praise on Colin, and thereby to

---

Blunderville, in answering the question, "What are Predicaments?" says: "Predicaments are certaine Titles or Tables containing all things that be in the world: for euery thing, whatsoeuer it be, is either a substance, or accident: and if it be a substance, it is found in the Table of substance hereafter following: if it bee an accident, it belongeth either to quantitie, qualitie, relation, action [Wilson's *manner of doing*], passion [Wilson's *suffering*], time, place, to be scited, or to haue" (p. 15).

66. In Blunderville's Table of Substances (p. 22), *deer* would be subsumed as a *substance* "with body . . . compound . . . liuing . . . sensible . . . reasonable . . . a 4 footed beast as a horse".

magnify his importance as a spokesman. The image cluster depicting the grief of nature, a topic thoroughly in the convention of pastoral elegy from classical times forward, has the additional merit of quickly identifying for the knowing reader the genre of the poem.

The river myth of Bregog and Mulla has been extensively studied as to its sources and analogues.[67] Yet beyond the autobiographical reference to the environs of Kilcolman and the vague attribution of the charming atmosphere lent by the myth, none of the critics has ventured to account otherwise for it.[68] If the myth is viewed as constructed from the predicament *relation* and elaborated from the common place of *adjuncts,* logical terms not materially different in their meaning from present-day denotations, a clue to the reason for the inclusion of the myth may appear. The reader will recall that the myth presents Old Mole (the mountain range, including the Ballyhoura Hills and the Galtee Mountains, located north and east of Spenser's Kilcolman estate in central Munster) and Mulla (the Awbeg river) in the relation of father and daughter. The *adjuncts* of fatherhood include the clear prerogative, in Renaissance domestic mores, for a father to choose a husband for his daughter, and correlatively to interpose obstacles to the free play of her fancies. The *adjuncts* of the love relationship are the countervailing desire of the lovers to unite at whatever cost. The outcome of the successful evasion of parental authority in the myth is naturally, in a moral writer like Spenser, disaster. This is precisely the outcome to the lovers, Bregog and Mulla. Thus, one may posit the hypothesis that Spenser intends the myth as an argument against the upsetting of hierarchy, of order, and an argument for permanence

67. The Commentary in the *Variorum* collects extracts from the important authorities on both literary parallels and apposite Kilcolman geography and topography (*Works,* VII, 454-7).

68. An apparent exception to this statement is Gottfried, "Spenser and the Italian Myth of Locality". Gottfried deals with the Bregog and Mulla tale as one of two Spenserian topographical myths which are "digressions apparently written from mere exuberance" (p. 107). He traces possible sources from Florentine and Neopolitan poets writing between the fourteenth and sixteenth centuries, differentiating Spenser's myths from those of his predecessors on the basis that Spenser "feels no compulsion to bring his story into visual consistency with real things" (p. 125). Thus Gottfried deals with the myths as examples of techniques—as "evidence of Spenser's literary character" (p. 107)—rather than as operative units within the artistic structure of a single poem or a single canto.

as opposed to mutability.[69] If this view is correct, the purpose of the myth is to adduce proof in the form of an *exemplum* for the validity of the principle—a conceptual function. The myth is introduced in answer to the final question of the "method"—"What exa[*m*]ple there is to proue it". Again, as with the nature-in-mourning passage, topographical fiction is ideally suited to pastoral or woodland setting, and so satisfies also the omnipresent demand of decorum.

Within the first third of the poem, largely given over to the pastoral ideal, the most elaborate image, also springing from logical methodology and furnishing thematic amplification, is the "marine pastoral" figure of Cynthia as "shepheardesse" of the sea (ll. 240-63). This allegory, transferring the terms of Elizabeth's guardianship of the sheep on land to a corresponding role at sea, proceeds by the standard logical predicament of *relation* and common place of *adjuncts*. Thus, the relationship of stewardship is transferred from sheep and cattle to "fishes with their frie" (l. 242). This same relation of "commandement" (l. 263) in pastoral-mythological terms applies as well to Triton and Proteus, lesser gods of the sea under Cynthia (daughter of the king of gods and men); to "I among the rest of many least" (l. 252)—the "shepheard of the Ocean", Sir Walter Raleigh; and to the water Nymphs, with the Nereids probably being subintended.

The adjuncts or attendant circumstances rounding out the concept of Cynthia as "Ladie" (l. 235), "Regent" (l. 235), and "shepheardesse" (l. 236) in relation to her charges are the "surges hie" (l. 240) in place of the hills, the setting sail and docking of the ships as parallels to the departure and return of the sheep "at euening and at morne" (l. 247), and the care of the ships after a voyage as a correlative of the washing and enfolding of the sheep by the Nymphs. It is to be remarked that the correspondence

69. Charles G. Smith, "Spenser's Theory of Friendship", *PMLA,* XLIX (1934), 496, points out among the parallels between the fourth book of the *Faerie Queene* and the *Cantos of Mutabilitie* the fact that the main characters in the latter, Nature and Sergeant Order, have their counterparts in Venus and Concord in the former. Now, two of Spenser's three main treatments, outside of *Colin Clout,* concerning the idea of love as a harmonizing and unifying force occur in Book Four of the *Faerie Queene* and in the *Cantos of Mutabilitie*. Therefore, the probable association in Spenser's mind of order with love supports the interpretation of the myth advanced here.

between the "real" in pastoral terms and the imagined in marine terms is by no means exact. For instance, the ships (the sheep) do not feed on water (hills and pastures), nor do they breed. Furthermore, the repair and refitting of the ships is only remotely comparable to the washing and enfolding of sheep after they have been shorn. The lack of correspondence between the terms of the tenor and the vehicle would be somewhat reduced if a subtle meaning is read into the reference to breeding in the "bosome of the billowes" (l. 243) and if the relationship is taken to be: in the same way that the fish "feed" (that is, increase, enlarge), so do the English ships increase by taking into themselves the booty from Spanish treasure galleons. If this explanation is accepted, then one would have to regard as significant also the reference to the care of the ships being similar to the washing and enfolding of the sheep "when they be shorne" (l. 258)—that is, when the increase in their value has been removed. It does not seem likely, however, that this hypothetical extension of the possible meaning is justified; such an interpretation would probably represent unwarranted extension, or overreading. The purpose served by the image—rendering direct praise to Elizabeth and reflecting indirect praise on Raleigh—does not require such an oblique interpretation. The fashioning of the image according to ordinary logical bases conventionally requires that the analogies need be exact in only a single quality or property.[70] The image permits Spenser to accord a graceful compliment to Elizabeth in terms of her relation as queen-shepherdess to subject-charges, with the addition of adjuncts naturally expressive of the respective roles of monarchs and shepherds.

The merit of the fusion of sea and pastoral terms is not in its originality but in its familiarity! The association goes back at least to the classical myth connecting Neaera, daughter of the sea god Nereus, with Sylvanus, the woodland satyr. The conception of Elizabeth as a sea "deity" had been growing since the famous entertainment in her honor at Kenilworth Castle in 1575, and, after the victory over the Armada in 1588, became a particularly fitting symbol. The designation of "Cynthia" as a name for Elizabeth appears in John Lyly's play *Endymion* (1588).[71] The "Ora-

70. Cf. Wilson, *Rule of Reason* (fol. 50r) on the place *similitude*: "A similitude is, when two thinges or more, are so compared together, that euen as in the first, there is one propertie: So in the other there is a like property, according to both their natures seuerally obserued".

71. E. C. Wilson, *England's Eliza,* p. 297.

tion of Nereus to her Maiesty", part of an entertainment furnished the Queen at Elvetham in September of 1591 and attributed to John Lyly by his editor, R. W. Bond, speaks of "Faire Cinthia the wide Oceans Empress",[72] and characters in the pageant mingle sea and pastoral terms. Two of these characters, moreover, are the sea nymph Neaera and her lover, Sylvanus, the god of the outdoors.

In the middle section of the poem (ll. 328-647), devoted mainly to praising the courtly ideal, Spenser has Colin describe, in response to "leading questions" by the interlocutors, his sojourn at court. Although the imagery in this section is related largely to post-Sicilian adulterated pastoral matter, it is intimately associated with those literary areas with which the courtier, as a man of learning, was presumed to be thoroughly conversant: classical myth; courtly love ideals of a knight's faithful service to his lady; Platonism and Neo-Platonism, with Ficino's *Commentarium in Convivium* and Hoby's translation of Castiglione's *Libro del Cortegiano* as representative media of transmission;[73] Petrarchism; and the Bible. The intermingling of these literary antecedents, besides being sanctioned by humanistic pastoral models, probably did not seem incongruous to a thorough-going eclecticist like Spenser.[74] Furthermore, as Earle B. Fowler points out, courtly love, the cult of the Virgin, and Neo-Platonism had already been syncretized in the *dolce stil nuovo,*[75] exemplified in its early vogue by Dante. Thus, it can be considered that these literary traditions, like those of pure pastoral, constituted for Spenser a kind of unified body of materials for image making. Let us look at a representative image or image cluster relating to these fused backgrounds.

72. *The Complete Works of John Lyly,* ed. R. Warwick Bond (Oxford, 1902), I, 442.

73. *Daphnaïda,* p. 209; see also Ernest Cassirer, *The Platonic Renaissance in England,* trans. James P. Pettegrove (Austin, 1953), p. 111. "His [Ficino's] commentary on Plato's Symposium was a source-book of English poetics throughout the whole of the sixteenth century".

74. Cf. Dodge, ed. *Complete Poetical Works of Spenser,* p. 90, commenting on this characteristic of Spenser in his discussion of *Mother Hubberds Tale*: "Nothing shows better the independence of his artistic eclecticism, his gift for taking here, there, and everywhere whatever appeals to his imagination, than the mediaevalism of this his one satire"; also, Henry Gibbons Lotspeich, *Classical Mythology in the Poetry of Edmund Spenser,* Princeton Studies in English, No. 9 (Princeton, 1932), p. 27: "His [Spenser's] poetry is the fullest and richest expression in English of the eclecticism which characterized the Renaissance".

75. *Spenser and the System of Courtly Love* (Louisville, 1934), pp. 1-5.

The following panegyric to Elizabeth at the outset of the section is in the rhetorical form of a *comparatio* or comparison, organized according to a balanced arrangement, *carmen correlativum* :

> I would her lyken to a crowne of lillies
> Vpon a virgin brydes adorned head,
> With Roses dight and Goolds and Daffadillies;
> Or like the circlet of a Turtle true,
> In which all colours of the rainbow bee;
> Or like fair Phebes garlond shining new,
> In which all pure perfection one may see. (ll. 337-43).

This passage, glanced at briefly before as visual imagery, is, in logical terms, a series of parallels in place *similitude* with respect to *quality* or *property*. Thus, Cynthia is *like* a regal wreath, the colored band around a turtle dove's neck, or the ring around the moon. The *property* of the wreath is lilies, roses, marigolds, and daffodils; the *property* of the circlet, colors; of Phoebe's garland, light. There is also, of course, the play on crown with its suggestion of *adjuncts* power and royalty.

The *Variorum* commentary for lines 336-9 invites attention to a line in *The Faerie Queene* (V.iii.23.5)[76] describing Florimell and using a comparison mingling roses and lilies. The commentary on the lines in *The Faerie Queene* quotes passages from Virgil and Ovid as possible sources for the conceit.[77] However, the purpose of the comparisons for the passage of *Colin Clout* under discussion, unlike that of the Florimell stanza, is not mainly to picture Cynthia's facial coloring by contrasting the red and the white, but to impart ideas of rule and éclat, bride-like purity, and radiant perfection. The likening of Cynthia to the dove's iridescent band and to the moon ring also support through Neo-Platonic and biblical associations the idea of Cynthia's being at one the symbol of chaste love and of regal glory. As regards the latter, Renwick quotes, in connection with this passage, an extract from *Libro del Cortegiano* on the sacredness of monarchy in terms of the sun and moon reflecting "a certeine likenesse of God".[78] As regards the former,

76. *Works,* V, 32.
77. *Ibid.,* p. 189.
78. *Daphnaïda,* p. 186.

the dove's neck-ring, in the repertory of *amour courtois,* is a familiar motif of outward beauty toward which the soul is drawn in love.[79] Lines 341-2 have symbolic associations with the Bible, too, although this hyperbole is not nearly so directly reminiscent of scriptural sources as is the later and even more elaborate encomium on the same monarch (ll. 596-615). Nevertheless, these associations, not hitherto pointed out, strengthen the view that the passage is part of the "persuasion" of the poem, and not a description or ornamentation *per se.* A standard guide to symbolical terms in the Bible gives for "dove" the following attribution: "The symbol of purity and innocence".[80] The author adds the comment, "Probably the emblem was borrowed from the history of Noah and his dove with the olive of peace, and might be intended to denote a pacific reign". In the story of Noah and the flood, the rainbow is also a symbol of the Supreme Ruler's benevolence toward mankind.[81] Perhaps enough has been said to show the control of meaning through literary legacy operating simultaneously from different sources and at various removes. All such literary associations lend conceptual values to the similes. While the comparisons do please by recalling to the "inward eye" attractive objects of the visible world, that is their incidental function. If it were their main one, the details would be amplified and made more sensuously vivid. The images in the present passage, then, deal with Cynthia-Elizabeth as a representative of ideal virtue, beauty, and glory, and not with her as a person—at the time of *Colin Clout's* publication a woman already in her sixties, of whom Ben Jonson was ungallantly to tell Drummond long after that she "never saw her self after she became old jn a true Glass. they painted her & sometymes would vermilion her nose".[82]

79. A seminal Arabic work in the transmission of the love traditions which helped build the courtly ideal of the Renaissance takes its title from this motif—Ibn Hazm's *The Dove's Neck-ring* (1022). See Andreas Capellanus, *The Art of Courtly Love,* ed. and trans. John Jay Parry (New York, 1941), pp. 8-10, for evidence of the Platonic cast of Ibn Hazm's concept of love in this work. For an account of the transmission to the Provençal troubadours of love themes in Arab prose and poetry, based ultimately on the same sources as those used by Ovid, see Ibn Hazm, *The Dove's Neck-ring,* trans. A. R. Nykl (Paris, 1931), Ch. IV.

80. Thomas Wemyss, *A Key to the Symbolical Language of Scripture* (Edinburgh, 1840), p. 141.

81. *Ibid.,* pp. 142, 348-9.

82. *Ben Jonson,* ed. Herford and Simpson, I, 141-2.

The laudatory verses just discussed are the first of a series of passages which a number of well-known Spenserians have roundly condemned as flattery which overpasses in its grossness the bounds of good taste, being not only *ultra fidem,* beyond credit, to borrow Puttenham's phrases, but also *ultra modum,* beyond all measure.[83] The criticism that Spenser exceeds the poetic license for praise to overreach a little has centered on this and a later passage (ll. 590-615) expressing sustained adoration of Cynthia. But it has also been applied to the encomiastic section on the twelve ladies of Cynthia's train (ll. 485-577). Though these two passages will be taken up in proper sequence, it may be remarked that they are similar to lines 337-43 in being replete with figurative images, logically based, which have the same type of valuative and symbolic referents. The tenor of the reproaches levelled against Spenser for the poetic tributes to Cynthia may be gleaned from a few illustrative quotations. Francis T. Palgrave says that "Elizabeth (here named Cynthia) [is] described in a style of what, however reluctantly, must be termed servile rapture".[84] Speaking generally of Spenser, Richard W. Church accuses the author of *The Faerie Queene* of sharing the propensity of the age to engage in "gross, shameless, lying flattery".[85] In a much alluded-to and damning indictment applied directly to the lines on the Queen in *Colin Clout* Church writes: "He [Spenser] had already too well caught the trick of flattery—flattery in a degree almost inconceivable to us".[86] Pauline Henley, after quoting lines 181-7, ending

> And wend with him, his *Cynthia* to see:
> Whose grace was great, and bounty most rewardfull,

comments: "Scattered throughout his works are grossly flattering passages which at the present day would evoke scorn and contempt".[87] Renwick, in his notes on lines 332-51, finds it necessary to excuse Spenser: "This seems exaggerated, even as conventional panegyric ... That Elizabeth was avid for the strongest flattery

83. Page 192.
84. "Essays on the Minor Poems of Spenser", in *The Complete Works in Verse and Prose of Edmund Spenser,* ed. Alexander B. Grosart (privately published, 1882-84), IV, lxxx.
85. *Spenser,* English Men of Letters (London, 1886), p. 137.
86. *Ibid.,* p. 98.
87. *Spenser in Ireland* (Cork, 1928), p. 75.

may be a stain on her character: we need not blame her men for giving her what she liked, nor need we call it insincere ... Also fashion changes."[88]

Observations like these tend to ignore the fact that the words of adoration are uttered, not by Spenser in his own person, giving, let us say, a deposition in a court of law, but by a fictive character speaking in an imaginative construct.[89] The strictures are largely beside the point, moreover, since they fail to take into account the depersonalizing character of the imagery. As already noted for the first panegyric on Cynthia and as will become increasingly plain from subsequent laudatory verses, that imagery serves to generalize the praise, to abstract the "lovely ideas from their earthly manifestations".[90]

To continue with the orderly canvass of imagery from the standpoint of its employment in support of logical functions. The familiar lore and machinery of classical mythology do not represent a sizeable element in image-making. But Spenser's complete assimilation of such materials,[91] together with a confident reliance upon the educated reader's familiarity with them, made their employment as the

88. *Daphnaïda,* p. 186.

89. See Ch. VI for a full discussion of this important concept.

90. E. C. Wilson, p. 153. Wilson's preceding comment that the "final rationale of this glorification of Elisa or Cynthia is to be found in the profoundly Platonic cast of Spenser's imagination" (*ibid.*) hits very close to the mark. Wilson does not, however, connect the abstracting effect of the praise with the imagery *per se,* nor does he make any distinction between passages, on the one hand, which secure their transfer of values from images of comparison, logically grounded, and passages, on the other, which secure their idealizing effect from other causes. Thus, Wilson applies his "rationale" to the second eulogy of Cynthia (ll. 590-615), where it is appropriate, but also applies it to the second part of the same tribute (ll. 620-47), where it is not. This latter passage is a pastoral hyperbole in which Platonic essences play no part whatever. This passage containing the lines, "Her name in euery tree I will endosse,/That as the trees do grow, her name may grow", which echo verses in Virgil's tenth eclogue, gets its abstracting effect not from transfiguration, but from the creation of aesthetic distance and from the conscious imitation of a famous classical conceit.

91. Cf. Lotspeich, pp. 27-8: "Classic myth, as it came to Spenser, was 'polyseme', rich in the meanings and associations given it by generations of poets and commentators. Much of it was ready-made for this purpose; all of it was plastic and adaptable ... It furnished him with a body of symbols that could be used for feelings and intuitions for which no other terms would do ... In all these ways it became organic and integral to his poetry, traditional and conventional to be sure, but also living and vital, because it expressed what was vital to him."

stuff of imagery virtually inevitable upon occasion. A good example of this sometimes rather casual use of the body of mythological lore is found in the long section devoted to Colin's qualified praise of the court poets (ll. 377-449). Two short passages in particular, lines 412-15 and lines 420-25, on Alabaster and Daniel respectively, exemplify the method for sub-themes. The first passage is the rhetorical *horismos*, or figure of difference, employing the logical common place *contraries* :

> Nor *Po* nor *Tyburs* swans so much renowned,
> Nor all the brood of *Greece* so highly praised,
> Can match that *Muse* when it with bayes is crowned,
> And to the pitch of her perfection raised.

Here the image (answering the "method" question, "What doe disagree or what contrarie") has the general function of discriminating between the genius of Alabaster, when writing in the heroic genre, and the genius of earlier epic poets. It should be noted that the terms of the distinction are, by modern criteria, loose in the extreme. For example, the reader of whatever period might well ask to which specific poets of ancient Greece and Rome and Renaissance Italy is Alabaster being contrasted. Perhaps the vagueness here is a kindness on the part of Spenser, even though the recollection of at least Homer, Virgil, and Ariosto is inevitable. The epithet of "swan", as everyone knows, had been applied even in Roman times to Virgil, the "Mantuan Swan", and to Homer, "the swan of Meander", the appellation in both cases deriving ultimately from the myth of Apollo's having been at one time metamorphosed into this bird.[92] The precise Muse intended appears to be Calliope, the muse of epic poetry, rather than Clio, the muse of history. The mention in line 404 of Alabaster's "heroick song" makes this identification virtually certain. The reference to "Crowning with bayes", the traditional method of proclaiming a poet's victory over his rivals in poetic contests, may, in the present instance, be more likely to mean that Alabaster is superior *when* under Calliope's inspiration. The phrase "pitch of perfection",

92. It has not been deemed necessary to document the items of classical mythology, which are familiar to educated readers even in our own day; nor is the exact form in which these myths and their accretions came to Spenser germane to this discussion.

with *pitch* being used in its sixteenth-century sense of "the height to which anything rises; altitude, elevation",[93] may connect with the next-following image, in which there is allusion to the Muse's taking flight. In any event, the point is that, for the purpose of praising one of a group of contemporary poets, the terms are adequate, since the mythological context is a familiar one to educated readers.

The succeeding metaphorical image (ll. 420-5), with reference to Daniel, relies again on the sure acquaintance of the reader with the commonplaces concerning the beings of the mythological world:

> Yet doth his trembling *Muse* but lowlie flie,
> As daring not too rashly mount on hight,
> And doth her tender plumes as yet but trie,
> In loues soft laies and looser thoughts delight.
> Then rouze thy feathers quickly *Daniell,*
> And to what course thou please thy selfe aduance.

The image utilizes the logical method of *adjuncts* in the speaker's advice to Daniel, who in turn is now assimilated to the Muse and exhorted to "rouze thy feathers" and ascend—that is, proceed to higher "kinds" like epic. It will be noted that a transfer is made from the Muse herself, who lacks wings, to her mount Pegasus, which possesses them. That is, the *adjunct* of the Muses is the winged horse, on which they frequently ride. The whole metaphor, while lightly and easily executed by means of the logical common place, is nevertheless adequate to support with reasonable effectiveness the hortatory commendation of Daniel.

From the praise of the poets at court, Spenser has Colin persuaded to comment upon the "Nymphs" through the device of a provoking remark by Lucida. The praise of the maids of the court is prefaced by a series of metaphors collected in a rhetorical unit of repetition and amplification known technically as *expolitio* or *exergasia*:[94]

> For that my selfe I do professe to be
> Vassall to one, whom all my dayes I serue;
> The beame of beautie sparkled from aboue,

93. OED, *s.v.,* pitch.
94. See Rix, p. 46, for a definition by Susenbrotus of this figure.

The floure of vertue and pure chastitie,
The blossome of sweet ioy and perfect loue,
The pearle of peerlesse grace and modestie. (ll. 466-71)

Puttenham comments upon the figure *expolitio* as follows: "So doth this figure (which therefore I call the *Gorgious*) polish our speech & as it were attire it with copious & pleasant amplifications and much varietie of sentences all running vpon one point & to one inte[*n*]t".[95] Logically, the images of lines 468-71 are based on the categories *substance* (beam, flower, blossom, pearl) and one of the concepts of *accident—quality*. The implied comparison in all cases is controlled by the conventional associations of such terms as commonly employed in the literary tradition of courtly love, much of which had long been absorbed by pastoral. The two elements (among many) of chivalric love which are germane to this passage are the relation of vassal (lover) to lord (beloved),[96] and the Platonic mode which connects beauty, love, virtue, and light. This second element, the purpose of which is to etherealize love and spiritualize its object, hearkens back to the basic Platonic conception that "every soul derives from the One, of which all beauty (both physical and abstract) is a radiation, and every soul potentially desires and can obtain reunion with the One".[97]

Passages in the fourth book of Castiglione's *Libro del Cortegiano* are replete with elaborations of this concept. For example, beauty and love are connected with light in this typical extract from Bembo's discourse on love:

> But speakyinge of the beawtie that we meane, which is onlie it, that appeereth in bodies, and especially in the face of mann, and moveth thys fervent covetinge which we call Love, we will terme it an influence of the heavenlie bountifulness, the whiche for all it stretcheth over all thynges that be created (like the light of the Sonn) yet when it findeth out a face well proportioned, and framed with a certein livelie agreement of severall colours, and set furth with lightes and shadowes,

95. Page 247.
96. Fowler, p. 61, quotes lines 466 and 467 in connection with his discussion of vassalage as a courtly love convention widely employed by Spenser.
97. Edwin Casady, "The Neo-Platonic Ladder in Spenser's *Amoretti*", *PQ*, XX (1941), 284.

> and with an orderly distaunce and limites of lines, therinto it distilleth it self and appeereth most welfavoured, and decketh out and lyghtneth the subject where it shyneth wyth a marveylous grace and glistringe (like the Sonne beames that strike against beawtifull plate of fine golde wrought and sett wyth precyous jewelles) so that it draweth unto it mens eyes with pleasure, and percing through them imprinteth him selfe in the soule, and wyth an unwonted sweetenesse all to stirreth her and delyteth, and settynge her on fire maketh her to covett him.[98]

Bembo later relates Beauty to Truth and to Virtue:

> For in case they, whan the soule is not nowe so much wayed downe with the bodyly burdein, and whan the naturall burning asswageth and draweth to a warmeth, if thei be inflamed with beawty, and to it bend their coveting guided by reasonable choise, they be not deceived, and possesse beawtye perfectly, and therefor through the possessing of it, alwaies goodnes ensueth to them: bicause beauty is good and consequently the true love of it is most good and holy, and evermore bringeth furth good frutes in the soules of them, that with the bridle of reason restraine the yll disposition of sense . . .[99]

The image sequence of the short passage under discussion reveals how completely Spenser had absorbed that peculiar blend of Platonic and court-of-love material so characteristic of the Platonic revival in Italy. The same associations of light, grace, and virtue with the love of a beautiful woman can be traced back even earlier than Castiglione to the sonnets of Petrarch's *Canzoniere*. In these one can find almost at random some phase of the concept. While Spenser's heavy indebtedness in the *Amoretti* to Petrarch is a critical commonplace, the closeness of the phraseology in *Colin Clout* to that of the *Sonnets* has apparently gone unnoticed. This similarity underscores Spenser's dependence upon the body of Neo-Platonic love poetry—with Petrarch as its fountainhead—for the significance of images in *Colin Clout*.

98. Baldassare Castiglione, *The Book of the Courtier*, trans. Sir Thomas Hoby (London, 1900), the Tudor Translations, Vol. XXIII, ed. W. E. Henley, p. 343.

99. *Ibid.*, p. 345.

A few resemblances between the concepts expressed in lines 468-71 of *Colin Clout* and those of Petrarch's sonnets will clarify the point: "The beame of beauty sparkled from aboue"—"When Love his flaming image on her brow/Enthrones in perfect beauty like a star";[100] "The floure of vertue and pure chastitie"—"But as thy beauty honours holiness,/Enshrining thy chaste soul in perfect praise";[101] "The blossome of sweet ioy and perfect loue"—"Love pours such flame of sweetness on the air";[102] "The pearle of peerlesse grace and modestie"—"And with her gentle gaze and step agree/Her mild, subdued and never froward air."[103] The use of an analogous combination of imagistic objects in *Colin Clout* and in a single sonnet of Petrarch's is strikingly exemplified by Sonnet LXVI, the octave of which is as follows:

> That which in perfume and lustre vied
> With the translucent odorous Orient—
> Fruits, flowers, herbs and leaves of every scent—
> Through whom the West obtained the wreath of pride:
> My lovely laurel which has deified
> All grace, all beauty, virtue's tower and tent,
> Lo, underneath its shadowy firmament
> God and my Goddess sitting side by side![104]

The passage under discussion reflects the faithfulness with which Spenser follows the main stream of Neo-Platonic doctrine arising in Italy (with tributaries also in France). The resemblances in terms have been drawn in some detail since the entire long passage on the ladies at court (ll. 559-615), which follows Spenser's literary bow to his inamorata, is a veritable sourcebook of comparable conventional conceits. Of these, the terms of light, illumination, and reflection are the most pervasive. Seven of the twelve ladies are figured in light imagery: Theana's "goodly beames . . . through that darksome vale do glister bright" (ll. 493-5); Marian, whose "beautie shyneth as the morning cleare" (l. 506); Mansilia, the "onely mirrhor of feminitie" (l. 513); Galathea, also possessed of

100. *The Sonnets of Petrarch,* trans. Joseph Auslander (London, 1932), Sonnet XII, p. 12.
101. *Ibid.,* Sonnet CCXXV, p. 225.
102. *Ibid.,* Sonnet CXXI, p. 121.
103. *Ibid.,* Sonnet CXXXII, p. 132.
104. *Ibid.,* p. 294.

"bright shining beames" (l. 518); Stella, by name already a "star"; Phyllis with her "beauties amorous reflection" (l. 546); and Charillis, "like a goodly beacon" (l. 562).

The most lavishly favored, imagistically speaking, is Charillis, who, besides being "like a goodly beacon", is an "ornament of praise" (l. 549), "the pride and primrose of the rest" (l. 560). These latter two areas of comparison, those of jewels and flowers, constituting the second terms of the images, vie with terms of light as vehicles. All gifts and riches, more "rich than pearles of *Ynde,* or gold of *Opher*" (l. 490) are lodged in the mind of Urania, whereas Theana is simply an "ornament of womankind" (l. 498). As for flowers, Neaera is the "blosome of grace and curtesie" (l. 528), and Phyllis is the "floure of rare perfection" (l. 544). The only other imagistic terms are those applied to Theana, "the well of bountie and braue mynd" (l. 496), and to Amaryllis, who has all previously-mentioned virtues "seald vp in the threasure of her hart" (l. 571). It is noteworthy that the last two ladies referred to, Flavia and Candida, have no imagery applied to them. This fact ties in with the suggestion by the editor of the *Variorum* that Flavia and Candida are introduced to avert injured pride on the part of the ladies-in-waiting who could, if they were so inclined, appropriate the praises as belonging to themselves.[105]

The images in the long passage on the ladies are figurational; they are in the form of metaphor or simile. Like the images of the passage on Rosalind immediately preceding, they are characteristically based on *substance* with the addition of *quality,* and—in a few instances—*adjuncts.* The application of these logical bases gives the typical image formation:

> Phyllis the floure of rare perfection,
> Faire spreading forth her leaues with fresh delight (ll. 544-5)

The *substance* is plant; the *quality* (or *attribute*) is perfection; the *adjunct* is the augmentation of the plant in foliation; to the *adjunct* is appended, in this particular case, another predicament of *accident,* namely, *manner of doing*—"Faire spreading . . . with fresh delight". In all cases the images are in essence valuative. Their primary function is to praise by bringing the names of the ladies into association with terms equated, in the vocabulary of

105. *Works,* VII, 477.

courtly love, with the idea of supreme merit. None of the images attempts or even approximates visual or physical representation of the ladies in question.

Incidentally, something of added tone is given to the passage by the entirely conventionalized classical type names with either Greek or Latin feminine endings. These names suggest another poet also renowned like Spenser for formal artistry—Horace, phrases from whose *Carmina* the *Variorum* commentaries show to be frequently echoed in other poems by Spenser. Though the names, to be sure, are not distinctive, it is nevertheless a point of passing interest that, in addition to the name "Cynthia", three of the names for the twelve ladies occur in the *Carmina* of amative tone. These are not the ones Horace delights most to sing about—Lalage, Lydia, and Chloe—but Galatea (3.27), Phyllis (2.4) and Neaera (3.14).

When at the conclusion of Colin's tribute to the ladies, Aglaura, one of the circle of admiring listeners, asks him to "finish the story" by telling of "*Cynthiaes* goodness and high grace," Colin obliges by giving voice to an effusive glorification of the Queen that tops in its hyperbole not only the praise of the ladies but the earlier profession of eternal service and devotion to his beloved, in which he had declared:

> And I hers euer onely, euer one:
> One euer I all vowed hers to bee,
> One euer I, and others neuer none. (ll. 477-9)

This passage, however, the last of three in honor of Cynthia, following the superlatives bestowed on a dozen of her maids and occurring as the climax of the entire section on the courtly ideal, manifestly demands a raising of style to the utmost limit. The massing of major rhetorical schemes in this series of four interlocked stanza (ll. 596-615)—*carmen correlativum,* or elaborate balance; *synathroismus,* Puttenham's "heaping figure"; *expolitio,* the amplification of a single idea with "other wordes, sentences, exornations, and fygures";[106] *distributio,* the division of the general into its parts; and *comparatio,* in this instance, a succession of similes—is buttressed by images exactly similar in their shaping principle to those in the passage on the ladies, and differing from

106. Rix, p. 46, quoting Peacham's definition from the *Garden of Eloquence.*

them only in their controlling frame of reference. Instead of connecting with the Italian-Platonic "Idea" of beauty, they go back to a literary antecedent of greater familiarity and more compelling authority to the contemporary reader. That source is, naturally, Holy Writ.

Grace W. Landrum presents as an Appendix to "Spenser's Use of the Bible and His Alleged Puritanism",[107] a complete listing of "Spenser's Biblical References and Allusions". These include for *Colin Clout* seven separate references for single or double lines scattered throughout the poem and one reference to John i.3 for one ten-line passage.[108] The ten-line passage (839-48) occurs in the opening section of the part telling of the creation of the world through love. Of the seven references, three are to lines in the present Cynthia passage (596-7, 605, and 608-9). However, since the comparable phrases are roughly analogous only and not identical with those of the Bible, it is somewhat surprising that Miss Landrum neglects to mention the parallels between the entire panegyric (ll. 596-615) and the Song of Songs. This resemblance is pointed out by another scholar, Israel Baroway. Baroway in his essay, "The Imagery of Spenser and the 'Song of Songs' ",[109] shows that though there are no exact verbal similarities between Spenser's lines on Cynthia and the biblical marriage song, the resemblances in phrasing and imagery are too striking to be fortuitous. In Baroway's article, incidentally the one previous treatment, with a single minor exception, dealing with imagery in *Colin Clout*,[110] the author states:

> It is sufficient evidence of his debt to the imagery of that poem [Song of Songs] to find him synthesizing the stuff of experience into pictures that are kindred spiritually; to find his

107. *PMLA*, XLI (1926), 517-44.
108. *Ibid.*, p. 543.
109. *JEGP*, XXXIII (1934), 23-45).
110. The one exception is the consideration of roughly the same passage, lines 596-611, by Davis on pp. 169-70 of his chapter on "Imagery" in *Edmund Spenser*. Speaking of Spenser's use of metaphor and simile, he makes the general observation: "In their simpler and less subtle usage the two figures are closely related, both supplying favorite spices to the banquets of Ovid and Petrarch" (p. 169). Davis prefaces his quotation of the illustrative passage with this statement: "Sugared comparisons fall thick and fast throughout the four stanzas to Cynthia dovetailed in *Colin Clouts Come Home Againe*" (*ibid.*).

imagination creating the same species of combinations which distinguish the biblical marriage song; to find in his lines the same kind of symbolism and the same kind of visual, olfactory and saporific imagery of the *grapes,* the *clusters,* the *vine,* and the *incense* that characterizes

> thy breasts are lyke clusters of grapes, *Song of Sol.* (7 : 8),
> thy breasts shall now be lyke clusters of the vine, (7 : 9),
> Let us get up early to the vines, let us see if the vine flourisheth, whether it had budded the small grapes, (7:13),
> I will get me to the mountain of myrrhe and to the hill of Frankincense, (4 : 6),
> Who is shee that commeth out of the Wilderness lyke pillars of smoke perfumed with myrrhe and incense and with all the spices of the marchant, (3 : 6),
> Thy plants are as an orchard ... with the trees of incense, (4 :13-14).[111]

Certainly Spenser's lines honoring Cynthia-Elizabeth are close in their wording to the portions of the Song of Solomon quoted by Baroway, as can be readily seen when the more comparable lines are cited:

> Her words were like a streame of honny fleeting,
> The which doth softly trickle from the hiue :
> . . . .
> Her deeds were like great clusters of ripe grapes,
> Which load the bunches of the fruitfull vine :
> . . . .
> Her lookes were like beames of the morning Sun,
> Forth looking through the windowes of the East,
> . . . .
> Her thoughts are like the fume of Franckincense,
> Which from a golden Censer forth doth rise.
> (ll. 596-7, 600-1, 604-5, 608-9)

Baroway insists that the imagery in this passage, in the "garden sonnet" (*Amoretti,* LXIV), in the "tradeful merchants" sonnet (*Amoretti,* XV), and in a few passages of the *Epithalamion* and

111. Baroway, p. 38.

The Faerie Queene, being largely derived from the Song of Songs, is formed in a manner different from the imagery employed by Spenser when his sources are other than the biblical hymeneal. Quoting R. G. Moulton, *A Modern Reader's Bible* (1920), Baroway states with reference to the Canticles-based passages of Spenser: "His poetic tradition 'combines with imagery, *the very different device of symbolism,*' an appeal 'to some analytical faculty or conventional association of ideas' rather than to the pictorial sense."[112] Calling Spenser's imagery drawn from the Book of Canticles "un-Spenserian, un-Elizabethan, un-Occidental",[113] Baroway attributes its uniqueness to Spenser's having copied not just the terms but the mode of its source. According to Baroway, the characteristic quality of the Hebraic imagery which Spenser imitates is the way in which the analytic approach modifies the sensory effect, causing the imagery in both cases to work as "an ingenious vehicle of qualitative transference".[114] Baroway avers further that Spenser copied the "one distinctive variation of symbolism—the grouping of excellences"[115] from the Song.

As has been repeatedly shown, however, especially in the discussion of the passage on the ladies at court, arising directly out of Neo-Platonic, not Hebraic, modes of thought, Spenser's images have been predominantly unsensuous, qualitative, conceptual, and characteristically controlled by conventional associations established by familiar literary antecedents. The derivation of the images from logical bases makes this conceptual, valuative effect virtually inescapable. As for the "grouping of excellences", the rhetorical schemes of *synathroismus, expolitio,* and *distributio* by their very nature demand such a grouping. The praise of Rosalind (ll. 468-71) beginning "The beame of beautie sparkled from aboue", whose terms are entirely Petrarchan, is precisely such a grouping. So also is the twenty-line passage cited by Puttenham as an illustration of the rhetorical figure "Merismus or the Distributer",[116] employed "when we may conueniently vtter a matter in one/entier speach or proposition and will rather do it peecemeale and by distributio[*n*] of euery part for amplification sake".[117] This passage is identified

112. *Ibid.,* pp. 25-6.
113. *Ibid.,* p. 25.
114. *Ibid.,* p. 26.
115. *Ibid.,* p. 27.
116. Page 222.
117. *Ibid.*

by Willcock and Walker, editors of the standard edition of the *Arte of English Poesie,* as from Puttenham's own collection of poems in honor of Elizabeth, *Partheniades,*[118] which they date *c.* 1581-82.[119] The passage, non-imagistic and indebted to no particular source, certainly not the Bible, for its terms, exemplifies no more than the conventionalized Elizabethan use of the figure which the author, like Spenser, very likely learned during his stay at Cambridge.[120] The figure of *distributio* naturally lends itself to the "grouping of excellences", as the first ten rather wooden lines of the commendation amply attest:

> Not your bewtie, most gracious soueraine,
> Nor maidenly lookes, mainteind vvith maiestie:
> Your stately port, vvhich doth not match but staine,
> For your presence, your pallace and your traine,
> All Princes Courts, mine eye could euer see:
> Not your quicke vvits, your sober gouernaunce:
> Your cleare forsight, your faithfull memorie,
> So sweete features, in so staid countenaunce:
> Nor languages, with plentuous utterance,
> So able to discourse, and entertaine.[121]

Accordingly, while Baroway's analysis (which he drew from Moulton) of the passage in *Colin Clout* interpenetrated with phrases strongly reminiscent of the Song of Solomon is substantially valid, his claim that the imagery in the Song furnished Spenser with an entirely new principle of image formation in this and other passages will hardly stand.

Aesthetic considerations necessitate a passage of diminuendo after the climactic extravagance of Colin's laudation of Cynthia. Accordingly, the ensuing division of the poem (ll. 648-794), dealing with the perversion of the courtly ideal—the other side of the coin, so to speak, furnishes such a change of pace. Glancing at England earlier in the dialogue, Colin had hinted that the ideal perfection attained by the poetic courtiers, the ladies-in-waiting, and the

118. *Ibid.,* p. 357.
119. *Ibid.,* p. ix.
120. The editors of the *Arte* state (p. xix) that Puttenham matriculated at Cambridge in 1546.
121. Puttenham, p. 223.

Queen herself was not a universal condition prevailing among those who inhabited the court:

> For God his gifts there plenteously bestowes,
> But gracelesse men them greatly do abuse. (ll. 327-8)

The castigation of bad courtiers, a passage which Renwick compares to *The Teares of the Muses* (ll. 67-108) and to *Mother Hubberds Tale* (ll. 581-942),[122] fairly direct and circumstantial, as befits the lowered style of satire, still contains a sizeable amount of figurative imagery.

The opening of the denunciatory passage retains Colin in the pastoral guise, employing with figuration the stock imagery of this tradition—"chose back to my sheep to tourne" (l. 672) . . . "and leaue their lambes to losse misled amisse" (l. 687). Since the remainder of the section is focused on the "enormities" (l. 665) at court, there is little further need for pure pastoral terms. Instead the passage employs the language of courtly love, as modified by the Platonic element, but in reverse, so to speak. That is, the dispraise is bodied forth in terms which contrast the whiteness of the courtly ideal with the blackness of its perversion. The result is a kind of parody of the courtly code pointed up by expressions of coarser grain. An analysis of one extended passage will serve to illustrate the satiric method.

In the part explaining why the intrigant is best fitted to get on at court, beginning, "For arts of schoole haue there small countenance" (l. 703), there is allusion to the misuse of these arts, to "professors" suborned to vile ends, and to the disgraceful necessity imposed upon "gentle wit" to stoop to sycophancy. The mention of these reversals of the true standard is followed by an image in the form of a simile:

> For each mans worth is measured by his weed,
> As harts by hornes, or asses by their eares. (ll. 711-12)

As pointed out in the second chapter, the comparison was proverbial in Spenser's day, the popular esteem of the ass's mental capacity being no different from that commonly entertained today. The first comparison, equating "weed" with "hornes" and "eares", becomes a springboard, as it were, for a related pair of analogies to follow: one making the point that as not all creatures with

122. *Daphnaïda,* p. 189.

exceedingly high horns are harts, neither do those men of "highest" (most elegant) appearance always possess the "highest" (best endowed) mind; the other, which in turn leads to two additional images in the form of similes, making the point that pompous words are like

> bladders blowen vp with wynd,
> That being prickt do vanish into noughts.
> Euen such is all their vaunted vanitie,
> Nought else but smoke, that fumeth soone away.

The logical bases of the vehicles of the first simile quoted immediately above are those of the predicament *substance* (bladders), followed by the places *adjunct* (blowen vp with wynd) and *cause and effect* (that fumeth . . . away) and the predicament *manner of doing* (soone). These virtually automatic-reflex projections of methods of logic into image formation delimit the applicability of the vehicles to a minimum of meaning and thereby better serve to elucidate the precise nature of something—in this case, the vainglorious emptiness of the "haughtie words" (l. 716) that come so readily to the lips of the charlatans. Again, the homespun terms *bladders, wind, smoke* underscore the gap between the pretentious and the genuine. The smoke figure, though used in Psalm lxviiii.2, had undoubtedly passed into popular idiom.

Colin's speech closes with one of the few personifications in the poem:

> Whiles single Truth and simple honestie
> Do wander vp and downe despys'd of all. (ll. 727-8)

Here the epithets "single" and "simple" are applications of the predicament *quality* to the personified virtues. The verbs and adverbs describe *manner of doing.*

Now the basic concept of this part (ll. 703-30) is the distinction between the true and false ideal. The images, through the employment of homely terms as the second element in the comparisons, serve to emphasize the differentiation. The dichotomy is an application of the familiar Platonic notion of essences underlying all created forms, which are, in turn, but shadows of the reality. The abuses at court arise, in the estimation of the speaker, largely from the confusion between the *appearance* of good and *good itself,* in that the *outward show* of virtue and worth is mistaken for *true* virtue and worth. In *Mother Hubberds Tale,* the same concept is not nearly so persuasive when stated in direct, non-imagistic language. There, the Mule advising the Ape and the Fox how to "get on" at court, declares:

> For not by that which is, the world now deemeth,
> (As it was wont) but by that same that seemeth.[123]

An explanation similar to the one given above for the imagery in lines 703-30 can be offered for the images in metaphoric form in lines 757-68, which characterize the charlatans in the learned arts —such arts being in themselves a worthwhile branch of human endeavor, "Whose praise hereby no whit impaired is" (l. 755)—who

> drownded lie in pleasures wastefull well,
> In which like Moldwarps nousling still they lurke. (ll. 762-3)

With their non-courtly terms of lying drowned in a well and burrowing moles, the images serve to intensify by their very dissonance the deplorable condition of "those that faultie bee" (l. 756)—to magnify their apostasy to the ideal which they falsely profess to follow.

Perhaps the high-water mark of Spenser's satiric vein, both within and outside of this poem, is reached in Colin's vehement denial of Corylas' suggestion that "loue" is confined to the fields and forests only:

> Not so (quoth he) loue most aboundeth there.
> For all the walls and windows there are writ,
> All full of loue, and loue, and loue my deare,
> And all their talke and studie is of it.
> Ne any there doth braue or valiant seeme,
> Vnlesse that some gay Mistresse badge he beares:
> Ne any one himselfe doth ought esteeme,
> Vnlesse he swim in loue vp to the eares. (ll. 775-82)

The metaphoric image of the last line is a defining or characterizing figure, employing, once more, the phrases of common currency.

Viewing as a whole the imagery of the section describing the falsification of the courtly code, one can see that the images contribute greatly to the conscious contrast of styles and thus support

123. Lines 649-50, *Works,* VIII, 123.

the conceptual plan to make a sharp distinction between genuine and spurious virtue.

The remainder of the poem embodies no imagery of a type not already exemplified. The paucity of figurative imagery in the cosmology (ll. 799-883) is traceable in large part to lack of such imagery in the poems of Empedocles and Lucretius, who seem likely sources for this section.[124] Moreover, Genesis i.20-26, containing substantially the same material as the Spenser passage,[125] has no metaphors or similitudes. Virtually the only image of a figurative nature in the part setting forth the concept of love as the great moving and unifying force of the Universe is the one in lines 871-4:

> For beautie is the bayt which with delight
> Doth man allure, for to enlarge his kynd,
> Beautie the burning lamp of heauens light,
> Darting her beames into each feeble mynd.

This, of course, is the familiar rendering of the Italian-Platonic light-beauty motif. Similarly, dearth of figurative imagery characterizes the final section devoted to Rosalind (ll. 903-51), which is thoroughly in the Petrarchan vein of chivalric love. The more mannered style of the poem, up to line 794, where Colin concludes his strictures on the courtly milieu, gives way to stylistic fluidity and directness in the sections on cosmological love and on Rosalind, which nevertheless are also rich in literary associations of classical and Italian Renaissance vintage.

In conclusion, when imagery with potential sensuous impact occurs, such imagery tends to be relatively weak in sensory stimulation for one of two reasons: either it lacks graphic detail, in which case its appeal is subordinated to a conceptual function; or its elaboration is mainly for fashioning an effective imitation or a rhetorical pattern.

124. Evelyn May Albright, "Spenser's Cosmic Philosophy and His Religion", *PMLA,* XLIV (1929), 715-59, while admitting some Lucretian influence, favors Empedocles as the chief source of Spenser's theory of origins. Apposite quotations from both these Epicurean philosophic poets given by Miss Albright, pp. 725, 726, 727, 735-6, 742-3, afford a convenient verification of the non-figurative character of the language.

125. *Ibid.,* p. 730. But see also above, n. 38.

In terms of kinds of content from which details are drawn, the imagery relates to, and depends for its rich overtones upon, matter and modes that had become conventionalized in pastoral literature during its long history from the third century B.C. to Spenser's era. The incorporation of earlier genre conventions like the singing match, the love plaint, the assembly and dispersal of shepherds—sometimes termed "pure pastoral"—makes the poem in its entirety a pastoral allegory. The inclusion of later genre conventions like the cosmology, the Neo-Platonic ideology, and the chivalric point of view—sometimes referred to as "adulterated pastoral"—modifies the force of the allegory. Together, the two content areas—pure and admixed pastoral—constitute the indispensable frame of reference for interpreting the individual images—descriptions, concretions, and figures, especially metaphors and similitudes. An important outcome of these interactions is to give a centripetal impulse to the poem.

The fact that the figurative structures, such as *comparatio, similitudo, icon, prosopopoeia, metaphora,* and *allegoria*—and these are the mainstays of Spenser's tropical language in the poem—utilize almost exclusively in their second terms subjects associated with early and late pastoral tradition further enhances the centripetal movement of the poem. These rhetorical figures of comparison which stud the poem have been seen to be formed largely by application of inventional modes practiced almost universally at the time in connection with the formal study of rhetoric and logic. The logical bases of the images thus formed serve to convey to the reader the intended relationship between subject and analogue (tenor and vehicle) and consequently to help illuminate the true nature of the thing discussed.

It is hardly necessary, in closing the chapter, to add that ascertaining the logical base of an image does not give one a mechanically sure clue to its full meaning, nor does the recognition that the function of an image may be logical imply that the image lacks emotional power. Imagery is, of course, only one aspect of style, which in turn is part of a still larger poetic universe, embracing as well, character, situation, and action, from all of which dramaturgical elements images pick up emotion. To the remainder of this poetic universe, which is conveyed *by words* but is not entirely *of words,* I shall now, in the succeeding chapter, turn.

CHAPTER V

THE TONE AND FEELING

The Neo-Aristotelian, Elder Olson, in an essay examining the critical method of Empson and of the "new criticism" generally, makes the interesting observation that some translations of poetry are unsatisfactory because the translator renders the dictionary meaning only, or the style, or the rhythm, and fails to convey the significance of the speech as action. In such cases, continues Olson, the translator "loses the passionate anger, or the fright; he loses the characteristic marks of nobility or meanness".[1] Oslon is here alluding to the ancient distinction between *lexis* and *praxis* as two conditions or spheres of meaning in a mimetic poem. Earlier in the essay he clarified the distinction between the former and the latter by this statement: "What the poetic character says in the mimetic poem is speech and has meaning; his *saying it* is action, an act of persuading, confessing, commanding, informing, torturing, or what not".[2] Because *Colin Clout* is cast in dramaturgical form, its mimetic features deserve consideration to the end that *praxis* may serve to give wholeness to *lexis*. The preceding chapters, except the Introduction, have in the main been devoted to the latter aspect of meaning—*lexis* as conveyed through words standing as signs, words joined as predications, and words grouped as linguistic and prosodic patterns. But if we as readers and interpreters neglect the complementary part of meaning—that inferable from the speeches as to the character, emotions, fortune, and situation of the *persona* who represents by speaking—we shall certainly be in like case with those translators who leave out of their renditions the attitude and emotions of the poetic speaker or speakers. Indeed, it is mainly such impressions that, in fictive works, engage our humanity.

Inferences as to the speaker's attitude and emotions—inferences of the kind we are constantly registering in real life—determine, in large measure, our interpretation of the language, particularly

1. Elder Olson, "Contemporary Criticism, and Poetic Diction", in *Critics and Criticism: Ancient and Modern,* ed. R. S. Crane (Chicago, 1952), p. 72.
2. *Ibid.*, p. 54.

on its emotive side. In registering the emotional coloration which words and speeches possess, we are guided by grammatical, rhetorical, logical, and prosodic arrangements and devices. These direct our attention in such a way as to control emotional response. The very position of a word in a sentence may, as we know, have an emotional bearing. Inasmuch as emotionality in a poem is as much a product of the medium of disclosure (*lexis*) as of that which is disclosed (*praxis*), emotional matters have necessarily been a part —though a relatively submerged one—of the previous chapters. The inseparable relationship of the rhetorical figures, the diction, the versification, and the imagery to such matters may be recalled by a brief highlighting. Chapter II draws attention to the employment of figures of rhetoric for the expression of strong emotion. When Colin's feeling is at a peak, figures multiply. Certain passages stand out, as has been seen, for the fervency of their emotion—a fervency which is accounted for by the inciting power of such figures as *synathroismus, anaphora, acclamatio,* and *apostrophe.* Chapter III reveals the role diction and versification play in setting the mood of the poem and in conveying and evoking emotion. The archaic locutions, for instance, impart a slight flavor of rustic remoteness; the courtly vocabulary adds elevation and dignity. A particular word may serve to illuminate a relationship. As a case in point, the word *fon* applied by Colin to Cuddy in the line, "Ah *Cuddy* . . . thous a fon", conveys both the idea of mild rebuke and the relationship of affection between the two characters. The choice of words and the prosodic devices induce the reader to *feel* the emotion that is being ideationally presented. A good illustration of this is the opening speech of Hobbinol, recalling the general despair occasioned by Colin's long absence. Here the monosyllabic words with their abundance of long vowels slow the pace to accord with the feeling of grief; and alliteration acts to underscore words that either name the emotion or suggest it : "dead in dole", "waters wept", "languour did lament", "painfull to repeat".

Chapter IV reveals that the imagery, too, is an important element of the affective character of *Colin Clout,* operating through its mediation between objective and subjective reality. Such mediation, to be effective, implies that the poet will provide a system of control or controls which will enable the reader to structure his response to the foci of experience we call images. In Chapter IV, also, we have seen how the poet has provided—or rather has used —such a system of controls by relating most of the images to topics and traditions quite familiar to his presumed readers and by elaborating the images by equally familiar modes of invention. The kind of audience Spenser envisaged for the poem is, naturally, a most significant factor in the determination of tone—the attitude of the writer toward his readers. The term *tone* and its correlative *feeling*—the attitude of communicator toward his materials—are not used in the preceding chapters because the focus of attention is elsewhere. I propose, in the present chapter, to deal directly with tone and feeling, which the reader will doubtless recognize as the two middle terms of I. A. Richards' now generally accepted division of meaning into four parts, namely, sense, feeling, tone, and intention. This division, together with an explanation of the terms, is succinctly set forth by Richards in "Meaning, Four Kinds of", an essay in the *Dictionary of World Literature*.[3] The concepts envisaged for the two middle terms with which this chapter is primarily concerned are there stated as follows:

> Feeling. But we also, as a rule, have some feelings about these items, about the state of affairs we are referring to. We have some special bias of interest towards it, some personal coloring of feeling; and we use language to express these feelings, this nuance of interest.
>
> Tone. The speaker has ordinarily an attitude to his listener. He chooses or arranges his words differently as his audiences vary, in automatic or deliberate consequence of his relation to them. The tone of his utterance reflects their relation, his sense of how he stands towards those he is addressing.[4]

I shall employ the concepts signified by these locutions to encompass the entire emotional range of *Colin Clout,* conceived now in mimetic terms as an exhibition of characters acting (thinking, speaking, and doing) and reacting in a self-contained dramaturgical milieu. By this analysis of emotional elements, I expect to reveal how the interior drama both helps clarify the poet's intention and heightens the centripetal movement.

3. Ed. Joseph T. Shipley, rev. ed. (New York, 1953), pp. 262-3. Richards' description of the four parts of meaning in the *Dictionary* is virtually identical, except for its being more concise, to that set forth in his *Practical Criticism: A Study of Literary Judgment* (London, 1929), pp. 181-3.

4. *Dictionary of World Literature,* p. 263.

To determine the tone in a poem of mixed speech, that is, in a poem in which there are numerous voices, one must ascertain the identity of the voices and also the precise mode of address.[5] Even though the reader retains awareness, naturally, that the poet is the creator of the whole, the reader needs to know, in cases where the poet is not speaking in his own person, the character of the person he is "imitating".[6] These phenomena of voice and address arise, in their more overt manifestations, out of the organization of the poem both in its structural and in its conceptual phases.[7] As a narrative, the structure of the poem is relatively simple—three episodes within a frame. The poem opens with a description by the "narrator" of Colin's piping to ten shepherds and shepherdesses who have gathered to listen to his recital of his recent adventures abroad. The poem closes with an account by the narrator of the dispersal of the group, whose members are reminded by darkening skies that it is time to bring their flocks into the fold. The three episodes are the visit of the "Shepheard of the Ocean", ending with line 195; the ocean voyage and the landing, ending with line 327; and the sojourn at court, ending with line 794. The part within the frame is technically a dialogue, but the narration of what transpires in the three episodes is carried almost entirely in the discourse of Colin. Thematically, the poem falls into a more complex pattern with less clear-cut divisions. These correspond only roughly

5. It is pertinent to note that much of what is now implied in the concept of tone was subsumed in ancient times under expositions regarding the mechanism of voice and address, of which, the Renaissance, however, seems to have made little explicit use. Plato differentiates narration into three types—simple narration, imitation, or a union of the two (*The Republic,* 392d-394c, in *The Dialogues of Plato,* trans. B. Jowett, 4th ed. [Oxford, 1953], II, 238-40). Aristotle is in substantial accord when he says that one may speak at one moment in narrative, and at another in an assumed character, or one may remain the same throughout, without any change (*Poetics,* 3, 1448a, trans. Ingram Bywater, Vol. XI of *The Works of Aristotle,* ed. W. D. Ross [Oxford, 1924]). As to address, Aristotle states that of the three elements in speech making—speaker, subject, and person addressed—it is the last one, the hearer, that determines for a good orator the end and object of the speech (*Rhetoric,* i.3, 1358, trans. W. Rhys Roberts, Vol. XI of *The Works of Aristotle,* ed. W. D. Ross [Oxford, 1924]).

6. Plato recognizes this dual relationship in the question he has Socrates pose to Adeimantus: "But when the poet speaks in the person of another, may we not say that he assimilates his style to that of the person who, as he informs you, is going to speak?" (*Republic,* 393c, II, 239).

7. These phases are expanded in the final chapter, where they enter into the discussion of overall unity.

to the narrative parts. The thematic units, already intimated in the previous chapter, may be given the following designations reflecting their approximate content: (1) the pastoral ideal (ll. 1-327); (2) the courtly ideal (ll. 328-647); (3) the perversion of the courtly ideal (ll. 648-794); (4) the Neo-Platonic notion of love as the great moving force of the universe (ll. 795-902); and (5) the praise of Rosalind (ll. 903-951). In common with the recitation of the episodes, the opinions and arguments presented are, in the main, those of Colin speaking directly.

In all there are eleven "voices" in the poem, including that of the narrator. The narrator's main functions are to set the stage at the beginning for the "action" to follow, to introduce and close the remarks of each of the ten speakers, and to conclude the action. The voice of the narrator appears in seventy-three lines at forty-four separate places, but, aside from the opening and closing passages—the frame proper—the narrator's voice in all but four passages is limited to conversational tags: "quoth he", "said then that bony Boy", "him *Thestylis* bespake", and the like.

Because charged language is so sparingly used by the narrator outside the frame, the four instances in which the reader is "led" by it deserves particularization. In line 36, "To whom the shepheard gently answered thus", the adverb *gently* hints at the amicability of relations between Colin and Hobbinol. In lines 52-55, emotional loading shows itself in the narrator's emphasis on the eagerness with which the listeners crowd around to hear the beginning of Colin's adventures. Their attitude of earnest, rapt attention, which is underscored by the metaphor "with hungrie eares" (l. 53) sets the mode of reception for the tale, with reference *both* to Colin's immediate audience and to the reader of the poem. In line 352, "With that *Alexis* broke his tale asunder", the charged verbal phrase betokens Alexis' heightened reaction to Colin's description of Cynthia. The last of the four passages, besides the frame, which utilize the voice of the narrator for other than mechanical purposes, is the comment regarding the effect on the shepherds of Colin's laudatory cadenza concerning Cynthia:

> Much was the whole assembly of those heards,
> Moov'd at his speech, so feelingly he spake:
> And stood awhile astonisht at his words,
> Till *Thestylis* at last their silence brake,
> Saying, . . . (ll. 648-52)

In this emotive language, the narrator conveys to the reader how Colin's audience received this elaborate flourish. The narrator's words further attest to the importance of Colin's final obeisance to Queen-Cynthia. If added evidence were needed of the significance of Colin's panegyric at this juncture, it could be found in the fact that the tribute stands at the end of the second thematic unit dealing with the courtly ideal and at the ideological turning point of the poem, where Thestylis poses to Colin the crucial question:

> Why didst thou euer leaue that happie place,
> In which such wealth might vnto thee accrew?
> And back returnedst to this barrein soyle,
> Where cold and care and penury do dwell. (ll. 654-7)

The contribution of the narrator to the orectic climate of the poem is most influential in the opening and closing passages, to which we now turn, because these set the mood of the whole by establishing a control to moderate the writer-reader relationship. At the outset the pastoral strain helps put the reader in a contemplative but not overly relaxed state of mind. The conclusion is calculated to leave him in relatively the same disposition. In the introductory passage, words strongly suggestive of pleasantness aid in setting up a euphoristic relationship between the writer and the reader or listener. These words afford favorable stimuli by conjuring up the pleasant emotions directly: love ("laies of sweet loue", "lou'd this shepheard dearest in degree"); desire ("greedie listfull eares"); joy ("play", "iolly groome"). Even the simile in which the swains are represented as "stand[ing] astonisht" ... "Like hartlesse deare, dismayd with thunders sound" does not act to nullify the pleasant association, since, as brought out in the last chapter, the figure conceptualizes the attitude of earnest, spellbound attention accorded Colin. The verbs of motion or action—"sate", "charming", "play", etc.—function as kinesthetic imagery to maintain alertness on the part of the reader.

The concluding passage of the poem, the completion of the narrative frame in the *chronographia,* appropriately calls forth a somewhat more relaxed attitude on the part of the reader than does the opening one. The liquids and sibilants, unusually abundant—

> So hauing ended, he from ground did rise,
> And after him vprose eke all the rest:

All loth to part, but that the glooming skies
Warnd them to draw their bleating flocks to rest— (ll. 952-5)

constitute sound imagery of smoothness and easy motion, which conduces to a mood of relaxation, a mood reinforced by the final emotive *rest*.

The voice of the narrator is thus seen to be important in creating the overall "atmosphere" that is to obtain between writer and reader and in assisting the reader to respond appropriately to Colin's speeches by reference to their effect upon the immediate audience of shepherds.

A like importance, however, can hardly be assigned most of the other voices. The exceptions to this general statement are, of course, Colin himself, who speaks 730 of the 936 lines in the body of the poem; Hobbinol, who speaks forty-two lines; Cuddy, thirty-two; and Thestylis, eighteen. Even though the roles of most of the shepherds are *individually* negligible in respect to number of lines assigned (Marin, five; Corydon, one; Corylas, six; Alexis, thirteen; Lucida, twenty-seven; Melissa, twelve; and Aglaura, five), the role of the interlocutors collectively is a major and vital one.

The first function served by the presence of the interlocutors is dramatic. Even the personages who do not emerge as distinct individuals are nevertheless members of an *interacting* group. Their presence makes possible the assembly, traditionalized in both pastoral and romance literature. The gathering of members of both sexes and the large number of interlocutors are characteristic of the pastoral romance, exemplified by Sidney's *Arcadia* and Lodge's *Rosalynde*. The assembly, the personalized setting *in toto,* justifies the emotional quality of Colin's presentation. Equivalent ideas set forth in characteristic philosophic exposition could not appropriately be emotionally oriented.

The second function served by the presence of the interlocutors is rhetorical. The interruptions of Colin's discourse help further expositional coherence by summarizing what Colin has just said and by pointing forward to what he is going to say. Such is Thestylis' comment which follows Colin's recital about Mulla and Bregog:

Now by my life this was a mery lay:
Worthie of *Colin* selfe, that did it make.
But read now eke of friendship I thee pray,
What dittie did that other shepheard sing? (ll. 157-60)

After Colin's compliance with this request, Marin observes:

> Right well he sure did plaine:
> That could great *Cynthiaes* sore displeasure breake,
> And moue to take him to her grace againe.
> But tell on further *Colin,* as befell
> Twixt him and thee, that thee did hence dissuade. (ll. 173-7)

Interposures to aid coherence are especially noteworthy when they occur between major divisions of the poem. Here they signalize the end of one episode or thematic unit and mark the beginning of another. In fact, the only division which does not have such an interruption is the sojourn-at-court episode, ending with line 794, where Colin makes a direct transition from a description of profane love at court to that of devout love among the shepherds. Otherwise, the speech of a shepherd always creates an "intermission" between the parts of Colin's discourse: Corydon, line 200; Corylas, lines 328-9; Thestylis, lines 652-9; Hobbinol, lines 903-6.

Finally, employment of a group of voices has an aesthetic function in that it helps to dispel the monotony which would result from having Colin's presentation in one solid passage. The participation of the ten "interspeakers", as men of the Renaissance sometimes call them,[8] gives a dramatic and dynamic character to the poem, which might otherwise tend to become rather static and hence lifeless.

Despite the great importance of the interlocutors, it still remains true, as stated before, that most of the personages who speak are not real "voices"; they are more in the nature of genre machinery or of rhetorical aids. That is to say, the reader does not really get to know these speakers as *persons,* does not become conscious of their distinctive personalities. As "persons" they are, in short, little more than their derived pastoral or mythological names. Besides Colin, only Hobbinol, Cuddy, and Thestylis actually emerge with any distinguishable flavor. Colin excepted, they are also the first three interlocutors to appear.

In analyzing the tone of the speeches by these important personages, and also that of Colin as the principal spokesman, one needs

8. E.g., the term is used to render "entreparleurs" in a translation of Pierre de la Primaudaye's popular *Academe Françoise* (*The French Academie,* trans. Thomas Bowes, *et al.* [London, 1618], sig. 1v).

to keep two things in mind: first, the relationship of the speaker to his addressee or addressees; and, second, the identity and character of the speaker himself. The speaker's consciousness of a relationship between himself and the audience powerfully affects the nature of the discourse. So also do his qualities as a person. These two phenomena of voice and address are reflected in details of the speeches. Hence the reader may expect to find in the ensuing discussion of the four main personages allusions to the social situation which environs each speech and to the character of the speakers, as revealed, for the most part, in what they say.

Hobbinol, to a degree beyond that of the other participants (Colin excepted), is accorded special recognition in terms of position (first speaker), in number of lines assigned (forty-two), and in explicit characterization by the narrator as

> One of those groomes (a iolly groome was he,
> As euer piped on an oaten reed,
> And lou'd this shepheard dearest in degree,
> Hight *Hobbinol*) ... (ll. 12-15)

In the first of his three speeches, Hobbinol addresses Colin in terms which, like those of the above characterization, go beyond the mere conventional. Not only does he express at some length the general grief occasioned by Colin's absence but he avers that he personally had "of many greatest crosse" (l. 18). Hobbinol's plea for Colin to narrate his "late voyage" (l. 34) is "gently" (l. 36) answered by the latter. Hobbinol's chiding of Colin for having made blame of the court too general is mollified by an explicit reminder to Colin of a past and presumably long-standing relation between the two:

> For well I wot, sith I my selfe was there,
> To wait on *Lobbin* (*Lobbin* well thou knewest). (ll. 735-6)

Since Lobbin is generally taken to be the Earl of Leicester, who was Spenser's patron almost two decades prior to the publication of *Colin Clout,* the allusion may be presumed to be to an association of long duration. In the three-way exchange among Melissa, Hobbinol, and Lucida—the single time, incidentally, that any of the interlocutors addresses directly another than Colin—Hobbinol is the only one who can on his own cognizance speak of Colin's past love life ("For hauing loued euer one most deare") (l. 904); Lucida must qualify her remarks with a reservation ("I haue often heard . . .") (l. 907).

Cuddy, the next interlocutor to speak, has a unique role—that of the ingenuous character. It is true that all of the interlocutors are set forth as shepherds, but of Colin's entourage only Cuddy expresses in any pronounced way notions that can properly be called naïve. Colin himself, as shall appear, assumes this role in one instance, but toward Cuddy his general attitude is one of affectionate superiority, like that exhibited by a fond parent who *expects* to find his offspring constantly engaged in wayward but essentially harmless acts. The *ingénu* note as such does not, however, occur in either of Cuddy's first two speeches: one asking Colin "To tell what thou didst sing, when he did plaie" (l. 84); the other, requesting Colin to recount his experiences abroad (ll. 96-9). Cuddy's role as an innocent first appears at the point when Colin concludes his account of the sea voyage with a statement of the travelers' setting ashore on "Cynthias land" (l. 289). Thereupon Cuddy takes up the cue immediately with the query:

> What land is that thou meanst . . .
> And is there other, then whereon we stand? (ll. 290-91)

Colin's reply is indulgent, lightly patronizing:

> Ah *Cuddy* . . . thous a fon,
> That hast not seene least part of natures worke. (ll. 292-3)

Later in the same speech Colin repeats the sentiment, "Nought has thou foolish boy seene in thy daies" (l. 303). It is at this juncture that the quality of naïveté pointedly attributed to Cuddy permits him to pose the seemingly artless question which goes unerringly to the heart of the major enigma:

> But if that land be there . . . as here,
> And is theyr heauen likewise there all one?
> And if like heauen, be heauenly graces there,
> Like as in this same world where we do wone? (ll. 304-7)

Colin's rejoinder, one of the key speeches in the poem, lacks all traces of his previous banter.

The subsequent two speeches by Cuddy in the latter part of the poem continue in a less obvious vein of simplicity. The first of these (ll. 616-19), just before the peroration of Colin's final encomium on Cynthia, reminds Colin of their common station as shepherds and suggests that Colin's praise is couched in language too lofty for a shepherd. The speech in which Cuddy makes his last appearance (ll. 823-34) also notes that Colin's eloquence exceeds the humbler shepherd's expectation. It concludes by praising Colin for giving voice to a conception of love hitherto beyond Cuddy's ken.

In his first two speeches, Cuddy's function is the same as that of most of the other interlocutors, particularly the minor ones: to objectify the dramatic setting and to canalize, for the benefit of the reader, Colin's long discourse. In his second two speeches, Cuddy's function is in part to lighten the tone by injecting bits of humor. A touch of irony, however, enters Cuddy's question as to the existence of heaven and heavenly graces in "that land". But the irony is on the writer-reader level, not on the level of the interior drama. Cuddy's seemingly childlike question is aimed over the heads of his immediate circle of addressees to Spenser's ultimate audience. Of course, as one might expect, Colin's own discourse is likewise pitched at two levels—the one for the "live" audience and the other for the sophisticated reader. When, as happens in Colin's grandiloquent praise of Cynthia or in his inspired testimonial to the power of love, the two levels tend to diverge too far, they are "adjusted". The two final speeches of Cuddy adjust, in the interest of decorum, Colin's supra-pastoral flights.

Just as the diction is only lightly flabored with rusticity, so is the shepherd's cloak casually worn by all the participants, but it is never entirely doffed. One of the previously unnoticed excellences of the poem is Spenser's maintenance of this dual level of address, which is accomplished by keeping a minimal difference between the perception and sophistication of the interior audience and that of the intended but removed audience—the courtly circle of readers. Accordingly, the comments and questions of the various speakers are not noticeably unsophisticated. In fact, they tend to be quite the opposite. Yet none of the remarks by any of the speakers is overtly "out of character". Aside from Cuddy, who has a major role, only two of the other participants—both minor figures—show the naïve tendency. Corydon has the single line, "And is the sea . . . so fearfull?" (l. 200). Corylas, given six lines in all, poses the question and makes the comment:

And is loue then . . . once knowne
In Court, and his sweet lore professed there?
I weened sure he was our God alone:
And only woond in fields and forests here. (ll. 771-4)

Both of these speeches, the one by Corydon and the other by Corylas, further illustrate the device of break-ins upon Colin's discourse; these interruptions serve at key junctures as a kind of rhetorical punctuation.

With further reference to the lack of simplicity on the part of most of the characters, Thestylis, the third shepherd to speak (not counting Colin), manifests a high degree of shrewdness. Thestylis has only eighteen lines, nine less than Lucida, but the reader is able to form a more distinct impression of his character than he can that of the shepherdess. For example, in his first speech, requesting Colin to disclose the substance of the "ditty" sung by "that other shepheard", Thestylis displays the ability to view matters with a certain detachment by generalizing on his own motives:

For I do couet most the same to heare,
And men vse most to couet forreine thing. (ll. 161-2)

Colin's exchanges with Thestylis, unlike those with Cuddy, never display raillery or condescension, nor does Thestylis ever appear in the guise of an innocent. As mentioned earlier, it is Thestylis who tears aside the veil imposed by Colin's extravagant praises of the court and penetrates to the central issue: Why did Colin leave the scene which so abounded in elegance and grace? Why does he choose to dwell amidst the penury and harshness of an essentially inhospitable land? That Thestylis could ask such personal and conceivably embarrassing questions suggests the closeness between the two. The final comment of Thestylis (ll. 676-9) intimating that Colin's censure of courtiers may arise from envy again bespeaks both the interlocutor's perspicacity and his sense of confidence as Colin's *fidus Achates*. The words employed by Thestylis here are sufficiently edged to provoke an angry response, but Colin evinces no such reaction; nor, in truth, does the reader who is responsive to the overtones expect him to.

Thestylis comes through to the reader as a person with a distinct character. Neither sentimental like Hobbinol, nor naïve like Cuddy, he is in a sense Colin's *alter ego*. Thestylis' asperity towards Colin, like Colin's critical view of some aspects of the court scene, helps prevent a poem largely devoted to praise from becoming overly saccharine, flavoring it with that dash of salt which Sir John Harington thought necessary to make verse last.[9] Thestylis' contribution goes beyond that of being a foil in a dramatic representation. If the main substance of the poem be thought of as an "argument"—that is, as a persuasion to justify Colin's concept of the good life, the speeches of Thestylis may then be considered to represent the opposition: whether that opposition is conceived as being external or internal is immaterial. The technique of anticipating objections and blunting their force in advance is as old as the art of forensics. The probability of the conscious use of this device by Spenser is strengthened by the recollection that the entire discipline of logic had been formulated in intimate association with forensics, with Cicero one of its leading theoretical as well as practical exponents.

In addition to those already named, the only other interlocutor in Colin's group to have a substantial number of lines is Lucida; however, neither one of her two speeches, totalling twenty-seven lines, reveals either her personality or any special relationship to Colin. The first (ll. 457-63) performs the familiar function of transition. In the longer speech near the end of the poem (ll. 907-26), she tells by hearsay Rosalind's cruelty towards Colin. She also recounts the *exemplum* of Stesichorus, who, according to the classical account, had been severely punished for reviling "fairest *Helene*". The speech furnishes a perfect platform for launching Colin into his concluding diapason of chivalric devotion to his mistress.

Like Hobbinol, Cuddy, Thestylis, Lucida, and the other shepherds, Colin is himself one of the "voices" in the poem. His mode of address is essentially the same as that of the others: direct discourse to a circle of immediate listeners. Like them, he too is a character in a drama-like setting. The pervasive atmosphere is one of cordiality. The group stands in a relationship of confident friendship, one with another. The intimacy of this relationship vis-à-vis Colin is interestingly reflected in one place (ll. 903-12) by the fact that two members of the group, Lucida and Hobbinol,

9. Epigram i.37, *The Letters and Epigrams of Sir John Harington,* ed. Norman Egbert McClure (Philadelphia, 1930), p. 163.

feel free to discuss Colin in the third person while he is himself on the scene. The subject of their conversation is none other than Colin's love affair with Rosalind! Thus Colin, as one of the group, addresses all of his words directly to its other nine members, who in turn respond to his thoughts and react to his manner of delivering them. To this extent, then, Colin is simply one more member of the pastoral gathering.

But in another and more significant sense, Colin stands apart from the group. Some of this difference in dimension between him and the others arises from a difference of tone; some, from the scale of his contribution; but the greatest part of the difference derives from the distinctive character of his discourse.

As to tone, Colin's relationship to the group is not really that of an equal. It is true that the others address him familiarly at times; they allude to their common situation as shepherds; they recall shared experiences; they even twit him a little about his unsuccessful love affair. It should be recalled, however, that the others have assembled to listen to him. They constantly urge him to tell about this or that. They continually praise highly his skill in discourse and stand in awe of his experience among the high and the mighty. Then, too, it should be noted that all of the members, with the one exception of the exchange between Hobbinol and Lucida mentioned above, address their remarks *directly* to Colin, employing variously the nominative of address, the second person pronoun, and the imperative form of the verb. The fact that all of the other members are understood to be listening intently heightens for the reader the importance of the exchanges. The narrator further aids this natural dramatic tension by stressing that the group is avid to learn the details of Colin's adventure abroad. When Colin brings his discourse to an unmistakable close, the group disperses.

From the standpoint of scale, Colin's contribution dwarfs that of the other members. As noted, he speaks 730 of the entire 955 lines in the poem. His nearest competitor in number of lines spoken is Hobbinol, who has forty-two. Colin as a person is the cynosure of the group; his speeches constitute the chief reason for the group to remain. His discourse in twenty-two separate parts, ranging from a minimum of eight lines to a maximum of eighty-nine and averaging thirty-three lines, is the core of the dialogue. In a very real sense, his discourse *is* the poem, for which the enveloping action and the speeches of the other characters constitute merely a setting.

The final and perhaps most telling difference between Colin's speeches and those of the others is that his words treat connectedly a series of themes arising from, and suggested by, his recollection of his experiences at court. While the other speakers frequently comment on some of the things Colin says, they never deal with independent topics; moreover, their remarks always center on, and relate to, Colin's presentation. In short, their contribution is peripheral; Colin's is central.

In view of the fact, then, that the poem exists mainly to embody a sequence of reflections and attitudes uttered by Colin, it is feasible to consider these utterances in the same way that one might examine the statements in a poem containing only one speaker—the poet himself, speaking either in his own person, or under a mask, or in a combination of the two. The questions of whether Colin is a mask for Spenser, the historical person, and to what degree the real and the fictive coincide are extremely important factors in interpretation. These questions have, accordingly, been given separate treatment in the chapter which follows. The conclusions there reached need not obtrude upon the present consideration concerning the affective character of Colin's discourse. Indeed, this consideration, to be most useful for a view of the poem as an operative artistic whole, should not be confused or prejudiced by real or fancied parallels between the posture of Colin's affairs as set forth in the poem and the posture of real affairs actually obtaining in the life of the empirical author. Consequently, the following analysis of the "feeling" in the poem proceeds, insofar as possible, on the basis of *internal* evidence only.

Parenthetically, one should note that this analysis cannot be carried on adequately in terms known to the Elizabethans themselves. The reason for this is twofold: (1) The utmost confusion and contrariety prevailed in Renaissance treatises on psychology, particularly with respect to the classification, terminology, and nature of the emotions.[10] (2) Many of the insights and techniques

10. See Louise C. Turner Forest, "A Caveat for Critics Against Invoking Elizabethan Psychology", *PMLA,* LXI (1946), 651-72, for a detailed picture of the chaotic conditions of both learned and popular psychology of the time. In "Elizabethan Psychological Literature", *Joseph Quincy Adams Memorial Studies,* eds. James G. McManaway, Giles E. Dawson, and Edwin C. Willoughby (Washington, D.C., 1948), pp. 509-22, Lawrence Babb, concurring in Mrs. Forest's sketch, ascribes the unscientific character of Renaissance psychological literature to the disposition of its writers who, thor-

helpful to this analysis were not formulated prior to the work of the semanticists in the first half of the present century.[11]

The formulation of one of these semanticists—Richards—on "feeling" as a distinct quality in a poem has already been quoted. It will be recalled that it is in terms of the communicator's (in the present case, Colin's) "special bias of interest", "personal coloring of feeling", "nuance of interest", toward the "state of affairs" or "items" he is referring to. The proper subject for this part of the chapter then is not the "state of affairs"—the ideas presented or even the emotions stated in the poem. Rather, the proper subject is characterizing the speaker's *attitude toward* these topics. It is relatively easy to identify the feelings presented for consideration

---

oughly in accord with the temper of the times, reverenced pronouncements of earlier authorities over regard for direct observation of human nature; generally eschewed systematic organization and close reasoning (though they frequently paid lip service to both); and viewed psychology primarily as a medium for inculcating ethical and moral truths.

11. In view of the fact, intimated in the previous note, that writers of leading Renaissance treatises on the passions founder helplessly when they attempt a logical and workable classification of the emotions (and this includes such widely-read authors and works as Thomas Wright, *The Passions of the Minde in Generall* [London, 1604]; Nicholas Coeffeteau, *A Table of Humane Passions,* trans. Edward Grimestone [London, 1621]; Marin Cureau de la Chambre, *The Character of the Passions,* trans. anon. [London, 1650]), it is worth observing that modern semanticists who have done so much to sensitize the reader to the emotional implications of words and to provide a vocabulary for describing these effects have declined attempting to categorize the human emotions. One looks in vain for a complete listing or classification of emotions in Richards' *Principles of Literary Criticism,* 5th ed. (New York, 1934); and in *The Meaning of Meaning,* 3rd ed. (New York, 1930), which he wrote with C. K. Ogden. Richards, in a footnote (p. 102) of *Principles,* refers to a more detailed discussion of pleasure, emotion and attitude to be found in C. K. Ogden, *The Meaning of Psychology* (New York, 1926). Ogden in this work does not present a complete list of the emotions either, but his theory of emotions as composite experiences may help to explain the absence on the part of either of the two Cambridge dons of any attempt to draw up a classified list: "Fear, disgust, anger, and love may seem at least to contain specific modifications of consciousness with as good a right to be classed among affective phenomena as pleasure or unpleasure. But when we look more closely these emotional characters turn out to be composite. We cannot reduce pleasure and unpleasure either to awareness or to striving or to pleasure, and conscious striving, and its peculiar character is given by what we are aware of, how we are striving, and, as a rule, unpleasure" (pp. 195-6).

because the speaker frequently uses names of the emotions, their equivalent adjectives, or verbal counterparts. Thus, in relating his first glimpse of land, Colin expresses the attitude of *fear* which the waters arouse in him (ll. 196-9). In recollecting the impression that Cynthia made upon him when he was first ushered into her presence (ll. 333-51), Colin gives voice to a feeling compounded of *wonder* and *admiration*. His declaration of *love* to "one, whom all my dayes I serue" (l. 467) depicts yet another emotion. In the section dealing with the perversion of the courtly ideal (ll. 648-794), Colin presents his various feelings of *anger, scorn, hatred* toward the courtiers. The emotions vocalized are part of the "sense" of the poem—the "state of affairs"—toward which the hearers' attention is being directed. But what is behind these vocalizations? What is the speaker's "bias of interest", his "personal coloring of feeling" toward them? Ascertaining this internalized element is manifestly a much more delicate task than pointing out the emotion expressed. It involves no less than attempting to discern in the written word the equivalents in face-to-face speech of intonation, facial expression, and bodily action. The ability of the reader to respond appropriately to the writer's subtle substitutions for oral tones and bodily gesture would be severely limited were it not for the fact that, in Richards' words, "Any lively, close, realistic thought of an emotion is so apt to revive it that most descriptions that are at all concrete or intimate, that do succeed in 'putting it before one', also reinstate it".[12] In any event, despite the self-evident delicacy of the operation, one must attempt to ascertain the orientation of the speaker toward his subject because the way the reader is to "take" Colin's utterances depends on the determination of "feeling", which is both a part of meaning and an integrating element of highest import.

The orientation of Colin toward his subject will be found to be one of seriousness, but this dominant attitude has, as shall be seen, numerous shadings. This inward "interest" pervades all the themes; it is a concomitant of all the emotions represented. Taken as a whole, it helps explain the highly persuasive quality of the praise and the dispraise.

The apparent lapses from the note of high seriousness, like Colin's assumption of the *ingenu* role in his account of the first sight of the ocean, in his description of the ship, and in his by-play

12. *Practical Criticism*, p. 223.

with Cuddy are adaptations to his part as one of the *dramatis personae*—a shepherd. While the entire dramatic situation conveys, as has been noted, an atmosphere of cordiality into which the reader is drawn, nevertheless maintenance of decorum in accord with the demands of the pastoral motif does not operate to diminish the fundamental earnestness of the poem.

In point of fact, the pastoral device facilitates the serious intent because it effects the reduction in scale necessary to discuss, both freely and in good taste, the affairs of state and the attributes of the reigning monarch in a period which took very seriously the doctrine of the divine right of kings—and of queens! Neither are the invective, the sardonic humor, the mordant wit, vented at times in rather coarse language, running through the satiric section on the perversion of the courtly ideal (ll. 468-794), an offset to the gravity of the treatment. On the contrary, the satire in *Colin Clout* deepens this gravity in the same way that, for instance, the ironic humor contained in Samuel Johnson's famous letter rejecting Lord Chesterfield's belated aid underscores the intensity of the feeling.

One indication of the importance with which Colin regards his subject is the absence from his entire discourse of elements which characteristically distinguish light handling. Thus, the poem has no jests in the sense of broadly humorous remarks or anecdotes. In fact, it has a paucity of humor in general. Colin's presentation is not calculated to produce laughter on the part of his *immediate* audience. It does occasion some degree of amusement on the part of his *removed* audience—the reader—in the part where, under the guise of an innocent, Colin describes the sea and the vessel. But even here the modern reader may make too much of the humor by overestimating the degree of familiarity and feeling of safety with which many Elizabethans regarded ocean voyages. Today one tends very easily to forget the comparative smallness of the vessels used in sixteenth-century Europe and the frequency of shipwrecks.

Likewise absent from *Colin Clout* is the representation of anything inherently implausible. The sea as meadow is metaphor. The story told by Colin concerning the love of the rivers Bregog and Mulla, even at the level of the interior audience, is fictive—a shepherd's song. At the level of the intended reader (or listener), the story is allegory in the form of a topographical myth. Nor is there any trace in the poem of the farce which makes *Mother Hubberds Tale* so amusing; nor, of the mock heroic which makes *Muiopotmos* so fanciful.

The imagery, moreover, contains no suggestion of levity. On the contrary, it reinforces the weighty tone. The figurative images so abundant in the poem have as their characteristic mode the relation of their second terms to areas of serious scholarly cultivation—pastoral poems, classic myths, Neo-Platonic dialogues, Petrarchan love lyrics, and biblical rhapsodies.

Having marked on the need to separate the speaker's "attitude to things" from his "thoughts about them"[13] and having characterized the general orientation of Colin's discourse, we may now proceed to specifics—to tracing the various nuances of feeling which Colin manifests toward what he is stating. This canvass will necessarily center upon expressions directly revelatory of emotional inherencies because locutions which are charged by the immediate context constitute one of the most palpable indications of the speaker's inner feelings toward his subject.

An attitude of pleasant restraint characterizes the opening two speeches by Colin (ll. 37-51, 56-79), with the quality of pleasure predominating over reserve. A similar attitude characterizes Colin's final speech (ll. 927-51), with the quality of restraint, of complex emotions held in check, predominating over pleasure. In the first speech, Colin expresses his willingness to comply with Hobbinol's request, averring that his recent experience at court still holds a pleasant place in his thoughts. The vocabulary here serves to reflect, express, and evoke feelings corresponding to the emotion named or suggested. The connotative value of some of these names is high: "full of my thoughts satiety" (l. 42), "sweet contentment" (l. 43), "lifes sole blisse" (l. 47). Similarly, the account of the meeting with the "straunge shepheard" contains an abundance of such loaded names: "pipes delight" (l. 61), "pleasant fit" (l. 69). In addition, what Richards calls "projectile adjectives" or "aesthetic adjectives" play an important part.[14] The reader registers such

13. The quoted locutions appear in Ogden, *Meaning of Psychology*. The context in which they occur is highly germane to the present matter: "It [ordinary language] reflects the thinker's attitude to things as well as his thoughts about them, and it is bent and twisted throughout in the interests of communication. For language, in addition to serving the thinker himself, is used in order to make other people go through the same thinking processes" (p. 233).

14. Of this class of words and corresponding abstract substantives, Richards observes: "In so far as they register the projection of a feeling into an object they carry a double function at least . . . We may take such a word as *beauty* either as standing for some inherent property (or set of

"value" adjectives as "blessed" (l. 40), "sweet" (l. 43), "glorious" (l. 46), "pleasing" (l. 62). Verbal equivalents of these same emotion-naming words have a like role in reflecting the pleasant mood felt by Colin. Examples of these are "couet" (l. 37), "desires" (l. 50), "allured" (l. 61), "plaie" (l. 69), "pleasd" (l. 71). The restrained joy implicit in Colin's two speeches derives from the fact that the pleasant experience is *retrospective* and the recollection of past pleasure is different from—less urgent than—anticipated pleasure.

The "satietie" of the opening passages shade into pensiveness in Colin's recital of the topographic myth, which was part of the exchange of songs between Colin and his visitor, the "shepheard of the Ocean". Colin explicitly tells his audience that the song suited his sad occasion both as an outcast lover and as an exile. It is true that Thestylis styles the myth "a mery lay" (l. 157), but he can hardly be using the word *mery* to mean that the tale is happy or cheerful in intrinsic content,[15] for, in truth, the myth is plaintive in tone to accord with the sad fate of the lovers, as well as with Colin's own situation. Thestylis' meaning is doubtless that the lay was well told and therefore pleasant or agreeable *to listen to.* The pensive cast of the imagery in such a passage as the following seems to defy description:

> And then besides, those little streames so broken
> He vnder ground so closely did conuay,
> That of their passage doth appeare no token
> Till they into the *Mullaes* water slide. (ll. 141-4)

One recalls for parallel the ineffable poignancy of Keats's line in the "Ode to a Grecian Urn":

> And, little town, thy streets forevermore
> Will silent be; and not a soul to tell
> Why thou art desolate, can e'er return.

properties) in the object said to be beautiful; or as standing for an emotive classification (i.e., placing the object in the class of things that affect us in a certain way); or, thirdly, as expressing the occurrence of a certain feeling in the speaker" (*Practical Criticism,* pp. 357-8).

15. The *O.E.D.* cites two Spenser quotations using the word *mery*: "Saint George of mery England, the signe of victoree' (*F.Q.I.*x.61.9, *Works,* I, 139); "To mery London, my most kyndly Nurse" (*Proth.* 128, *Works,* VIII, 260). In both cases the word means "pleasant, delightful in aspect or condition".

The concluding quatrain of the myth depends heavily for its nostalgic strain on the suggestive quality of the long *os* and the repetition of the liquids:

> So of a Riuer, which he was of old,
> He none was made, but scattred all to nought,
> And lost emong those rocks into him rold,
> Did lose his name: so deare his loue he bought. (ll. 152-5)

The evocative character of such locutions as "old", "scattred all to nought", "lost", and "lose" also plays a part in the reflection of the mood. One turns again to that later master of verbal melody for a similar type of magic—this in "The Eve of St. Agnes":

> And they are gone: aye, ages long ago
> These lovers fled away into the storm.

The reader will scarcely need to be reminded that the emotional texture of the topographic myth, which is one of *melancholy* in the modern sense, is quite different from what it would be if the underlying emotion were *grief*. In contrast to grief, which is one of the strong emotions, melancholy tends to be a pleasant type of self-regarding emotion—a species of mild self-flagellation in keeping with the Shelleyean sentiment that "Our sweetest songs are those that tell of saddest thought".

Colin's subsequent two speeches (ll. 163-71, 178-99), the one describing "that other shepheard[s] ... lamentable lay" and the other inviting attention to his own "lucklesse lot", evince emotions of sympathy and self-commiseration respectively. Implicit in the reference to the plight of his friend whom Cynthia "from her presence, fautlesse him debard" (l. 167), are the speaker's projection of self into the situation of the sufferer and a consequent active appropriation of his grief. With reference to self-commiseration, Colin's plaint is imaginatively bodied forth in the passage:

> He gan to cast great lyking to my lore,
> And great dislyking to my lucklesse lot;
> That banisht had my selfe, like wight forlore,
> Into that waste, where I was quite forgot. (ll. 180-83)

The auditory imagery here, particularly with respect to the *o* with *r* coloring recalls Edgar Allan Poe's explanation of "Nevermore" as the choice of the refrain in "The Raven":

> That such a close, to have force, must be sonorous and susceptible of protracted emphasis, admitted no doubt, and these considerations inevitably led me to the long *o* as the most sonorous vowel in connection with *r* as the most producible consonant.
>
> The sound of the *refrain* being thus determined, it became necessary to select a word embodying this sound, and at the same time in the fullest possible keeping with that melancholy which I had predetermined as the tone of the poem.[16]

Though both Spenser and Poe use similar harmonic and imagistic devices, the results are not comparable. In "The Raven" the reader fails to sense any genuine sincerity on the part of the speaker—the "I". The failure of "The Raven" is largely one of "feeling" and is not necessarily a result of the mechanistic theory by which Poe afterwards explained its composition. In contrast, the passage from *Colin Clout* just quoted rings true. The reader feels the coloration of self-commiseration and responds to it.

The presence of stronger emotion on Colin's part than those of satiety, melancholy, and others just alluded to is first evident in his reply to Cuddy's question as to whether heaven and heavenly graces also exist in "that land"—England. The passage embodying Colin's answer (ll. 308-27) has been noted in the chapter on rhetorical figures as illustrative of the power of major schemes like *synathroismus* or congeries and *acclamatio* or summing up to signalize forceful emotion. These figures, aided by the *anaphora* of "No" at the beginning of five lines, heightens emphasis by repetition and climax. The lines containing the indirect description of Ireland (312-19) abound in locutions of highly emotive suggestibility, calculated to conjure up fear-inspiring images. The fact that these accompaniments of the Irish scene alluded to by Colin—the "bloodie issues", the "griesly famine", the "raging sweard", the "nightly bodrags", the "rauenous wolues", the "outlawes fell"—were familiar to Elizabethan readers both by repute and from experience gives added point to the emotions underlying the raised utterances.[17]

16. "The Philosophy of Composition", *The Works of Edgar Allan Poe,* ed. John H. Ingram (Edinburgh, 1875), III, 271.

17. Renwick mentions that the bodrags or raids are alluded to in documents among the Irish papers. He also makes the comment, "The Irish wolves were almost a proverb in Elizabethan England" (*Daphnaïda,* p.

Colin's description of Cynthia inspired by his first sight of her (ll. 333-51) has been treated in the chapter on imagery as a series of parallels based on logical categories of likeness. The Queen is shadowed in terms of her resemblance to certain objects—a crown of lilies, the circlet of a turtle dove, and the like. Since these objects have symbolic meaning, the praise is largely conceptual in nature. Opening the passage with explicit reference to Cynthia's "glory" and "greatness", Colin does not attempt to express an observer's sensual response to the subject's physical or womanly attributes. Accordingly, regarded from this point of view, the description is not emotionally toned. One can, however, subsume without difficulty a great part of this description under the rubric of "aesthetic emotions", which Maher, writing in the modern period, has defined as "sentiments awakened by the contemplation of the Beautiful and the Sublime".[18] Conceding the large part that the reason plays in the human appreciation of beauty, Maher states: "The most universal feature in the various kinds of beautiful or pleasing objects, the generality of philosophers have held to consist of unity amid variety ... Symmetry, fitness, harmony, and the like, are but special forms of this unity".[19] Inasmuch as virtually all the qualities indirectly attributed to Cynthia by means of the images—

> I would her lyken to a crowne of lillies,
> Vpon a virgin brydes adorned head,
> With Roses dight and Goolds and Daffadillies;

---

186). According to him, moreover, those who, like Spenser, lived near the famous fastnesses of the Glen of Aherlow and the Great Wood, "knew something about outlaws". Spenser, in an oft-quoted passage of *A View of the Present State of Ireland, Prose Works,* p. 158, has Eudoxus speak of the extremes of privation to which the wars had reduced the Irish peasants: "Out of euerie Corner of the woods and glinnes they Came Crepinge forthe vppon theire hands for theire Leggs Coulde not beare them, they looked like Anotomies of deathe, they spake like ghostes Cryinge out of theire graues, they did eate the dead Carrions, happie wheare they Coulde finde them, Yea and one another sone after, in so muche as the verye carkasses they spared not to scrapte out of theire graves".

18. Michael Maher, S.J., *Psychology: Empirical and Rational,* 9th ed., Stonyhurst Philosophical Series (London, 1933), p. 435. Maher employs as the foundation of his influential work originally published in 1890 the Thomist synthesis of Aristotelian and Stoical doctrines on the passions.

19. *Ibid.,* p. 436.

Or like the circlet of a Turtle true,
In which all colours of the rainbow bee;
Or like faire *Phebes* garlond shining new,
In which all pure perfection one may see— (ll. 337-43)

can be contained under this elaboration of the formula "unity amidst variety", one need not belabor the observation that aesthetic emotion pervades the passage.

The figures of *occupatio,* or pretending to pass over, and of *meiosis* or diminution, both of which express Colin's doubt as to his ability to render suitable homage to such a high personage as Queen-Cynthia, suggest the presence on his part of a more rarefied emotion than that of the Beautiful alone; they suggest the presence of the Sublime. The *occupatio* stands at the beginning of the section where Colin, speaking of Cynthia's glory, says, "Such greatnes I cannot compare to ought" (l. 335). He goes on, nevertheless, to compare it to many things! The *meiosis* occurs toward the end of the passage:

But vaine it is to thinke by paragone
Of earthly things, to iudge of things diuine:
Her power, her mercy, her wisedom, none
Can deeme, but who the Godhead can define.
Why then do I base shepheard bold and blind,
Presume the things so sacred to prophane? (ll. 344-9)

The ornate splendor of the imagery framed by *occupatio* and *meiosis* conveys a direct intimation of the thrill felt by Colin as a beholder of such grandeur—a thrill compounded of admiration, awe, and sympathy.[20]

The long passage paying homage to the maids of honor (ll. 486-577) is similarly constructed of figurative imagery relating to abstract notions of the Beautiful and of the Sublime. This being so, attribution of aesthetic emotion to the roll call of the ladies is equally appropriate. Again, Colin's declaration of chivalric devotion and adoration to his lady (ll. 466-79), which follows Petrarchan concepts of beauty and perfection, can be construed as aesthetically oriented. But, as indicated in the chapter on figures of rhetoric,

20. "The emotion [of the Sublime] involves admiration, fear, or awe, and a certain sympathy with the power manifested" (*ibid.,* p. 438).

the elaborate rhetorical texture signalizes exceptional fervency, causing the declaration to surpass in emotional force Colin's previous graceful bow to the gentlewomen in the royal circle. To a still greater degree the aesthetic substratum of the first part of the final disquisition on Cynthia's glory (ll. 590-615) is overlaid, as is also noted in Chapter II, by a dazzling panoply of figurative patterning. The chapter on imagery, moreover, draws attention to the use of biblical parallels from the Song of Solomon to generate affective power in this tribute.

The four speeches alluded to above—the first sustained praise of Cynthia, the tribute of vassalage to Rosalind, the notice of the ladies at court, and the final laudation of Cynthia—all evince, to a greater or lesser extent, aesthetic emotion of the Beautiful and the Sublime.

In the succeeding section of the poem, the series of speeches encompassed under the thematic heading, perversion of the courtly ideal (ll. 648-794), have been treated in the latter part of the chapter on imagery. There it is pointed out that in the representation of false courtiers and the abuses of which they are charged, Colin employs terms which contrast, because of their relative bluntness and coarseness, with the elegance of those used in describing the courtly ideal. From this section a long list of locutions which carry a heavy cargo of adverse emotional loading can easily be compiled. To mention only a few here, they range from the somewhat abstract words and phrases like "enormities" (l. 665), "that liues painted blisse" (l. 685), "foule disgrace" (l. 691), "lewd speeches and licentious deeds" (l. 787), and "sordid vses" (l. 792); through terms of sharp disapprobation applied directly to the evil courtiers, like "wretches" (l. 675), "guilefull hollow hart" (l. 699), "instruments of others gaines" (l. 766); to concrete words of strongly pejorative connotation used by Colin in the context of the passages, like "asses by their eares" (l. 712), "bladders blowen vp with wynd" (l. 717), "drownded lie in pleasures wastefull well" (l. 762), and "swim in loue vp to the eares" (l. 782). The barrage of venom-dripped words of the type just quoted is perhaps the main factor contributing to the reader's consciousness of intense feeling suffusing this section. In addition, the very scale of the fulmination—about one-fifth of Colin's entire discourse—makes for cumulative force. The relative simplicity of the syntax, the concrete character of the language, and the comparative paucity of tropical devices all play a part, too, in the unmistakable attitude of conviction which invests this diatribe.

While the posture of concern, of involvement, is implicit in this part, if one were to attempt to single out one specific emotional ingredient, he might well be at a loss to do so. I do not refer now, of course, to the emotional states represented, which are a combination of anger, scorn, derision, contempt, indignation; nor to the mode of presenting these states, which is irony. Actually, the overriding impression one gets with respect to these speeches is that of *suppressed* emotion. The language as a whole seems to reflect a surcharged affective state on the part of the speaker. If this identification of the orectic inherency is correct, the existence of a condition of general disturbance furnishes the most reliable index of the speaker's impulsion, since such a state could well be the outward manifestation of an inward affective disequilibrium. One must, to be sure, temper the application of this commonplace of contemporary psychology—the effect of emotion on the entire bodily consciousness—when dealing with expression in a work of conscious literary art; nevertheless, the pertinence of such an explanation to the nature of the "feeling" in the section under review can scarcely be doubted.

With reference to the long section dealing with the nature and power of love (ll. 795-902), the fusion of literary sources found in this part is richly reflected in the vocabulary. In particular, the terms used to set forth the various concepts of love hark back to the commonplaces of medieval court-of-love poems and Neo-Platonic writings, which were staples of aristocratic learning. Some of these concepts, with their associated vocabulary, are: Love as a god—"So we him worship, so we him adore" (l. 815); love as a feudal lord—"Ah my dread Lord, that doest liege hearts possesse" (l. 793); love as a universal cohesive force—"And so great enemies as of them bee,/Be euer drawne together into one" (ll. 844-5); love as one whose wounds can be healed only by her whose beauty inflicted them—"But being hurt, seeke to be medicynd/Of her that first did stir that mortall stownd" (ll. 877-8); and love as the ally of chastity—"Thus ought all louers of their lord to deeme:/And with chaste heart to honor him alway" (ll. 887-8). The expression of sentiments such as these evoked, particularly for the learned reader of Spenser's day, a mood of elevation and dignity appropriate to a recall of literary and philosophic associations. The evocative power of these passages is necessarily more limited for most modern readers.

Examining more closely the speeches in this sequence, one finds that the praise of love opens with a somewhat detached air:

> But we poore shepheards whether rightly so,
> Or through our rudenesse into errour led,
> Do make religion how we rashly go,
> To serue that God, that is so greatly dred. (ll. 795-8)

After Cuddy's comment on "these oracles so sage,/Of that high powre" (ll. 825-6), Colin continues in a rather philosophical vein, employing language that is especially direct and concrete. The following passage is typical of the movement:

> And shortly after euerie liuing wight,
> Crept forth like wormes out of her slimie nature,
> Soone as on them the Suns life giuing light,
> Had powred kindly heat and formall feature,
> Thenceforth they gan each one his like to loue,
> And like himself desire for to beget,
> The Lyon chose his mate, the Turtle Doue
> Her deare, the Dolphin his own Dolphinet. (ll. 859-66).

With the summing up by the proverb, "So loue is Lord of all the world by right", the speech gains emotional momentum. Colin's miniature "Hymne in Honour of Love" concludes with a castigation of base lovers. Here the speaker manifests unusually strong animus. He evinces no trace of the ironic smile evident earlier when he discusses a related topic, the disreputable side of court life.

Taken as a whole, the section on love maintains an attitude of devotion and humility appropriate to the conceptualization of the power in terms of divine and feudal lordship. At the same time, the section exhibits the directness, clarity, and eloquence suited to philosophical discourse. It is a kind of emotional plateau between two peaks: that of vehemence in the philippic against the depraved court followers and that of fervency in Colin's parting affirmation of exalted devotion to his beloved.

This parting speech, mentioned earlier in the present chapter, is discussed in some detail near the end of the chapter on diction and versification. The extremely skillful employment of metrical and harmonic aids to intensify the speech, which is one of high emotional potency, is there pointed out. The part in the second chapter dealing with the role of the rhetorical figures in expressing and evoking excitement invites attention to the *apostrophe* which ends Colin's final plea on a note of impassioned eloquence. Here, as in some of the other sections, no precise designation exists for the speaker's "nuance of interest" toward the protestation of undying love contained in the passage. Despite its intensity, the passage does not let out all stops. In it there is a quality of restraint, of powerful emotion held in reserve—the whole gaining richness from what has gone before—that makes it a well nigh perfect climax for the dialogue.

The present chapter has viewed *Colin Clout* in its mimetic aspects to permit consideration of *praxis* as a sphere of meaning complementary to *lexis*. Such a consideration places primary emphasis on speech as action, oriented in emotion. Examination of the orectic spectrum shows how the poet has established a setting in the form of a narrative frame to provide a medium for focusing, in an atmosphere of cordiality and permissiveness, a sequence of ideas and attitudes projected by one main spokesman, Colin Clout. By the device of a *conversazione* carried on along lines of familiar pastoral and romance types, Colin's presentation operates at two levels of address: direct discourse to the immediate gathering (the interior audience) and communication beyond the immediate audience to the polite readership of the court and other aristocratic circles (the exterior audience). The drama-like setting, which involves the participation of a mixed group of ten persons figured as shepherds and shepherdesses, serves the dual function of vitalizing Colin's discourse and of controlling it rhetorically.

Though Colin's speeches are set within an atmosphere of pastoral simplicity and cordiality, an hitherto unnoticed emotional vibrancy exists on or close to the surface of his utterances. The orientation of these affective impulses is one of basic concern vis-à-vis the speaker's subject—a seriousness free from all traces of grimness or despair. The gravity has a range of shadings, consisting of the following emotional nuances: a posture of dignity and a sense of restraint, counterpointed in one part by a vein of irony and satire; a tendency toward pensiveness; a sense of pity for others and commiseration for the speaker himself; an aesthetic sensitivity and responsiveness; a coloring of animus toward immoral persons and abhorrent practices; and, finally, impulses of attraction to others, blending elements of warmth, affection, admiration, and love.

These varied but logically-flowing emotional currents must be "felt" by the reader in order for him to respond to them; however, they are by no means products solely of a given reader's introspection. On the contrary, the poet has throughout employed definite, conscious, and artistically manipulated means to externalize this orectic potential: syntax, diction, prosody, imagery, and rhetorical figuration.

So prominent (but not unfavorably obtrusive) are these means of expressing and evoking feeling that the reader who has been alerted to them gains from the perusal of the pastoral a peculiarly powerful sense of the poet's deliberate control exercised from beginning to end. Because the emotional impetus, discharged (as in life itself) in currents of varying force, is never allowed to get out of hand, the reader receives an overall impression of poised reconciliation on the part of the speaker. This impression is reinforced by the fact that the narrative frame permits the poem to begin and end on a note of relative tranquillity. The emotional fervency is further tempered by the circumstance that the "story" of the poem is told retrospectively by Colin. Casting the narrative in the past tense, moreover, works to enhance the atmosphere of contemplation. The additional fact that the poem consists predominantly of praise —a pleasant emotional consciousness—makes it reasonable to read into the attitude of the speaker a posture of contentment—a state of mind gained through a resolution of conflicts.

CHAPTER VI

THE USE OF PERSONAL MATERIAL

The dedication of *Colin Clout,* under date of 27 December 1591 at Spenser's Kilcolman estate in central Munster, to Sir Walter Raleigh, presents the poem as a "simple pastorall . . . agreeing with the truth in circumstance and matter". This explicit statement over the signature of the poet, plus the manifest correspondence of factual elements in the poem to persons, places, and incidents known from other sources to appertain to the historical Spenser, has led scholars and critics, past and present, to accept an unusually close relationship between the matter in the work and the biography of the living person who wrote it.

The existence of this relationship has tended to distort readings of the poem by causing distinctions between Colin Clout as a *persona* and Edmund Spenser as a person to be blurred. The result has frequently been to overrate the importance of the autobiographical elements as shaping forces and to neglect or understate the importance of fabrication. Indeed, perusing the scholarship concerning the poem—not all of it literary—one is rather surprised to note how much of it holds, by implication at least, that the orientation is principally factual—that the poem is an authentic record of the acts, sentiments, and personal associations of the author, under the *nom de plume* of the title character, during the period from the autumn of 1589 to the date of the dedication; and, conversely, to note how little of the scholarship emphasizes the basic orientation as imaginative. Considerations presented in this and in the succeeding final chapter will doubtless aid in redressing the balance.

The view of *Colin Clout* as a kind of "verse diary"[1] appears in three main forms or versions. In a given study, these may or may not be distinct. The first version accords, by implication, almost literal acceptance to data referrable to external fact, principally

1. Frederick Ives Carpenter, *A Reference Guide to Edmund Spenser* (Chicago, 1923), p. 25.

the three narrative episodes: the visit to Kilcolman of the Shepherd of the Ocean (Raleigh); the crossing of the Irish Sea by Colin (Spenser) and the Shepherd; and the sojourn at court of the title character. The second version, an extension of the first, regards—also by implication—the feelings and thoughts of the title character as a direct reflection of those held by the quill-holding author. The third version sees the poem as a construct fabricated in part from variations on an autobiographic theme. It takes cognizance, in various degrees, of the way in which events in private life and actual thoughts and feelings of the empirical author may be—to paraphrase Ben Jonson—cast in new and altered form when such material is struck upon the Muses' anvil.[2]

I question the propriety of giving virtually unqualified credence to the first two versions, which the preponderance of scholarship favors. I concur in the third view, which has hitherto lacked both clarification and amplification. Accepting the pastoral as an expression of deep artistic sincerity on Spenser's part, I would place major stress on the oblique and refracted way in which reality appears.

With reference to the first view, the prefatory "Life of Spenser" given in the earliest variorum edition—that of Henry Todd in 1805—cites the poem as first-hand evidence of the visit, of the resulting voyage by the two poets to London, and of Spenser's audience with the Queen.[3] Spenser's later biographers, too, with certain minor exceptions to be noted, seem not to question the authenticity of the events as depicted in the poem. E. de Sélincourt, making a special effort to interpret the biographical material in Spenser's works, concludes that Spenser recounted his recent experience in *Colin Clout*—"Ralegh's visit to him at Kilcolman; their journey to London, his reception at court, and his impressions of all he saw there".[4] In a work dealing solely with Spenser's Irish experiences, another biographer speaks of the proximity of Kilcolman to the main road and its consequent convenience to travelers to Kilmallock or to Limerick. Thereupon she goes on to

2. "To the Memory of My Beloved, the Author Mr. William Shakespeare: and What He Hath Left Us", *Ben Jonson,* eds. C. H. Herford, Percy and Evelyn Simpson (Oxford, 1947), VIII, 392.

3. *The Works of Edmund Spenser,* ed. Henry John Todd (London, 1805), I, lxiv-lxv.

4. *The Poetical Works of Edmund Spenser,* eds. J. C. Smith and E. de Sélincourt (London, 1912), xxxv.

observe: "But of the interesting guests we have no record, with one exception—Sir Walter Raleigh, whose visit, memorable in many respects, took place towards the end of 1589. The circumstances are immortalised in *Colin Clouts Come Home Again* . . . Spenser describes the meeting with this famous Undertaker, who had come over from Lismore."[5] Still another assiduous student of Spenser's activities during the Kilcolman period voices the opinion that in *Colin Clout* "the poet becomes frankly autobiographical and tells the story of his meeting with Ralegh in Ireland, that nobleman's delight in Spenser's poetry, and the subsequent journey to the court where the *Faerie Queene* was presented to Elizabeth".[6] The author of the latest full-scale biography of Spenser, A. C. Judson, likewise considers the poem substantially as primary historical material. "With the arrival of Raleigh at Kilcolman," he states, "we enter upon a well-documented period of Spenser's life, for this famous visit, and the subsequent journey of the two men to England, are faithfully portrayed in *Colin Clouts Come Home Againe*."[7]

Biographies of Raleigh, as well as those of Spenser, are virtually unanimous in accepting the narrative episodes as almost wholly authentic in detail. These include the still-standard nineteenth-century works by Edwards and Stebbing. The former in his *Life*, based according to the title page on contemporary documents, states that Raleigh "went to Kilcolman Castle, and his visit had a memorable result for English literature. Spenser has given us his own poetised account of this visit, in the beautiful Pastoral which he entitled 'Colin Clout's come Home again'."[8] Stebbing, in his *Biography*, asserts that Spenser described the visit of his neighbor to

5. Henley, *Spenser in Ireland*, pp. 73-4.
6. Koller, "Spenser and Ralegh", p. 37.
7. Judson, *Life*, p. 136. Significantly, William Nelson, who in his recent study devotes a chapter to the life of Spenser "stripped as far as may be of the mass of conjecture that has accumulated about it", pointedly refrains from endorsing the authenticity of biographical details, employing such clauses as, "If the account in that poem [*Colin Clout*] be taken as historically true", and, "Colin is said to have accompanied the Shepherd to the royal court" (*The Poetry of Edmund Spenser: A Study* [New York, 1963], pp. ix, 5).
8. Edward Edwards, *The Life of Sir Walter Ralegh* (London, 1868), I, 120. Edwards does note that the poem depicts the friendship of the two men as originating at the time of the visit, whereas, according to him, they were "well acquainted with each other, some ten years earlier than 1589" (p. 122).

Kilcolman "in the tenderest and least artificial of his poems".[9] Chroniclers of local Irish history, writing in archaeological journals and other periodicals of the past century, typically describe the present states of Youghal or of Lismore, quote lavishly from the poem, and elaborate freely with details of oral tradition, but add no documentary evidence of the Spenser-Raleigh visit of 1589.[10] Biographers of the present century follow more or less closely the lines set by their predecessors in taking over the entire narrative account given in the poem.[11]

The weight of authority in favor of the reliability of the poem as a source for biography is indeed imposing. Certainly no positive evidence is at hand to contradict the factual parallels within the poetic version. The account of the episodes given there is, one must concede, both possible and plausible. It should be noted, however, that while the citations which have been presented above—and many similar ones which have been excluded for the sake of economy—help convince one of the existence of a virtually exact correspondence between Spenser's life and the episodes of the poem involving Colin, they do not actually validate such an hypothesis because they do not *prove* the facts; they tend to *assume* the details to be true. The plausibility of the factual parallels and the weight of authority notwithstanding, one must allow for the possibility that the poem may not be so minutely faithful an account of what actually transpired as the Dedication professes and the biographers espouse.

9. William Stebbing, *Sir Walter Ralegh: A Biography* (Oxford, 1899), p. 71. Stebbing, like Edwards, alluding to the time the acquaintance began, suggests the poem may be departing here from the literal truth (*ibid.*).

10. Cf. Samuel Hayman, "Ecclesiastical Antiquities of Youghal", No. III, *Journal of the Kilkenny Archaeological Society,* N.S., I (1856-57), 25-26; Sir John P. Hennessy, "Sir Walter Ralegh in Ireland", *Nineteenth Century,* X (1881), 678; Louise Imogen Guiney, "Sir Walter Raleigh of Youghal in the County of Cork", *Atlantic Monthly,* LXVI (1890), 784-5; and M.R.S.A., "Sir Walter Raleigh at Youghal", *Journal of the Cork Historical and Archaeological Society,* I (1892), 129-30.

11. See, e.g., Muriel Clara Bradbrook, *The School of Night: A Study in the Literary Relationships of Sir Walter Ralegh* (Cambridge, Eng., 1936), p. 5; Edward Thompson, *Sir Walter Ralegh: Last of the Elizabethans* (London, 1935), pp. 63-4; Hugh Ross Williamson, *Sir Walter Raleigh* (London, 1951), pp. 50-5; and Willard M. Wallace, *Sir Walter Raleigh,* pp. 68-9. Walter Oakeshott, *The Queen and the Poet,* pp. 82-4, in a synopsis of what *Colin Clout* says about Raleigh's visit and its aftermath, does not question the veracity of the details.

One reason that renders this hypothesis supportable is the fact that the meeting in 1589 at Kilcolman between Spenser and Raleigh is not corroborated by any known contemporary accounts or documents. Acceptance as to the actuality of the meeting with the attendant circumstances described rests solely upon the account in the poem. The same lack of substantiation by any other source applies to the voyage across the Irish Channel which the poem represents Colin-Spenser as taking in company with Shepherd of the Ocean-Raleigh. Even Spenser's audience with the Queen and his activities at court, except for the poem, depend for their authentication not upon positive proof but upon indirect and circumstantial evidence, such as the entry of the first three books of *The Faerie Queene* on the Stationers' Register by Ponsonby on 1 December 1589;[12] publication of *The Faerie Queene* in the spring of 1590,[13] with its "Letter of the Authors" and its dedicatory and commendatory poems; entry of the *Complaints* volume on 29 December 1590 and publication by 19 March 1591;[14] and the grant of Spenser's pension of fifty pounds on 25 February 1591.[15]

That the Raleigh visit to Kilcolman either did not take place or was not as detailed in the poem is a possibility. Another possibility is that the poem alters the actual case by making it appear that there was only a *single* visit rather than a series. Yet there is a strong likelihood that there may have been several visits. To assess properly the possibilities in this regard, it is necessary to authenticate the presence in Munster of the peripatetic Raleigh during the summer and autumn of 1589. Fortunately, official records are available to substantiate Raleigh's residence in Ireland during the above-mentioned period. There is, moreover, a possibility that he may have been in Cork and Waterford counties some three months longer than has been commonly supposed. The longer the duration of Raleigh's stay in Ireland in 1589, the more likely it is that Spenser and the knight exchanged a *number* of visits. A certain amount of evidence can be adduced to support the belief that Raleight's sojourn in Ireland was closer to five months than to three in duration. A hitherto unnoticed letter in this connection written by Lord Deputy Fitzwilliam to Burghley, the Lord Treas-

12. Judson, *Life,* p. 139.
13. *Ibid.,* p. 143.
14. *Ibid.,* p. 151.
15. *Ibid.,* p. 155.

urer of England, of 29 April 1589, indicates that Raleigh may have already been in Ireland by that date, for the letter expresses the view that, although the appointment of commissioners to hear controversies between the country people and the undertakers will be very good for the province, the undertakers are not likely to perform their part of the agreements.[16] The Lord Deputy then speaks of one Patrick Condon (an Anglo-Irishman, whose ancestral lands were near those assigned to the English planters and who resented their encroachment)[17] as still being a prisoner in Dublin Castle, although some lesser prisoners had escaped. Thereafter follows the comment which, taken in the context of the whole, lends weight to the probability of Raleigh's presence in Munster as early as April of 1589, some two or three months sooner than customarily thought: "But how Sir Walter Raleigh may conceive thereby either cause of complaint or any doubt to receive trouble in his lands by Patrick Condon, I know not, both because I am not well acquainted with that matter . . ."[18]

Two other items calendared in the *State Papers for Ireland,* not elsewhere noted in this connection, lend strong support to the evidence of Fitzwilliam's letter that Raleigh was in Ireland by the early spring of 1589. One is the two-page form, dated 12 May 1589, in which Sir Walter answers by marginal notations questions of Her Majesty's Commission concerning peopling of the attainted lands. In that document Raleigh also refers to Patrick Condon as one of the few remaining dangerous Irish.[19] The other item, listed under the same date, is a six-page abstract containing the names of authorized residents upon Raleigh's lands and possessions in Waterford and Cork counties.[20] The note is signed "W. Ralegh".[21]

In any event Raleigh was certainly in Ireland by August, since a letter of Sir Francis Allen's to Anthony Bacon dated in that month mentions Raleigh as being "confined . . . into Ireland".[22] Besides

16. Great Britain, Public Record Office, *Calendar of State Papers Relating to Ireland of the Reign of Elizabeth,* IV: 1588-92 (London, 1885), 154-5, No. 45. See below, n. 23, for further reference to the time of Raleigh's arrival in Ireland.
17. Judson, *Life,* pp. 120, 132.
18. *CS*PI (1588-92), IV, 155.
19. *Ibid.,* IV, 170, No .27.
20. *Ibid.,* IV, 170-2, No. 28.
21. *Ibid.,* IV, 172.
22. Edwards, I, 119.

Lismore Castle, thirty miles east of Kilcolman, Raleigh resided during his stay in Ireland in a manor house some forty miles from Spenser at Youghal, presumably so that he could be near his 42,000 acre estate of Inchiquin. Authority for possession of this estate was granted him by a warrant recorded in the *State Papers for Ireland* under date of June 1589.[23] Renwick cites the *Calendar of Carew Papers, 1589-1600,* for evidence of Raleigh's presence at Lismore on 26 September 1589 and for his presence in London on 12 November 1589.[24] Renwick's first reference from this *Calendar* is to a note added to a letter by Lord Deputy Fitzwilliam to Sir George Carew, which reads as follows: "This letter I [Carew] received at Lysmore, Sir Walter Ralighe being present, the 26th of September 1589".[25] The second reference is to a letter of Sir Walter's to the Lord Deputy of Ireland bearing the subscript: "London, 12 November 1589".[26] The letters in the Carew papers prove that Raleigh voyaged to England in the interval between the dates given; since neither letter mentions Spenser, they do not prove that Spenser accompanied him.

Now the poem tells of a single meeting between the principals at Kilcolman, which Spenser first occupied between 3 September 1588 and 24 March 1588/89.[27] Suppose, despite the lack of substantiation outside the poem for the meeting described, one assumes the probable—that it actually took place. Let us now return to the further possibility mentioned before—that *more than one meeting occurred.* If such appears to be the case, then the poem departs from strict historicity, for nowhere in the poem is mention made of a return visit on the part of Spenser to the Warden's house at Youghal or to Lismore Castle. Yet in view of the relatively short

23. Koller, "Spenser and Ralegh", p. 41. This warrant is apparently the basis for Miss Koller's confirmation of the traditional view that "Ralegh was in Ireland from at least July 1589 to the following November". She hints at the possibility of an earlier month of arrival in connection with "a message of January 25, 1589, from the Privy Council to the Lord Deputy" to the effect that Raleigh had undertaken to raise two hundred of the six hundred men appointed to be levied in Ireland (*ibid.*). Miss Koller, however, must have misread the date of this letter. It should be 25 January 1590 (*CSPI,* 1588-92, IV, 297).

24. *Daphnaïda,* p. 181.

25. Great Britain, Public Record Office, *Calendar of the Carew Manuscripts,* III: 1589-1600 (London, 1869), 12, No. 30.

26. *Ibid.,* III, 14, No. 35.

27. Ray Heffner, "Spenser's Acquisition of Kilcolman", *MLN,* XLVI (1931), 497.

distance involved and the convenience of the well-traveled Cork-Limerick road just off Spenser's estate, one finds it just as easy to assume that in the five months of clement weather from May to the following November, or, according to Miss Koller, during the three months from July to November, several meetings instead of just one took place. This assumption becomes stronger in view of the community of interests which the two shared—their enjoyment of patronage under the Earl of Leicester at the same time and their common service under Lord Grey.[28] Miss Koller further comments on the many things which might have drawn the two colonizers together during the period: their nearness to each other and to the city of Cork, a central point for the English; their unanimity of political interests; and their concern with conditions in Ireland.[29]

If there were a number of meetings—as seems likely—then the version in the poem exhibits a selective omission on the part of the poet and, to that extent, sacrifices historical accuracy. Another probable case of selective omission with a consequent blurring of historical exactitude appears in the poem. The poetical narrative alludes to only one homecoming on the part of the traveler, Colin. This is presumably the one that occurred, as the Dedication shows, by 27 December 1591.[30] Yet one scholar has invited attention to an extract in the accounts of the Treasurer at Wars in Ireland, Sir Henry Wallop, recording an authorization of 30 May 1590 to draw money in advance. The discoverer of this entry in Rawlinson Manuscript A. 317 is of the opinion that the bill was made out to Spenser in person, not to an assignee.[31] Judson, who believes that Spenser's permanent return to Ireland (i.e., until his revisit to London of 1595) followed shortly after the grant of his pension on 25 February 1591,[32] concurs with Wilson in the view that Spenser made a hasty trip to Ireland in the spring of 1590 to deal with Lord Roche, who was creating difficulties over Spenser's title to Kilcolman.[33]

Other elements of the poem not directly a part of the episodes also afford room for questioning the view prevailing among most

28. Koller, "Spenser and Ralegh", p. 38.
29. *Ibid.*, p. 42.
30. According to Renwick, Raleigh never returned to Ireland, and the date of Spenser's return (presumably in 1591) is not known (*Daphnaïda*, p. 181).
31. F. P. Wilson, "Spenser and Ireland", *RES*, II (1926), 456-7.
32. Judson, *Life*, p. 155.
33. *Ibid.*, p. 144.

students of Spenser's life and letters to the effect that the poem possesses virtually complete topical accuracy—that it is a thinly disguised history with the story "almost as clear as a chronicle".[34] Yet many of these same students call attention to details which, strictly interpreted, are inconsistent with such a view. These details have to do with revisions. The concensus of scholars is that *Colin Clout* was completed, except for revisions, late in 1591;[35] the reader of the poem must then consider the meeting, the crossing, and the sojourn at court to have taken place between the autumn of 1589 and the date of the dedicatory letter, 27 December 1591. The logical inference on the part of the reader who holds to the theory of topical accuracy must be that all of Spenser's activities described in the poem under the guise of Colin took place during this interval. A further inference must necessarily follow that Spenser's remarks by way of Colin apply only to experiences of the two-year period ending 27 December 1591. But such is by no means the true case, for the poem contains emendations bearing on happenings occurring during a four-year period between the dedication date and 1595, the year of publication for the *Colin Clout* volume.

The certain revisions deal with altered circumstances between 1591 and 1595 in the lives of two of the three Spencer sisters with whom Spenser claimed kinship: Anne (Charillis), Elizabeth (Phyllis), and Alice (Amaryllis). These ladies are among the twelve nymphs of Cynthia's train to whom Spenser pays special tribute (ll. 485-584). The complete evidence for these revisions need not be reviewed here. The fact of later addition is hinted at by Spenser himself for one of these changes. He alludes to the change in the elegiac passage (ll. 432-43) on Ferdinando Stanley, fifth earl of Derby, known as Lord Strange, whose death occurred in April of 1594.[36] Similarly, line 543 is an addition or an altered line because Alice (Amaryllis) did not become "highest in degree" until her husband was made Earl of Derby on the death of his father in 1593.[37] The passage referring to the husband of Anne (Charillis),

> Thrise happie do I hold thee noble swaine,
> The wich are of so rich a spoile possest,

34. *Complete Works of Spenser,* ed. Dodge, p. 686.
35. Koller, "Spenser and Ralegh", p. 51; Judson, *Life,* p. 6.
36. *Works,* VII, 472.
37. Ernest A. Strathmann, "Lady Carey and Spenser", *ELH,* II (1935), 52-3.

And it embracing deare without disdaine,
Hast sole possession in so chaste a brest, (ll. 552-5)

represents a third interpolation subsequent to 1591, since Anne married the "noble swaine", Robert Sackville, on 4 December 1592.[38]

Still another revision has been suggested which, if validated, would constitute a discrepancy between the account in the poem and strict historical fidelity. The matter concerns the much-vexed question of what, in point of fact and evidence, was the "lamentable lay" (l. 164) detailing the "great vnkindnesse" and "vsage hard" (l. 165) directed against Raleigh by "*Cynthia* the Ladie of the sea" (l. 166), which the knight read to Spenser in the fall of 1589. It has been urged that the sad and bitter poem alluded to in *Colin Clout* had not as yet been written by 1589, since it could not be the same one as that referred to by Spenser several times in *The Faerie Queene* volume of 1590, most strikingly as

. . . sweet verse, with Nectar sprinckeled
In which a gracious seruant pictured
His *Cynthia* . . .
That with his melting sweetnesse rauished.[39]

The proposal is that in *Colin Clout* Spenser may be referring instead to four poems or poetic fragments in Raleigh's autograph discovered during the 1860s among the Cecil papers at Hatfield House. The Hatfield fragments or Hatfield Poem, often titled from the headings of the last two portions as *The Ocean's Love to Cynthia,* are widely believed on the basis of internal evidence to have been written during 1592. If the passage in *Colin Clout* does refer to the Hatfield Poem (or, more specifically, to the long fragment) and that poem does date from 1592 (which the reader will recall as the time of Raleigh's disgrace and imprisonment in connection with the Elizabeth Throckmorton affair), then lines 164-75 (and probably lines 428-31 also) would have to be regarded as emendations made subsequent to the dedication date. Cogent

38. Judson, *Life,* p. 5. For further reference to this revised passage, see *Daphnaïda,* p. 181; Koller, "Spenser and Ralegh", pp. 54-5; Strathmann, pp. 52-3. Strathmann cites evidence correcting the date of the marriage (given by Renwick as 4 September 1591) to 4 December 1592 (p. 52, n. 64).

39. *F.Q.* III. *Pro.* iv. 4-7, *Works,* III, 2.

arguments, however, can be brought against the validity of this conclusion, and the matter can be regarded as less than settled.[40]

One final passage, first noted by Collier, has since been widely held to contain insertions later than 1591.[41] This is the notice of Spenser's younger literary contemporary, Samuel Daniel (ll. 417-27). The "well tuned song,/Which late he sung vnto a scornfull lasse" has been taken to refer to Daniel's *Sonnets to Delia,* published in 1592. The evidence that this passage postdates the dedication letter is, however, by no means conclusive.[42]

Even discounting the Cynthia passage and the hortatory lines to Daniel, there still remain three clear-cut instances of changes necessarily made after 1591. The point to be stressed about them is simply this : If Spenser under the *nom de guerre* of Colin is narrating, upon the occasion of his return to Kilcolman from overseas in 1591, an account of his recent sojourn at the English court, as the narrative frame makes so abundantly clear, how do events that occurred *subsequent* to his return get into the recital at all? That

40. The case for the 1592 dating is advanced by Miss Latham in *Poems of Sir Walter Ralegh,* pp. 172-9; evidence against the late dating and for a 1589 composition of the Hatfield Poem is marshalled by Alexander M. Buchan in "Ralegh's *Cynthia*—Facts or Legend", *MLQ,* I (1940), 461-74. Philip Edwards, in *Sir Walter Ralegh*, p. 98, concludes: "The dedication to *Colin Clout* is dated 1591, and although the poem was not published until 1595, there is no reason to suppose that the references to Ralegh were changed after the original composition and before publication". The problems of the dating of the poem in Hatfield MS 144, containing particularly the main fragment of 522 lines entitled, "The XIth and Last Book of the Ocean to Cynthia", and the relationship of these poems to references in *Colin Clout* are taken up most recently by Oakeshott in *The Queen and the Poet.* Oakeshott holds that the long poem, together with the other three found in Lord Salisbury's library, "dates from 1592, and is associated with Raleigh's imprisonment in that year, whatever its relationship to the *Cynthis* of *Colin Clout*" (p. 136). He conjectures that allusions to "lamentable lays", like those in *Colin Clout,* are to an earlier series of Raleigh's occasional verses to Elizabeth written between 1587 and 1592 (pp. 141, 170-1).

41. *Works of Edmund Spenser,* ed. John Payne Collier (London, 1862), I, xciv.

42. Koller, "Spenser and Ralegh", p. 54, follows Collier in accepting the passage as a later addition, but she disregards Renwick's contention that Spenser very likely saw the sonnet sequence *Delia* in manuscript. Renwick advances this possibility because "the passage can scarcely be a later interpolation, since lines 420-7 [recommending that Daniel try his hand at tragedy] must be earlier than Daniel's tragedy *Cleopatra,* published in 1594" (*Daphnaïda,* p. 187).

they do countervails the common view of the poem as a substantially *bona fide* account in fictitious guise. What is the explanation for this discrepancy? Is it not simply that Spenser was never particularly concerned with historical consistency? Is it not most likely that he was concerned, rather, with shaping a creative work which, though drawing freely on the real, need not be bound by the facts or chronology of what may have transpired in real life?

The discussion up to this point has shown the first form in which acceptance of the "verse diary" idea manifests itself—that of apparent acceptance in key biographical works of the poet's professed intention to body forth the "truth" with respect to the matters treated in the poem. Further, the discussion has questioned the feasibility of placing too literal an interpretation on Spenser's dedicatory remarks in view of the fact that the main episodes depicted—the meeting with Raleigh, the joint crossing, and so much of the sojourn at court—lack documentary or other corroborating evidence. It has invited attention to certain items of fact and presumption which, though seemingly pertinent to the complete record, find no place in the poem. This selective treatment argues a kind of subject limitation which accords better with a fabricated work of the creative imagination than with a sober history. And, finally, the discussion has further emphasized the flexible handling of factual material by citing the revised passages, which constitute an overt chronological discrepancy between the "story" as presented in the poem and the happenings of actual life.

Construction of the poem as a substantially faithful transcript of its creator's own experiences takes a second form, which manifests itself in works of primarily literary rather than biographical orientation. Exponents of this second point of view go beyond acceptance of an almost literal correspondence between historical events and data found in the poetic version that are of verifiable nature. Advocates of the first point of view tend to equate Spenser and Colin in respect to their acts; those maintaining, by implication, the second point of view go even further and, to all appearances, equate Spenser and Colin in respect to their thoughts and feelings. In conformity with this implicit predicate, they are prone to read into the poem attitudes, ideas, and even states of mind deemed to have been held by the historical Spenser during the period 1589-91.

The influence of Émile Legouis in promoting this by no means uncommon point of view continues to be powerful. The tendency to interpret the poem as a direct record of its author's mental life is clearly demonstrated by the eminent literary historian both in *Edmund Spenser* (1923), a critical biography; and in *Spenser* (1926), an English volume based in part on the French work and reproducing the text of six lectures delivered at Johns Hopkins University in 1922. In recent years a new edition of the critical biography has appeared.[43] In a chapter of this revised work, Legouis uses *Colin Clout* as support for the judgment that Spenser's temperament was mercurial in the extreme :

> Mais sa nervosité lui faisait parfois trahir sa tâche de moraliste. Il vacillait entre le dithyrambe et la satire, et c'était trop souvent le hasard de ses propres sentiments, satisfaits ou rebutés, qui en décidait. Rien n'est plus saisissant à cet égard que ce poème du *Retour de Colin Clout* commencé dans l'allégresse, plein d'éloges hyperboliques de la Cour, des seigneurs, des dames et des poètes qui en font la parure, puis, brusquement, passant à la plus vive attaque contre cette mème Cour, séjour des basses intrigues et des impudiques amours. Dans l'intervalle le poète n'a-t-il pas été déçu dans son espérance de quelque haute fortune?[44]

The same point about *Colin Clout* as an exhibition of the author's nervous instability is made somewhat more emphatically in another chapter dealing with Spenser's sojourn in England : "La brusquerie du revirement est telle que le même poème, celui du *Retour de Colin Clout,* qui commence par un joyeux enthousiasme s'achève en invectives violentes. Il en devient incohérent. La fin contredit le début."[45] A passage parallel in sentiment to this one occurs in Legouis' English work. It is still more explicit about the shortcomings of *Colin Clout* which arise from the poet's presumed failure to get a firm grip on himself :

43. *Edmond Spenser,* Les Grands Écrivains Étrangers, rev. ed. (Paris, 1956). This work was slightly revised by the author in 1936 and subsequently updated (in the notes only) by his son Pierre. The original work was praised by W. L. Renwick for the excellent way it relates Spenser's poems to their author's life (*Essay,* p. 3). In a review of the new edition, Renwick calls the work "the best single book on Spenser in any language" (*Études Anglaises,* XII [1959], 242) and testifies to its importance as "one of the main inspirations of the greatly widened study of Spenser since its first appearance" (*ibid.,* p. 243).

44. *Edmond Spenser,* p. 223.

45. *Ibid.,* p. 163.

> The whole beautiful palace erected by his naive enthusiasm seems to crumble to pieces before the reader's eyes. The satire is without warning substituted for the panegyric. The condemnation is as excessive as the preceding praise had been exaggerated. The nervousness of the author is obvious. He has jumped from love to hate, from admiration to scorn in the course of composition, without even taking pains to hide the inconsistency.[46]

Aside from the apparent acceptance of a direct equation between the title character and the historical Spenser, two assumptions implicit in Legouis' interpretation of material in the poem seem open to question. The first is that the praise of court life followed by dispraise necessarily reflects a correspondence to reality and is directly ascribable to one particular period in the life of the author. The second assumption is that Spenser felt himself obligated to make the poem conform to his actual state of mind vis-à-vis his experiences at court, irrespective of whether such a transcript of reality would benefit or damage the poem. Underlying the late French scholar's interpretation appears to be the notion that an obligation or compulsion existed requiring Spenser to hew to the autobiographical line and causing him to jump "from love to hate, from admiration to scorn in the course of composition, without even taking pains to hide the inconsistency".

The first assumption is rendered suspect by the fact that the contrast between the favorable and unfavorable aspects of court life was a common theme of sixteenth-century poetry.[47] Spenser, moreover, gives a bipolar representation of court life in poems written during various periods of his life. *Mother Hubberds Tale,* for example, combines the portrait of the perfect courtier (ll. 717-

46. *Spenser* (London, 1926), p. 13.

47. Cf. Edwin A. Greenlaw, "Spenser and the Earl of Leicester", *PMLA,* XXV (1910), 548: "The first story [of *Hub.*] is a general satire on court life, such as we find in Wyatt, and frequently in sixteenth-century literature in England and on the continent. The theme is at base a familiar incident in the Renard stories, with certain conventional Renaissance accretions, such as the contrast between the noble courtier and the base, and the satire on suitors' delays." See also W. D. Elcock, "English Indifference to Du Bellay's 'Regrets' ", *MLR,* XLVI (1951), 180, n. 1, for the view that Spenser's version in *Colin C*lout of the disreputable side of court society is conventionalized and medieval, as compared to the depiction of the same kind of milieu in Du Bellay's *Les Regrets.*

93)[48] with a description of the sad lot of the seeker after royal preferment (ll. 891-914).[49] Even if one allows that this latter passage dates from 1590 as part of the revision prior to publication,[50] it is worthy of note that, contrary to the order in *Colin Clout,* a passage of diatribe against the court (ll. 642-716)[51] *precedes* the pleasant picture of the brave courtier. This being the case, the question naturally arises : If the sequence of Spenser's states of mind is realistically set forth in *Colin Clout,* as Legouis seemingly assumes, why is there a different order in another poem relating to the same period? Works subsequent to *Colin Clout* continue to contrast the two sides of court life. Book VI of *The Faerie Queene,* published in 1596, similarly contains, in the prologue and in the initial stanza of Canto I,[52] explicit commendation of the court milieu, whereas the twenty-fourth and twenty-fifth stanzas of Canto IX of the same book[53] present Meliboe's unflattering recollections of the royal court in the days of his youth. Even *Prothalamion* (1596), celebrating the marriage of the two noble sisters at Essex House, opens, in the first person address of the narrator, with a passage of the familiar carping comment on the disappointments inseparable from attendance at a "Princes Court".[54]

Both the conventionality of Spenser's dichotomous versions of the court with its good and evil sides and his own frequent use of the theme elsewhere than in *Colin Clout* makes plausible an explanation for the shift from praise to blame different from that entertained by Legouis, who believed that it reflects a sudden plunge from "hope to despondency on Spenser's part".[55] The more likely possibility, one feels, is that both representations are traditional and generalized and do not necessarily correspond to the author's precise attitudes during the course of his London sojourn of 1589-91.

The second assumption which seems inherent in Legouis' comments on *Colin Clout* quoted above—that the poet would adhere

48. *Works,* VIII, 124-6.
49. *Ibid.,* pp. 128-9.
50. *Complaints,* ed. W. L. Renwick (London, 1928), An Elizabethan Gallery, No. 1, p. 229.
51. *Works,* VIII, 122-4.
52. *Ibid.,* VI, 1-4.
53. *Ibid.,* p. 108.
54. *Ibid.,* VIII, 257.
55. Legouis, *Spenser,* p. 12.

to the strict biographical truth without regard to the demands of unity and internal consistency—becomes, when so stated, palpably unacceptable. The final chapter on unity seeks to show that the ordonnance of the poem can be explained without reference to biographical verisimilitude or strict historicity. The same chapter will also undertake to bring out that the beginning of the poem is not contradicted by the end.

Other exponents of the second view, a view which makes Colin the counterpart of the flesh-and-blood Spenser, frequently differ from Legouis in being less assured in their attribution to the empirical author of feeling states discoverable in Colin, but the difference in outlook is largely one of degree rather than of kind. Certainly, the manifest correspondence between Spenser's life and letters exerts a tremendous pull in the direction of this second view. For example, Renwick himself stresses in numerous places the elusive nature of some of the apparently personal allusions in the poem and warns against too literal an identification between the man and the book. [56] Yet, in a collection of Tudor lives, he still makes the categorical statement: "From *Colin Clouts Come Home Againe* we can gather what Raleigh thought of Spenser and of his situation in 1589".[57]

The remarks of two prominent authors of comparatively recent literary histories give every indication of interpreting the poem as a fairly reliable revelation of the poet's own attitudes. These remarks may perhaps suffice to illustrate the second view or form in which opinion on the poem crystallizes. Tucker Brooke, author of the Renaissance section in a widely-used literary history, comments as follows: "The poignant disquisition on love and the sentimental memories of Rosalind with which *Colin Clouts Come Home Again* concludes suggests that the poet's homecoming, pleasant as it evidently was for him, was not unmarred by loneliness".[58] C. S. Lewis apparently feels justified in drawing conclusions about Spenser's private feelings from the poem. His observations take note of the dual view of the court which Legouis, as has been indicated, seems to regard as evidence of inconsistency in the poem. Lewis, however,

56. See, e.g., *Essay,* pp. 3, 130; *Complaints,* pp. 183-4; *Daphnaïda,* pp. 180-1.

57. W. L. Renwick, "Edmund Spenser", in *The Great Tudors,* ed. Katharine Garvin (London, 1935), p. 528.

58. C. F. Tucker Brooke, "The Renaissance", in *A Literary History of England,* ed. Albert C. Baugh (New York, 1948), p. 489.

inclines to the belief that this duality reflects an ambivalent mood on the part of Spenser:

> Under a thin disguise of pastoral this is the most familiar and autobiographical of Spenser's poems. Its mood is ambivalent. On the one hand, England is a paradise governed by a goddess, and the court a constellation of excellent poets and bright nymphs: on the other, that same court is a den of false loves, backbiting and intrigue, no place "for any gentle wit", from which Colin "rather chose back to his sheep to tourne". This is very natural. Thus many an exile feels when he comes back (he had almost said "comes *home*" to his post after the longed for, the exciting, and yet ultimately disappointing holiday in England. Doubly disappointing, because he has failed to get the job in England that he hoped for, and also wonders whether there are not, after all, many consolations for living abroad. I think that with Spenser these consolations were now more valuable than he fully realized, for though the poem contains bitter lines the prevailing air is one of cheerfulness.[59]

With respect to statements like those just quoted assigning Colin's ideas and feelings to Spenser, one need not maintain that they are entirely unfounded to suggest that the rationale on which they are based very likely leads to a misconstruing of the actual way the poet uses personal material in the poem. At the very least, the burden of proof would seem to rest on those who can boldly make such assertions as, for instance: "The sea and its associations inspire Spenser, as they have inspired all the greater English poets, but with something of the mingled terror and fascination expressed by Colin at his home-coming".[60] In any event, when two scholars, both of whom manifestly attempt to read the poem as literal autobiography, arrive at opposite conclusions, then the propriety of transferring the title character's attitude to his creator becomes extremely dubious. A case in point is the question of Spenser's stay in Ireland. Did he regard it as a kind of exile, or was he reasonably

59. C. S. Lewis, *English Literature in the Sixteenth Century, Excluding Drama* (Oxford, 1954), pp. 370-1.

60. Davis, *Edmund Spenser,* p. 176. Curiously enough, one biographer has it that *Raleigh* rather than Spenser "was apt to be seasick and disliked the sea" (Wynyard Browne, "Sir Walter Raleigh", in *The Great Tudors,* p. 605).

contented with his lot there? According to Greenlaw, "the positive evidence of *Colin Clout* proves contentment with his lot rather than bitter disappointment",[61] whereas Mounts feels that to regard the Irish years as anything but cause for sorrow is to "discredit Spenser's own most explicit testimony in *Colin Clout,* lines 180-183".[62]

To construe the emotions and attitudes of a character as identical to those of the author who created him is certainly to oversimplify the relation between the private life and the work as one of direct cause and effect, which most likely it is not. It is presumably to overlook the difference between a letter, a diary, a history on the one hand, and an imaginative work on the other. That both Spenser and his one-time patron, Sir Philip Sidney, were perfectly aware of the distinctions between narrative poetry and history is evident from their writings. In *An Apologie for Poetrie,* Sidney distinguishes carefully among the three main classes of discourse: philosophy, history and poetry. Philosophy, Sidney holds, depends on precept to "win the gole" but the philosopher tends to be too vague: the historian, on the other hand, "wanting the precept, is so tyed, not to what shoulde bee but to what is, to the particuler truth of things and not to the general reason of things". On this issue Sidney concludes that poetry is superior to both philosophy and history because the poet "coupleth the generall notion with the particular example". The "particular example" of poetry is, of course, not tied to "the particuler truth of things"; poetry gets its effects by creating a "perfect picture"—"an image of that whereas the Philosopher bestoweth but a woordish description".[63]

Spenser, too, in the "letter to the Authors" appended to the first three books of *The Faerie Queene* in 1590, indicates his complete awareness of the difference between narrative poetry and what would now be termed history. "For the Methode of a Poet historical is not such, as of an Historiographer. For an Historiographer discourseth of affayres orderly as they were donne, accounting as well the time as the actions, but a Poet thrusteth into the middest, euen where it most concerneth him, and there recoursing to the

61. Edwin A. Greenlaw, "Spenser and British Imperialism", *MP,* IX (1912), 350.

62. Charles E. Mounts, "Spenser and the Countess of Leicester", *ELH,* XIX (1952), 196.

63. Quotation and paraphrase of the *Apologie* are from *Eliz. Critical Essays,* I, 164.

things forepaste, and diuining of thinges to come, maketh a pleasing Analysis of all."[64]

The reference in Spenser's letter to the reordering of data suggests the freedom with which the poet operates in contrast with the historiographer. The upholders of the first and second views of *Colin Clout* tend to make of Spenser "an historiographer" rather than a poet. The upholders of the third view, tentatively advanced, to which attention will now be given, see *Colin Clout* more in the nature of a construct fabricated in part from variations upon an autobiographic theme.

The third and last approach discernible in the scholarship for interpreting the abundant personal material in *Colin Clout* takes into consideration the comparative latitude available to the poet for shaping his material. While the third way, in common with the other two, acknowledges the connection between the contents of the poem and the author's objective and subjective experience as an empirical person, it differs from the other two approaches in more adequately recognizing the complexity of the relationship between the *res* and the *verba.* Adhering to the third view, the reader does not simply make substitutions of names and places and then read the poem as a well-nigh literal transcript of what Spenser as a man did or felt in a specified place or during a circumscribed time.

Some notion of a more complex approach to reading Spenser is advanced by Renwick in *Edmund Spenser: An Essay on Renaissance Poetry* (1925). His edition of *Daphnaïda and Other Poems* (1929) contains comments enlarging upon the same general theme. In the Introduction to the *Essay,* Renwick stresses the importance of Spenser's scholarly training as a central fact in the formation of his art. "We must," he asserts, "regard his work as part of a cultural movement of European extent, as fruit of general and not merely personal experience."[65] A helpful particularization of this statement for purposes of understanding *Colin Clout* occurs in Chapter V of this work. Here Renwick illustrates a quotation from Ascham's *Scholemaster* by referring to the poet's practice in *Colin Clout*. The quotation is: "This *Imitatio* is *similis materiei dissimilis tractatio* and, also, *dissimilis materiei similis tractatio*".

64. *Works,* I, 168-9.
65. *Essay,* p. 4.

> Thus in *Colin Clouts Come Home Againe,* for instance,—and the same process may be observed in all his work—Spenser was treating of actual people and actual happenings in his own life, and at the same time, even discounting the pastoral scheme, every episode in the poem is a well-known theme of poetry. The meeting of the poets, the Ovidian horror of the sea, the panegyric upon a monarch, the courteous commemoration of friends and brother-poets, the attack on court life, the celebration of a mistress—in all these passages literary and personal motives and interests are inextricably bound up together.[66]

The implication of Spenser's literary borrowing, as here described, seems necessarily to be that the treatment of his own experiences would be colored and modified by the literary precedents—the common *materies.* Thus, Colin's celebration of Rosalind must be couched in the language of *amor courtois* and his suit must be represented as unsuccessful if Spenser is to follow the grand tradition of Petrarch in his well-heralded but hopeless love for Laura.

Renwick could well have adduced some further cases from *Colin Clout* to illustrate *similis tractatio*: the pastoral convention of mourning nature in the opening lament by Hobbinol; the *topographia* of the ill-fated love of Bregog for Mulla (ll. 104-55); and the *prosopopoeia* in which Colin, in the role of a naïve shepherd, describes the ship in terms of a living thing (ll. 212-22), recalling another shepherd's reaction, as described by Cicero in a famous passage from the *De Natura Deorum,* when that classical swain first caught sight of the *Argo.*[67]

In all of these cases, the "truth in fact and circumstances"—the expression of sadness occasioned among Spenser's friends in Ireland by his long absence; the Bregog, blocked by boulders and gliding underground to join the Awbeg; the ship on the east coast of Ireland that stood waiting to take Raleigh, and perhaps Spenser, too, back to England—has been refracted, as it were, through the prism of literary convention; or, to change the metaphor, the *imitatio* of earlier writers residual in these passages, and in many more, has caused the original stuff of Spenser's experience to suffer

66. *Ibid.,* p. 125.
67. Jortin, *Remarks on Spenser's Poems,* pp. 137-8, cited in *Works,* VII, 460.

a sea-change into something perhaps richer and stranger than the original—but, certainly, *different* from it.

In addition to imitation of treatment and theme, another aspect of the literary tradition having an important bearing on the interpretation of personal allusions in *Colin Clout* is the convention of the artificial pastoral which, according to Renwick, meant not merely that "the poet should write about shepherds, but that, writing about shepherds, he was at liberty to write about himself and his friends".[68] E. K., in the "Dedicatory Epistle" to *The Shepheardes Calender,* advertises that in composing that pastoral "this our new Poete" was following in the footsteps of Theocritus, Virgil, Petrarch, Boccaccio, and Mantuan.[69] One modern authority on the pastoral as a genre stresses that Petrarch, who along with his younger friend Boccaccio founded the Renaissance eclogue, was keenly aware of the value of pastoral for "covert reference to men and events of the day, since it is characteristic of the form to let its meaning only partially appear".[70] Both in the *Calender* and in the later pastoral, Spenser adheres to the well-established tradition of the Italian and French practitioners of the form in making references to men and events of his own time, usually under sundry kinds of disguises. To *The Shepheardes Calender,* Spenser, through the medium of E. K., left a key in the form of Glosses, which, however, are themselves either incomplete or far from clear.[71] To the personal allusions in *Colin Clout,* Spenser left no clues beyond those provided in the poem itself.[72] Speaking in general about these personal and political allusions which abound in all of Spenser's poems, Renwick declares :

Many of these allusions are extremely obscure. Their inter-

68. *Essay,* p. 38.
69. *Works,* VII, 10.
70. Greg, *Pastoral Poetry and Drama,* p. 18, n. 1.
71. For a complete treatment of the identifications in the *Calender,* see Paul E. McLane, *Spenser's Shepheardes Calender: A Study in Elizabethan Allegory* (Notre Dame, 1961).
72. No keys to the identity of veiled person in *Colin Clout* are known to have circulated, as they apparently did for the *Arcadia,* Sidney's prose romance first published in 1590, which was generally regarded as a *roman à clef.* For references to keys to Sidney's pastoral romance, see Renwick, *Essay,* p. 140; Kenneth Orne Myrick, *Sir Philip Sidney as a Literary Craftsman,* Harvard Studies in English, Vol. 14 (Cambridge, Mass., 1935), pp. 233-4; and Ralph M. Sargent, *At the Court of Queen Elizabeth: The Life and Lyrics of Sir Edward Dyer* (London, 1935), p. 65.

> pretation is uncertain and liable to be upset by chance discovery, and so many deductions except the most obvious are insecure and possibly dangerous . . . as their very obscurity proves, these allusions were intended for Spenser's contemporaries, not for posterity, and are therefore of secondary moment for the critic of his art.[73]

In the opening of his Commentary on *Colin Clout* in the *Daphnaïda* edition of the shorter poems, Renwick elaborates on these general dicta. He avers that the details of allegory are obscure because "Spenser was not concerned to be more explicit".[74] He then goes on to describe Spenser's characteristic method of dealing with such material:

> In this poem [*Colin Clout*] we find on a smaller scale just that variation from clarity to obscurity which makes the personal allegories of *The Faerie Queene* so hard to disentangle. Some of his names are the merest pastoral commonplaces, *Alexis, Corydon*; some have identifications appended, like *Mansilia* and *the Shepheard of the Ocean* himself; some are real names, *Alabaster* and *Daniel,* and some, like *Aetion,* seem to contain a hint that we have not yet contrived to follow to a certain conclusion. *Hobbinal* [sic] and *Cuddy* appear in *The Shepheardes Calender,* but may represent different people here. Even the river names are treated with the same uncertainty: *Mulla* is a feigned name, *Bregog* a real one borne by the stream to this day. There is throughout the poem a sort of oscillation between the complete pastoral disguising and the straightforward personal story.[75]

Perhaps the "pastoral disguising" to which Renwick alludes in this passage is no more devious nor more difficult to connect with external reality than is the "straightforward personal story". Considerations already introduced in this chapter—the historical obscurity shrouding the main narrative episodes, the apparently selective omission on Spenser's part of certain segments of the "record", the distortions caused by the revisions, and adaptations

73. *Essay,* p. 3.
74. *Daphnaïda,* p. 180.
75. *Ibid.,* pp. 180-1.

for the sake of literary echoes—suggest that any notion of anything such as a "straightforward" account may itself be a partial illusion!

Further weight is certainly lent to the possibility if not the probability of this conclusion by the circuitous mazes along which searchers have been led in their pursuit of parts of this supposedly forthright account. Perhaps the most sought-after quarry in the hunt has been the identity of Rosalind, who originally appeared as Colin's sweetheart in *The Shepheardes Calender* of 1579. There her name figures in six of the twelve eclogues. In *Colin Clout,* dated twelve years afterwards, a total of seventy highly fervent lines are devoted to her in the speeches of the title character (ll. 464-84, 903-51). Is she in *Colin Clout* the same Rosalind as the one Colin lost to Menalcas in the plaintive *June* eclogue? Various answers—yes, no, maybe—have been forthcoming. For the real-life counterpart of Colin's fickle mistress in the earlier pastoral, the reader can take his choice among some half-score possibilities suggested by commentators to the time of publication of the *Variorum* edition, *Minor Poe*ms Volume I (1943), where they are assembled as Appendix IV.[76] Subsequent scholarship adds two more alternatives: Rosalind is the name intended to cover all the ladies from the Queen downwards to whom Spenser might be supposed to wish to address.[77] Rosalind is Mary Sidney.[78]

Aside from the question of whether the two Rosalinds in the earlier and later pastorals refer to the same person, the problem has also been raised as to whether the unnamed lady accorded Colin's profession of vassalage in the middle passage of *Colin Clout* is the same as the Rosalind to whom, although unreachable, the hero vows eternal devotion in the concluding flourish. Two careful students of Spenser's life, in recent treatments of the matter, do

76. *Works,* VII, 651-5.

77. Margaret Galway, "Spenser's Rosalind" [London] TLS, 19 July 1947, p. 372. This article is chiefly concerned with the Rosalind of the *Calender;* however, discussion of that Rosalind can seldom proceed without reference to the Rosalind of *Colin Clout.* The same conclusion about the identity of Rosalind is also taken to apply to the later pastoral.

78. Ruth Mohl, "The Glosses Concerning Spenser's Rosalinde", *Studies in Spenser, Milton, and the Theory of Monarchy* (New York, 1949), pp. 1-14. Miss Mohl, writing primarily about the Rosalind of the *Calender,* likewise extends the finding to the one whom Colin as an adoring vassal pays tribute in ll. 464-79 and ll. 907-51 of *Colin Clout* (pp. 12-13).

not think she is the same person in both parts.[79] Both agree that the panegyric of the central section refers to Spenser's second wife, Elizabeth Boyle. One of them feels that lines 903-51 refer to the Rosalind of the *Calender*: "Let us not forget that the Rosalind of the *Calender,* though largely a poetic fiction, was probably to some extent a compliment to Machabyas Chylde, the poet's first wife".[80]

Thus, it is evident that researchers, despite the most diligent effort and the exercise of almost unbelievable ingenuity, cannot agree upon whom Rosalind was meant to represent. They have failed to track down the elusive game. The identity of Rosalind, which is of importance because of her "coming into close contact with Colin Clout himself"[81] is still a mystery.[82]

Another puzzle in some respects like that of Rosalind and likewise concerning a character close to Colin is posed by Hobbinol. E. K., the glossator of the *Calender,* identifies Hobbinol in that pastoral as Gabriel Harvey,[83] whom the reader will recall as the friend of Spenser's Cambridge days and with Spenser a fellow protégé of Lord Leicester in London during the years 1578-80.[84] Yet Harvey is not known to have ever been in Ireland.

Still a third crux is raised by the inclusion of Cuddy in *Colin Clout,* where, like Hobbinol, he is one of the principal interlocutors. Like Colin and Hobbinol also, Cuddy is a name which appears prominently in the *Calender,* which has an English setting. Since reference in line 300 to the river Funcheon seems to localize Cuddy in the later pastoral, Renwick tentatively identifies him as Arthur Hyde, a neighbor of Spenser's who held land along the river Funcheon.[85] Another scholar, however, argues that this character in the *February, August,* and *October* eclogues of the *Calender* is

79. Raymond Jenkins, "Rosalind in *Colin Clouts Come Home Againe*", *MLN,* LXVII (1952), 1-5, and Charles E. Mounts, "Two Rosalinds in 'Colin Clouts Come Home Againe' ", *N&Q,* N.S. II (1955), 283-4. Miss Mohl, on the other hand, thinks the two passages are about the same person: "He [Spenser] could scarcely declare his undying love for more than one lady in the same poem" (p. 12).

80. Mounts, "Two Rosalinds", p. 284.

81. *Shepherd's Calendar,* ed. Renwick, p. 166.

82. Cf. Judson, *Life,* p. 148.

83. Gloss to *Sept.,* 176, *Works,* VII, 93-4.

84. Eleanor Rosenberg, *Leicester: Patron of Letters* (New York, 1955), p. 337.

85. *Daphnaïda,* pp. 183-4.

Edward Dyer, a contemporary court poet of the Sidney-Pembroke circle, and that he is probably the Cuddy of *Colin Clout* as well.[86]

The point to be made about these biographical puzzles is that if Spenser had been penning a history or other kind of factual discourse, the elusive hints and seemingly contradictory leads would be inexcusable. But since he was writing a poem, the lack of any clear-cut conformity to external fact is not of itself a flaw. Indeed, in the present poem Spenser was not drafting a memoir nor a deposition for a court hearing, but was creating an imaginative construct; in so doing he was conforming to standard Renaissance poetic theory as enunciated, for instance, by Ronsard, leading poet of the French Pléiade in *Art Poetique* : "The subject of good poets is fable and fiction".[87]

Besides Renwick, Leicester Bradner reveals himself, in *Edmund Spenser and the Faerie Queene* (1948), to be representative of the surprisingly small third group which recognizes that personal interest material must be interpreted with extreme circumspection. In Chapter III, "Spenser's Poetic Method (*The Shepherds' Calendar*)", Bradner addresses himself, like Renwick, to the key problem of the people and events behind the covert allusions. With reference to the *Calender,* he cautions : "Therefore a reader approaching this poem must ask himself how he is to interpret the figures presented to him. When is he to look for relationship between the real and imaginary worlds, and how exact is this relationship going to be? It must be admitted immediately that Spenser makes uses of several different levels of relationship."[88] Bradner proceeds to group the characters under three main heads : absolute identifications—Colin (Spenser), Hobbinol (Harvey), etc.; real people for whom no direct clues are given as to their precise identity—Cuddy, Rosalind, Dido, etc.; decorative characters—Thenot, Perigot, etc.[89]

Now a similar classification could, of course, be made for *Colin Clout.* In the first group there would be only three members of the interior drama proper—that is, the convocation of shepherds : Colin (Spenser), Hobbinol (Harvey), Thestylis (Bryskett). To these may be added two personages who come in for prominent mention :

86. Paul E. McLane, "Spenser's Cuddie: Edward Dyer", *JEGP,* LIV (1955), 230-40.

87. Quoted by Renwick, *Essay,* p. 38.

88. Leicester Bradner, *Edmund Spenser and the Faerie Queene* (Chicago, 1948), p. 54.

89. *Ibid.,* pp. 54-5.

Cynthia (Queen Elizabeth) and the Shepherd of the Ocean (Raleigh). In addition, there would be ten of the twelve ladies briefly alluded to in the composite passage acknowledging the "Nymphs" (l. 578) of Cynthia's court who "me [Colin] graced goodly well" (l. 485).[90] Of ten contemporary poets to whom Spenser renders qualified praise, besides Alabaster and Daniel, named outright, only Alcyon (Arthur Gorges), Amyntas (Ferdinando Stanley, Earl of Derby) and Astrofell (Sidney) can confidently be put into the category of absolute identifications.[91] The second group in Bradner's classification, real people insufficiently identified, would include for *Colin Clout* the five remaining poets; Cuddy, one of the principal interlocutors of the pastoral coterie; and Rosalind, who, in an important middle and closing passage, is the subject of Colin's warm avowals of everlasting devotion. In the last group, following Bradner's formulation of levels of characters, those put in "merely to fill out the picture and to provide interlocutors where needed", are found most of the members of the interior dramatic group, the seven remaining shepherds and shepherdesses. Here also would be placed the two last-named members of Cynthia's retinue—Flavia and Candida, probably catchalls for those distaff readers who would like warrant, no matter how tenuous, for considering themselves among the foremost ladies of court society.

As for the second group of "real people" who are not given sufficient clues for identification, the two most prominent ones—Rosalind and Cuddy—have an insubstantiality of their own, as the literally scores of fruitless efforts to pin them down to living counterparts show. But even those named in the first group of "absolute identifications" do not necessarily conform either in their deeds or personalities with any degree of exactitude to what is known of their existential models. Gabriel Harvey, as previously pointed out, is never known to have been in Ireland. Queen Elizabeth, as the chapter on imagery indicates, is bodied forth in a camouflage of Petrarchan, Neo-Platonic, and Hebraic imagery so that any resemblance between the Cynthia of the three passages of apotheosis and the sexagenarian who sat on the English throne when *Colin Clout* appeared in the book stalls is hardly more than symbolical.

90. Judson, *Life,* p. 147, gives the names of the ladies alluded to in the famous passage. They are now well-nigh universally accepted.

91. The findings of the various scholars on these poets are brought together in the Commentary on *Colin Clout, Works,* VII, 463-74.

That "absolute identification" is no guarantee of absolute correspondence between the character and the man is clearly recognized by Bradner:

> There remains the question of the relation of the poet to his imaginary world. This is a particularly interesting question about Spenser because Colin Clout was adopted by him as a permanent poetical projection of himself, appearing in *Colin Clout's Come Home Again* and the *Faerie Queene* as well as in the *Shepherds' Calendar*. To what extent is Colin actually Edmund Spenser, and to what extent is he an imaginary character with freedom to do and say things not meant to represent the life of his creator?[92]

Though, of course, no categorical evidence can be brought forward to give a final answer to these important questions, the weight of probability is to the effect that the Colin of the poem is in essence an imaginative character. To regard him as anything else is to disregard his role as a fictive creation operating in an invented dramatic setting—a role which, as the preceding chapter demonstrates, exerts a powerful influence on Colin as a character: one who must necessarily adapt a great part of his discourse and behaviour to the expectations of the interior audience.

To read into Colin's utterances a direct reflection of Spenser's personal feelings at a given time is to slight or set at naught the pressures exerted upon an outstandingly bookish poet—the professed follower of Tityrus or Virgil,[93] the most learned of the Roman poets—by literary traditions and conventions. These precidents, as has been continually seen, operate to help determine the behavior and sentiments of all the *dramatis personae,* including Colin.

Thus, it becomes increasingly evident that the third way in which the concept of *Colin Clout* has tentatively manifested itself in the scholarship is closest to the true explanation of how Spenser deals with the personal interrelations. I have attempted to provide substance for this view which recognizes the oblique and refracted way in which reality appears. In the process, I have underscored the nature of the poem as a fabricated construct.

92. Bradner, p. 56.
93. "Letter of the Authors", *Works,* I, 167.

To emphasize the poem's nature as imaginative fashioning is by no means to imply that there is nothing of the real Spenser in Colin, nor to maintain that none of the author's actual feelings are allowed to intrude upon the pastoral scene. But the relationship between the "maker" and the title character, whose acts and attitudes are bodied forth, must certainly be envisaged as being on a different plane from that inferable from locutions characterizing the composition as "verse diary", "least artificial of his poems", "almost as clear as a chronicle", and the product of his "minutely biographic pen". Such phrases as these tend to misrepresent the poem for two reasons: first, the private experience behind it has been too greatly reordered and objectified to be recoverable from the poem itself; second, the biographical facts that can be reconstructed from parallels in the poem by the aid of external documents are relatively few.

In the order of their appearance, the particulars of persons, places, and actions that can be verified historically come down substantially to the following: The Shepherd of the Ocean is represented as coming from the "main-sea deepe" (l. 67). Raleigh had a residence at Youghal on the east coast of Ireland. The "Home" alluded to in the title is Spenser's Cork County estate of Kilcolman, identified by the accurate topographical details in the myth of Bregog and Mulla. The poem depicts the Shepherd of the Ocean as reciting to Colin a song concerning his harsh treatment at the hands of Cynthia. Raleigh, who by 1589 was already established as a personal favorite of Queen Elizabeth's, did write a poem or poems which complain of mistreatment by Queen-Cynthia. The poem narrates a voyage by the Shepherd of the Ocean and Colin to "*Cynthias* land" (l. 289). Raleigh crossed the Irish Sea to England during the fall of 1589. The Shepherd of the Ocean tells Colin during their voyage that he has "in the Ocean charge to me assignd" (l. 253). The Queen granted Raleigh the title of Vice Admiral of Devon and Cornwall in 1585.[94] Presumptive evidence places Spenser in London during the years 1590-91. A substitute, one Chicester, was appointed to take over his duties as Clerk of the Council of Munster.[95] Early in 1590, prior to 6 April, Spenser

94. One biographer of Raleigh suggests, not altogether facetiously, that Spenser was undoubtedly aware that "the pastoral charge of 'the Shepherd of the Ocean' was Spanish merchandise that strayed within range of his privateering hook" (Thompson, *Sir Walter Ralegh,* pp. 63-4).

95. Judson, *Life,* p. 137, and n.

added seven dedicatory sonnets to the first edition of *The Faerie Queene,*[96] published in London by Ponsonby. The new poems honor prominent members of Queen Elizabeth's government and the Countess of Pembroke. Five of the ten shepherds "in faithfull seruice of faire *Cynthia*" (l. 381) are contemporary poets, with known literary works. Ten of the twelve "Nymphs" of Cynthia's retinue selected for glorification are ladies of rank and prestige in Elizabethan court society. All but two of these have dedications addressed to them in subsequent poems of Spenser's.[97] Colin claims kinship with the three sisters of the "noble familie" (l. 537). The family alluded to is the Spencers of Althorpe, who did acknowledge the connection.[98] Spenser's exact genealogical relationship to this family, however, has not yet been ascertained.[99]

While the foregoing biographical facts having correlatives in the poem are naturally of interest to the reader, then and now, they are not necessary to either the interpretation or the enjoyment of the poem. Indeed, the poem would be less successful as a public performance if knowledge of biographical details were a prerequisite to understanding it. The personal material has been so abstracted and generalized as effectively to depersonalize the poem. As has been observed, Renaissance poetic theory applied to *Colin Clout* would make inevitable a separation between the title character and the author. Colin is a fictive personage, with relative freedom to do and say what it pleased the author to have him do and say. His speeches and acts need be compatible only with the demands of internal consistency. The experience of Spenser as an empirical person with a *given* past history may be no more than a point of departure for the depiction of the imaginary character, Colin.

To advocate the existence of such a separation between Spenser and Colin does not necessarily lessen the importance of the poem as a vehicle for the expression of artistic sincerity, which functions on a different level from autobiographic fidelity. Thus to contend that for Spenser, *Colin Clout* was an important poem of his full maturity embodying significant truth in Sidney's sense of "the general reason of things" is to acknowledge, in its proper perspective, the man behind the work. To stress the arduous labor and

96. *Ibid.,* pp. 142-3.
97. *Ibid.,* p. 147.
98. *Ibid.,* p. 6.
99. *Ibid.,* p. 7.

meticulous care lavished by the author upon it is to betoken the measure of his concern for it.

Even to draw attention to the repeated use of the pseudonym Colin, in works spanning an adult lifetime, is to underscore Spenser's implicit involvement in the poem, an involvement validated by the seriousness of tone and emotional vibrancy which pervade it. The pride which Spenser took in this *nom de plume* is evident from his having heralded his poetic career with it as "*Colin* . . . the Southerne shepheardes boye"[100] and having closed his career in a poem published posthumously by a reminder of the fame which he had bestowed upon the Munster river "Mulla",

> That Shepheard *Colin* dearely did condole, [in *Colin Clout*]
> And made her lucklesse loues well knowne to be.[101]

And to pass briefly in review the themes which Spenser kept coming back to time and time again is to give fitting recognition to his enduring interest in these topics—praising the attractions of the Kilcolman environs; glorifying England, her Queen, her gracious ladies, her courtiers, both adventurous and literary; excoriating malevolent court followers and warning against the vicious side of court life; and extolling both personal and abstract ideals of love and beauty.[102]

All things considered, one comes to believe that the "truth" of Spenser's "Dedicatory Letter" to *Colin Clout* is of an ideal rather than a literal kind, embodied in a fundamentally imaginative rather than a factual formulation. The nature of this formulation will be examined in the ensuing final chapter. This chapter will reveal that *Colin Clout* possesses an order of arrangement imposed, not by the necessity to conform to historicity, but by the demands of its own integrity. That the poem manifests such a self-contained unity as an independent work of creative art goes a long way in itself toward substantiating its essentially imaginative texture.

100. *S.C., April,* l. 21, *Works,* VII, 37.
101. *F.Q.* VII.vi.40.5-6, *Works,* VI, 161.
102. For parallels and contrasts between Spenser's treatment of the philosophy of love in *Colin Clout* and in the *Foure Hymnes,* see Nelson, *Poetry of Edmund Spenser,* pp. 97-104.

CHAPTER VII

UNITY

Perhaps the severest stricture to date on the alleged lack of unity in *Colin Clout* is the opinion of Émile Legouis quoted in the last chapter. Legouis, it will be recalled, claims that Spenser, by jumping from one emotion to another—from love to hate, from admiration to scorn—exhibits pronounced instability of temperament, and that these swings of passion on the author's part lead to palpable inconsistency in the poem: "Le fin contredit le début". Another critic, B. E. C. Davis, in *Edumnd Spenser: A Critical Study,* follows Legouis in equating directly and minutely the views of the author with those of the title character. But he attributes a lack of purposefulness in Spenser's fashioning of the poem not so much to his whirligigs of feeling as to the insouciant mood experienced by the author at the time of composition. Davis holds that *Mother Hubberds Tale* which he asserts to be a "personal manifesto"[1] against Lord Burghley and *The Ruines of Time,* both published in the *Complaints* volume of 1591, rendered Spenser ineligible for further preferment and caused him to abandon completely all hope for additional benefits of a material nature from the Crown. He discovers that *Colin Clout* evidences a spirit of "genial submission"[2] on Spenser's part, "proved" by the alleged freedom from the demands of logical design. He concludes the topic with the following statement: "Untied by argument or ulterior object, for once he rejoices in pure irresponsible self-expression, 'agreeing with the truth in circumstance and matter', humouring his fancy with favorite devices—the singing match, light burlesque, courtly eulogy and a hymn in honour of love, centred upon the person of his first mistress, Rosalind".[3]

Davis' evident representation of the pastoral as an unrestrained outpouring of the author's emotions might not seem so implausible

1. Page 45.
2. *Ibid.,* p. 47.
3. *Ibid.*

if *Colin Clout* were a nineteenth-century poem of the Romantic period. One recalls Byron who, if he was not precisely autobiographical in *Don Juan,* did at least find satisfaction in carrying the "pageant of his bleeding heart" around the European continent. But maintaining Davis' view for a poem written by a sixteenth-century poet who consistently displays originality within, rather than outside, the conventions appears to fly directly in the face of Renaissance poetic theory and practice as we have come to know them. That theory assuredly conceives of poetry, not as direct self-expression, but as an art of imitation—in the words of that epitome of Elizabethan literary theory, Sidney's *Apologie,* "a speaking picture: with this end, to teach and delight".[4] The "favourite devices" to which Davis alludes are literary conventions. Their use does not need to be that of diverting either the writer or the reader from serious considerations. These traditional forms of utterances—and others like them, including myth and the pastoral form itself—are devices serving two main purposes: to further the allegoric conception of poetry which "more than anything else, colored critical theory in Elizabethan England";[5] and to facilitate the expression of general truths under the veil of fictitious persons and pleasant fables. In Spenser's day, the pastoral genre, which *Colin Clout* represents, was regarded as an appropriate medium for serious discourse. From Virgil onward pastoral had been "persistently allegorical"[6] and especially fitted, in E. K.'s phrase, "to vnfold great matter of argument couertly".[7] In his classic of criticism Sidney accords recognition to pastoral as a means of conveying matters of high moment under the guise of shepherds' talk.[8]

Spenser's own practice in the poem, as thus far observed, harmonizes with the tenets of received Renaissance theory. The serious tone consistently maintained by Colin toward his subject strikingly confirms the weighty import which literati of the era deemed pastoral capable of sustaining. Moreover, all of the elements of the poem examined up to the present—rhetorical figures, diction, versification, imagery—reveal remarkable care and indefatigable

4. *Eliz. Critical Essays,* I, 158.
5. J. W. Spingarn, *A History of Literary Criticssm in the Renaissance,* rev. ed., Columbia Studies in Comparative Literature (New York, 1908), pp. 261-2.
6. *Shepheards Calender,* ed. Herford, p. xxxvi.
7. "Dedicatory Epistle" to *Shepheardes Calender, Works,* VII, 10.
8. *Apologie,* in *Eliz. Critical Essays,* I, 175-6.

effort on the part of the poet. The elaboration of such effects alone would certainly place the creation at the furthest remove from "pure irresponsible self-expression", unrestricted by any necessity for design or developed reasoning.

The smoothness with which the finished product reads—a fluidity aided by sensitive punctuation—is perhaps what misleads Davis and others to construe *Colin Clout* as an occasional piece, tossed off by the poet as relaxation from the more arduous labor of composing *The Faerie Queene*. Close study of the poem's elements belies this view. Certainly the sweat of which Ben Jonson speaks as constituting a necessity for him "who casts to write a living line", [9] is not evident in the completed version. If it were, the labor would to that degree be misspent. The studied felicity of the whole is a tribute to Spenser's poetic powers in imaginatively fusing the varied materials and devices.

Davis' opinion as to the lack of design and serious purpose in *Colin Clout*—and views in some ways similar to his, though less extreme[10]—seems plausible to many modern readers but is suspect for two main reasons: first, it fails to take sufficiently into account the conventions of a literary milieu quite different from our own; and, second, it virtually disregards the evidence of the constituent elements, which throughout the poem are so carefully wrought into a complex of interlaced structures. For one to demonstrate fully the falsity of the charge that *Colin Clout* lacks unity of design and purpose, however, he must necessarily go beyond an examination of the ingredient elements *per se*. He must examine the parts in relation to one another and to the whole. The crucial questions are:

9. "To the Memory of My Beloved, the Author Mr. William Shakespeare", *Ben Jonson*, eds. Herford and Simpson, VIII, 392.

10. E.g., Adolphus Alfred Jack, *A Commentary on the Poetry of Chaucer and Spenser*, p. 248: "In the whole poem [*Colin Clout*], moreover, there is no sufficient sustaining narrative, and if we say that structurally it is pleasantly discursive, we have exhausted judicious praise". McNeier, "Spenser's 'Pleasing Alcon' ", p. 138, quotes part of Jack's comment: "It [*Colin Clout*] was not all written at one time, or all in one piece; 'structurally it is pleasantly discursive' ". Nelson, *Poetry of Edmund Spenser*, pp. 59-60, grants a considerable measure of unity to the poem based on the unbroken flow of the quatrains, the pastoral atmosphere, and the narrative frame. "These unifying characteristics," he asserts, "bind together a tremendous variety of mood and subject ... The effect would be merely chaotic were it not for the easy run of the verse, the skillfully handled transitions, and the repeated reference to the pastoral setting of Colin's discourse" (*ibid.*).

Does the poem have a coherent structure? Does Colin's discourse relate to a single idea or problem or to a set of related problems? Is there a way in which the juxtaposition or opposition of the various sections operates to produce a meaningful pattern? Is there a universal quality in the poem? Do the various elements of style and tone contribute to the oneness of the poem? If so, in what way?

Before one proceeds to a consideration of these vital questions, it seems hardly necessary to observe that Spenser can confidently be accounted entirely familiar with the critical tradition that requires an author to have an overall principle of construction in a work. That he had himself authored a critical treatise entitled *The English Poete* is well known to Spenserians. In the renowned "Letter of the Authors" appended to the 1590 edition of *The Faerie Queene,* not only does Spenser speak familiarly of the reigning critics from Aristotle on down to his own times, but he takes pains to reconcile the order of narration for his *magnum opus* with tenets of the received literary tradition.[11]

Of the three luminaries whose pronouncements on the subject of unity were most widely disseminated—Plato, Aristotle, and Horace—perhaps those of the Augustan poet set forth in the *Ars Poetica* were most influential upon Spenser.[12] The firm hold that Horatian studies held in the schools of the Renaissance is strikingly evident from Sidney's rhetorical question in the *Apologie*: "who is it that euer was a scholler that doth not carry away some verses of *Virgill, Horace,* or *Cato,* which in his youth he learned, and euen to his old age serue him for howrely lessons?"[13] There is, moreover, direct evidence that the *Ars Poetica* was part of the curriculum at the Merchant Taylor's School,[14] which Spenser attended. Additional confirmation of Spenser's first-hand acquaintance with the work is furnished by the fact that in a playful Latin epistle dated 5 October 1579 and addressed to his friend Gabriel Harvey at Cambridge University, he skillfully works into the context of his letter the Horatian line, "*Omne tulit punctum,* qui miscuit vtile dulci".[15]

11. *Works,* I, 167-70.
12. See *Eliz. Critical Essays,* I, lxxiv-lxxv, for a forceful statement by the editor regarding the critical dominance of the famous "Epistle to the Pisos" in Spenser's time.
13. *Eliz. Critical Essays,* I, 183.
14. T. W. Baldwin, *William Shakespeare's Small Latine and Lesse Greeke* (Urbana, 1944), II, 497-8.
15. *Prose Works,* X, 11, l. 202.

The most explicit references to unity by Plato and Aristotle occur in the *Phaedrus* and the *Poetics,* respectively. Apposite brief quotations from these authors may conveniently preface notice of allusions to the subject in Horace's *Ars Poetica.* In the *Phaedrus,* which the reader will recall as concerned largely with rhetoric, Socrates is represented as saying to Phaedrus: "At any rate, you will allow that every discourse ought to be a living creature, having a body of its own and a head and feet; there should be a middle, beginning, and end, adapted to one another and to the whole?"[16] In the *Poetics,* Aristotle makes it clear that the most important unity is that of action. "We have laid it down," he tells us in words that Spenser, like ourselves, doubtless knew by heart, "that a tragedy is an imitation of an action that is complete in itself, as a whole of some magnitude ... Now a whole is that which has beginning, middle, and end."[17] Later Aristotle elaborates on what he means by "one action": "The truth is that, just as in the other imitative arts one imitation is always of one thing, so in poetry the story, as an imitation of action, must represent one action, a complete whole, with its several incidents so closely connected that the transposal or withdrawal of any one of them will disjoin and dislocate the whole".[18]

Turning now to the *Ars Poetica,* one finds that Horace devotes the first thirty-seven lines of this verse letter to his concept of unity. In this opening section, he likens a work whose parts are incongruous to a painter's representation of a horse's neck to which are joined a human head and face. He tells us that details presented in a poem must be relevant to the subject as a whole. Elaboration, he goes on to say, should not be at the expense of consistency. Although Plato's remarks apply originally to oratory, Aristotle's to tragedy, and Horace's to poetry generally, the similarity of the ideas is striking. One slight difference is that Horace has joined the conception of decorum to that of unity. But "the Philosopher" himself, discussing decorum in his treatise on oratory, had led the way to Horace's merging of the two concepts of unity and appropriateness. In the *Rhetoric,* Aristotle considers decorum as contributing to a consistency of style in relation to three elements: the nature of the subject, the kind or quality of emotion represented,

16. *Phaedrus,* 264c, in *Dialogues,* ed. Jowett, III, 172-3.

17. *Poetics,* 7, 1450b, trans. Ingram Bywater, Vol. XI of *The Works of Aristotle,* ed. W. D. Ross, 12 vols. (Oxford, 1934).

18. *Ibid.,* 8, 1451a.

and the circumstances and disposition of the speaker.[19] As will appear, Renaissance theorists of poetry enlarge classical concepts of decorum to a point where it becomes very close to the modern acceptation of unity as overall harmony and integrity in a work of literary art.

With reference again to the Latin epistolary critique, one should note also a significant later passage which deals both with matter to be imitated and with unity. This passage of the *Ars Poetica* contains the famous phrase "in medias res", which Spenser paraphrases as "thrusteth into the middest".[20] The significant lines from Horace are:

> Atque ita mentitur, sic veris falsa remiscet,
> Primo ne medium, medio ne discrepet imum.[21]

Howes's translation for these lines is given below since it conveys the sense with emphasis more appropriate to the matter at hand than do any of the contemporary translations, like those of Queen Elizabeth's or Ben Jonson's, for example.

> And so [the poet] adroitly mingles false with true,
> So with his fair illusions cheats the view,
> That all the parts—beginning, middle, end—
> In one harmonious compound sweetly blend.[22]

The previous chapter affords numerous illustrations of the way in which Spenser "mingles false with true" in the poem. It is now time to ascertain whether he joins "beginning, middle, end" into "one harmonious compound". If he does not, the lack must certainly be attributed to failure of execution, not to want of authoritative precept!

The Shepheardes Calender, Spenser's earlier pastoral, is set in a time-frame of the yearly seasons. *Colin Clout,* a kind of sequel to

19. *Rhetoric,* iii.7, 1408b, trans. W. Rhys Roberts, Vol. XI of *The Works of Aristotle,* ed. W. D. Ross, 12 vols. (Oxford, 1934).
20. "Letter of the Authors", *Works,* I, 169.
21. Lines 151-2.
22. *The Art of Poetry: The Poetical Treatises of Horace, Vida, and Boileau,* ed. Albert S. Cook (Boston, 1892), p. 12.The classical translations of Francis Howes (1776-1844) were published between the years 1806 and 1846, inclusive (*DNB*).

the *Calender,* is set in a time-frame of a shepherd's day. The more concentrated time span of the later pastoral helps to focus and give compression to the action. The third person narrator opens with a description of Colin piping to his bucolic companions. He closes the poem with the statement that Colin, having finished, rises and departs, followed by the other shepherds, who are reminded by the onset of darkness that it is time to lead their flocks into the fold for the night.

With the enveloping action, totalling nineteen lines at the beginning and end, there is the colloquy, technically a dialogue, between Colin and the other nine shepherds and shepherdesses. In this colloquy Colin is the principal speaker, reciting 730 of the poem's eight hundred dialogue lines. Colin begins his discourse in response to a request by Hobbinol to tell of his recent adventure abroad. The remainder of his discourse is a *single* sequence of thoughts. This sequence describes the circumstances leading up to Colin's visit to court, the ocean voyage, the activity at court, and the reflections arising from that visit.

The enveloping action presented in the words of the third person narrator provides a framework for Colin's speeches. The interplay between Colin and the other shepherds gives a dramaturgical cast to the poem and serves to focus attention upon Colin as the leading actor and spokesman. So large a portion of the entire dialogue, in truth, is given over to Colin's discourse that his speeches are in effect a monologue. The fact that his discourse is relatively closed in the sense that questions and remarks volunteered by the group do not really cause Colin to alter his views makes the monologue character of the poem more pronounced.

The mediation of the "interspeakers" at strategic places in Colin's "monologue" serves to structure his discourse, making its continuity clear to the reader. Accordingly, once the framework has been established—once the scene has been set, so to speak—the poem needs a minimum of intervention by the third person narrator. His role is pretty much reduced to providing conversational tags.

With reference to the near monologue by Colin, does this monologue, the core of the entire poem, relate to a single subject? The chapter on imagery brings out that the substance of Colin's complete discourse is unified in one sense by being matter that can be termed either pure pastoral or adulterated pastoral. If it belongs in the latter category, it is material that prior eclogists like Virgil, Mantuan, Petrarch, Marot, and others, had assimilated to pastoral poetry. The reputation achieved by these users of the medium provided ample warrant for Spenser to incorporate the same topics into his bucolic composition.

But since a collocation of topics even if related in various ways to a single genre can hardly of itself add up to any meaningful unity, one must go further and inquire into the way Spenser employs this material in Colin's speeches. One way that this material does *not* appear is as a succession of abstract truths. It occurs rather as the natural expression of Colin's character. Colin seeks to formulate his own sentiments in such a way as to influence others. The material thus takes on a distinctly personal and emotional coloration appropriate to the speaker's character, as revealed in the poem.

What, then, is the fictive character of Colin Clout? He is first of all a follower of Tityrus—the common designation for Virgil, the scholar poet *par excellence,* in the Augustan's capacity as a pastoralist. A disciple of the most learned poet of the Golden Age of Latin Literature, Colin is passionately interested in knowledge. As a poet Colin takes delight in vying with the Shepherd of the Ocean in an exchange of songs. Moreover, he judges and encourages Cynthia's shepherd-poets. The spokesman of the poem is in turn an amorist who pays court to the lady of his choice in the stylized vocabulary of chivalric love. The Colin of the poem is also a moral philosopher. As such he expresses in Neo-Platonic and biblical terms surpassing admiration for true virtue as realized principally in the person of the Queen and her gracious ladies; as such, in virulent language, he denounces vice as incarnated in the servitors of depraved love at court. And, finally, Colin is a religious man who speaks feelingly of God's bestowal of gifts upon the land, gifts which graceless men shamelessly abuse. Elsewhere in the poem he praises, in terms largely of pagan mythology, the divine power which out of love created the earth and peopled it through the sacred institution of marriage. The diverse topics are seen to be polarized around Colin's person in his respective roles of poet, lover, moral philosopher, and religious believer. His utterances come to the reader or listener in the *vox humana* of one soul striving to formulate his own response to problems having both a personal and a universal relevance.

The problems center on love in a broad conception fusing classical and medieval elements with Christian belief. The associations which directly link the doctrinal content of Colin's speeches—and equally those of the other interlocutors—with love, in an extension of that term beyond its common acceptation today, are not dependent on esoteric or private symbols. These associations arise naturally from the backgrounds of the poem—backgrounds of pastoralism, Platonism, classical mythology, court-of-love conventions, and biblical allusions. They are projected throughout the poem in recurrent images.

The opening lines describe the title character as the shepherd's boy

> That after *Tityrus* first sung his lay,
> Laies of sweet loue, without rebuke or blame. (ll. 2-3)

It is with an eloquent testimonial of lifelong love that Colin ends his disquisition. The passage in the middle section contains an equally fervent pledge to the lady of his election:

> And I hers euer onely euer one:
> One euer I all vowed hers to bee,
> One euer I, and others neuer none. (ll. 477-9)

The remaining parts are likewise variations on the theme of love. One of these variations takes the form of a "rebuke or blame" of love.

Hobbinol's speech, which begins the dialogue, addresses Colin in terms of deepest affection—"my liefe, my life" (l. 16). Non-sentient as well as sentient elements of nature share in this feeling for Colin. When he is gone love causes the woods to wail, the birds to stop singing, the fields to mourn, running waters to weep, and fish to lament. Colin's reply to Hobbinol is concerned largely with an expression of his feeling for another human being—who happens also to be his Queen. In Colin's words, she is "my lifes sole blisse, my hearts eternall threasure" (l. 47).

The ensuing section narrating the visit of the Shepherd of the Ocean deals with friendship—a modified form of love—between the two congenial poets, who spend their time exchanging songs—

> each making other mery,
> Neither enuying other, nor enuied. (ll. 77-8)

The lay of Bregog and Mulla which Colin recites to his friend also has love for its subject, but this time it is the improper love of Mulla, "Vnto whose bed false *Bregog* whylome stole".[23]

23. *F.Q.* VII.vi.40.4, *Works,* VI, 161.

The myth is of significant length, occupying 55 of the poem's 955 lines. The love affair which is its subject ends in tragedy because Mulla and Bregog conspired to disobey the express command of the latter's father, Old Mole. Such wilful disobedience on the part of the lovers was no trivial matter. The reader learns from the cosmology near the end of the poem that love, set forth in a mythopoetic conception paralleling Genesis, is the central force in the universe. It had brought harmony and order out of the chaos of warring elements. Now the unquestioned authority of God over monarch, of monarch over noble, of superior over inferior down through the social strata, and including, particularly, the authority of parent over offspring, is, in Renaissance thinking, an extension of the original hierarchical order which love established in the beginning. The maintenance of such an order in precarious Elizabethan times was regarded, particularly by the aristocratic class, as a prime necessity for the continuance of the stable state.[24] Of necessity, those who set themselves in opposition to that order are deemed guilty of a most serious transgression and must be punished. In the myth the transgressors are punished. That is why Spenser speaks elsewhere of Mulla's "lucklesse loues".[25]

Another luckless love is the one Colin's visitor, the Shepherd of the Ocean, sings about—

> Of great vnkindnesse, and of vsage hard,
> Of *Cynthia* the Ladie of the sea, (ll. 165-6)

whom the Shepherd apostrophizes as "my loues queene, and goddesse of my life" (l. 170).

While the voyage that the two friends subsequently take does not concern itself with love as such, it does dwell, to a surprising extent, on order. The account of the voyage is replete with references to titles and relationships expressive of the places, superior

24. Ulysses' speech on degree and order (William Shakespeare, *Troi.* I.iii.75-137) is the most famous contemporary statement of the idea upon which men of the Renaissance placed such great weight. It is worthy of note that in this speech Ulysses also mentions the flouting of parental authority ("And the rude son shall strike his father dead" [l. 115]) as an illustration of that potentially rapid disintegration of society which can occur "when degree is shak'd" (l. 101).

25. *F.Q.* VII.vi.40.6, *Works,* VI, 161.

and inferior, which various persons hold. The Shepherd tells Colin that the sea is

> the Regiment
> Of a great shepheardesse, that *Cynthia* hight,
> His liege his Ladie and his lifes Regent. (ll. 233-5)

Even the ocean has its greater and lesser gods. The Shepherd makes reference to his own relative position of "commandement" :

> And I among the rest of many least,
> Haue in the Ocean charge to me assignd. (ll. 252-3)

Colin, a little later in the poem, answering Cuddy's question about the land reached by the voyagers after their crossing, refers to the evidence of God's love toward mankind and also its rejection by men of ill will :

> For end, all good, all grace there freely growes,
> Had people grace it gratefully to vse :
> For God his gifts there plenteously bestowes,
> But gracelesse men them greatly do abuse. (ll. 324-7)

Continuing with his experiences at court to which the travelers later proceeded, Colin descants on the shepherd-poets who "do their *Cynthia* immortall make" (l. 453). Of these worthy men Colin speaks familiarly and in tones of warm friendship, despite the fact that they are potential rivals for recognition and rewards. The criticism which he intermingles in a few instances with the praise bespeaks the frank and solicitous friend.

The eulogies of the Queen and of the elegant ladies which occupy such a large part of the section dealing with the courtly milieu express respect on Colin's part for the high position which these representatives of aristocratic society hold. The praises also express unbounded admiration for these ladies. While admiration can be considered a mild form of love, the real significance of this section vis-à-vis the subject of love is the introduction on a large scale of Platonic conceptions of it. Although flesh-and-blood women are the objects of Colin's praises, he lauds them to the skies not as attractive members of the opposite sex but rather as embodiments of idealized virtue. This transmutation of desire away from humans and toward abstract qualities originates in Platonic thought. In the *Phaedrus* and more importantly in the *Symposium,* love, as we all know, is not just affection or passion felt for another human being. It is an ascending scale of desire running through all nature. It ranges from the physical passion of animals to the aspiration of man for the highest vision of truth. In the Neo-Platonic form of this conception—somewhere along this ascending scale or ladder of love—desire becomes spiritualized and transfigured into a quest for the reflection of the heavenly beauty that resides in every human body as an immanence of its divinity. Imagery of luminosity, so abundant in the section under discussion, is the verbal sign for this "influence of the heavenlie bountifulness".[26]

The satirical section that follows Colin's glorification of court life is a "rebuke" of love. In it, Colin employs Neo-Platonic terms to denounce perverted court followers. With love in its higher stages directed toward the pursuit of virtue—the good, the true, and the beautiful—the reverse of the force at the same conceptual level is vice—the inclination toward the bad, the false, and the ugly. The "misfaring" (l. 758) resulting from this evil inclination on the part of the courtiers is the burden of Colin's obloquy. The section closes with Colin's diatribe against the most flagrant of the evils practised at court—licentious love.

Contrasted with Colin's depiction of depraved love is his account of sacred love in the ensuing section. According to Colin, this latter kind of love preceded creation, itself forming the world by the power of concord. With beauty as the bait, men and women are drawn to each other for the purpose of multiplying their kind. Love, Colin goes on to say, is lord of the world by right and rules it by his powerful commands. The "vaine votaries of laesie loue" (l. 766) described earlier are "outlawes" (l. 890),

> For their desire is base, and doth not merit,
> The name of loue, but of disloyall lust. (ll. 891-2)

It is interesting to note that Melissa, in a characteristic passage of graceful transition, sums up Colin's long speech (ll. 835-94) as devoted to "loue and beautie" (l. 897)—elements which she explicitly equates with the moral quality of virtue, when she says

26. Castiglione, *Book of the Courtier,* p. 343.

all women are thy debtors found,
That doest their bountie still so much commend (ll. 901-2)

Bountie is here used to denote "goodness in general, worth, virtue",[27] a meaning of the term now obsolete.

Colin's discourse explores the subject of love in the traditional Renaissance acceptation of the word. The love treated here, though spiritualized, is largely a personal love, which finds its outlet in human associations. The conception in *Colin Clout* never extends to the uppermost heights of the ladder as it does in *The Hymnes of Heavenly Love and Beauty*. It is worthy of remark, however, that love on the level of the world is accorded full and favorable recognition for its own values.

The foregoing sketch shows how the poem centers on the subject of love. This conclusion, however, is in disagreement with that of one modern critic, Hallett Smith, who states that the poem is mainly concerned with the relationship between the poet and society. He declares: "the principal subject of this eclogue [*Colin Clout*], the relationship between a poet and his society, is a continuation and extension of 'October' ".[28] That this relationship enters into the poem is undeniable. But there are simply too many large blocks of material that cannot be subsumed under it to warrant calling the poet's relationship to society the *principal* subject. Unfortunately, the critic does not follow up his observation on the paramountcy of the poet-society theme. Instead he virtually leaves the matter with the somewhat vague statement: "His [the poet's] problem is always to build Jerusalem in England's green and pleasant land, and Colin first pays tribute to the fundamental beauty and promise of English life".[29] Smith then proceeds to

27. *OED, s.v., bounty,* derives the word from L. *bonitat-em,* goodness. The latest *OED* quotation for the meaning here given is from Drummond of Hawthornden's *Cypress Grove* (1711). De Sélincourt, in the glossary of his one-volume Oxford edition of the *Poetical Works,* s.v., *bountie, bounty,* also gives "goodness, virtue" as the meaning of the word occurring in two books of *The Faerie Queene.* Another form of the word has the same obsolete sense in the phrase "influence of the heavenlie bountifulness", quoted a few pages back from Hoby's translation of the *Book of the Courtier.* Opdycke translates the identical Italian phrase "effluence of divine goodness" (*The Book of the Courtier,* trans. Leonard Eckstein Opdycke [New York, 1903], p. 289).
28. *Elizabethan Poetry,* p. 55.
29. *Ibid.*

discuss the poem briefly in terms of the criticism of life which the pastoral convention makes possible. This criticism, he states, facilitates a contrast between the simple and the ambitious life and between pastoral love and love at court. But the subject of the poet's or artist's relationship to society receives no further mention.

A short canvass of the poem relative to the poet-society nexus will tend to show that this connection, though worthy of notice, is not the overriding theme. Part of this relationship, as set forth in the poem, is an *aspect* of the dominant love motif. The shepherd's role as a poet, for example, is linked with the second of two passages expressing eternal devotion to his mistress. Colin is proud to use his poetic gifts to give the world "This simple trophe of her great conquest" (l. 951). But the emphasis of the passage closed by this line is on *love,* not on poetry. The gift of song is only a *means* to an end—that end being the glorification of the speaker's beloved. The connection between the praise of Cynthia and the Neo-Platonic concept of love has been discussed. In two instances Colin pledges to devote his verse-making talent to eulogizing Cynthia. The first of the instances is the one in which Colin attempts to arouse himself by this incantation:

> Wake then my pipe, my sleepie *Muse* awake
> Till I haue told her praises lasting long. (ll. 48-9)

The second instance occurs in the extravagant promises Colin makes to "endosse" (l. 632) Cynthia's name in every tree and to teach the speaking woods and murmuring waterfall to vocalize it. Colin declares that his lays will immortalize Cynthia's fame.

The other part of the relationship of the poet vis-à-vis society is an aspect of more generalized matters. There is in *Colin Clout* no extended consideration devoted to the particular problem of the poet *qua* poet which is to be found in the *October* eclogue of the *Calender* or in *The Teares of the Muses.* The main lines of the sequence in *Colin Clout* which deals with Colin's poetic ambitions can be quickly summarized. The Shepherd of the Ocean recognizes Colin's superb poetic gift. He urges him to leave that waste where he is "quite forgot" (l. 183) and proceed to Cynthia's court. There he may expect to win fame and fortune. This advice Colin heeds. Once at court, he is privileged to read his poetry to Queen-Cynthia herself, who finds delight in it. Colin praises the poets at court and at the same time advises them to raise their sights to higher genres so that they may merit still greater recognition.

When Colin completes his recital of praise for the distinguished inhabitants of the court, Thestylis poses the inevitable and crucial question:

> Why *Colin,* since thou foundst such grace
> With *Cynthia* and all her noble crew:
> Why didst thou euer leaue that happie place,
> In which such wealth might vnto thee accrew?
> And back returnedst to this barrein soyle,
> Where cold and care and penury do dwell. (ll. 652-7).

Colin's reply, in essence, is that evils of the most abhorrent kind coexist along with the good at court. His comparatively brief experience, he assures his auditors, enabled him to witness enough of these "enormities" (l. 665) so that he

> Durst not aduenture such vnknowen wayes,
> Nor trust the guile of fortunes blandishment. (ll. 670-71)

The particulars regarding the "misfaring" (l. 758) of the base courtiers which Colin presents are of such nature as to discourage *anyone* who wants to make his way in court society. Only a few of these abuses or circumstances, like the small regard for learning, disadvantage the poet *qua* poet. In this connection, it is instructive to note that Hobbinol does not construe Colin's castigation of the court as applying exclusively or even mainly to poets. He takes issue with Colin on the ground that the latter's condemnation is too sweeping; he reminds Colin that some physicians, translators, teachers of science, and others, have fared rather well at court. If Colin were concerned with the status of poets alone, his natural reply would have been, "Yes, members of these other professions succeed at court, but not poets!" Instead, he concedes the truth of Hobbinol's remonstrance, agreeing that

> amongst them bee
> Full many persons of right worthie parts,
> Both for report of spotlesse honestie,
> And for profession of all learned arts. (ll. 751-4)

Colin speaks, then, of the failure of worthy men in general to receive their just deserts at court. This being the case, one can hardly subsume the long section of satire mainly under the topic of the *poet's* relationship to society.

While the details bearing directly on this relationship do not loom large, it is possible, of course, to maximize their significance. One can contend that, after all, the central narrative episode, Colin's sojourn at court, springs from this motif. The trip to the court is the result of his decision to try his fortune as a poet at court. The environment there, he assumes, is more conducive to winning fame and fortune than that "waste" (l. 183) where, according to his visitor, he had been banished "like wight forlore" (l. 182). This line of argument, though plausible, has the fundamental weakness that it fails to account for the conjunction of Colin's *entire* discourse with love. Hallett Smith appears to be the only reader who has voiced an opinion on the matter in print, but there are undoubtedly other readers who, like him, tend to overvalue the poet-versus-society role in *Colin Clout*. Such a tendency may arise from their assuming, without sufficient warrant, too close an identification between Colin Clout, the title character, and Spenser, the historical person, who is now generally remembered as a poet only.

The discussion up to this point has shown the unified design of the poem. In it the reader's attention is confined to a single group of characters who are involved in a particular situation for an unspecified portion of a single day. The situation remains the same throughout: Colin's presentation, before a group of attentive and responsive listeners, of circumstances leading up to his sojourn at court and the reflections arising from the recollection of that stay. Colin's presentation, set forth with emotional fervor appropriate to his protean pastoral role as shepherd, poet, lover, and moral philosopher, explores the problem of love. The conception of love explored in Colin's discourse is that which finds its associations in the world of men. Elsewhere Spenser epitomizes this conception in the statement, "loue is the lesson which the Lord vs taught".[30] The basis of the poem's organization thus set forth seems eminently logical. But is there also, one wonders, a larger unity going beyond this dialectic and extending the matter exploited into the realm of

30. *Am.*, Sonnet LXVIII, *Works,* VIII, 223.

the "general reason of things", which Sidney refers to as coming within the special province of the poet? I believe that there is.

To present this view, it is necessary to recapitulate what in the fifth chapter on "Tone and Feeling" were called the *thematic* divisions of the poem. Since it has now been revealed that the contents of the entire poem pertain directly or indirectly to love, it becomes more helpful to term these divisions *schematic* units. They are, it will be recalled, five in number as follows: (1) the pastoral ideal (ll. 1-327); (2) the courtly ideal (ll. 328-647); (3) the perversion of the courtly ideal (ll. 648-794); (4) the Neo-Platonic notion of love as the great moving force of the universe (ll. 795-902); and (5) the praise of Rosalind (ll. 903-51).

The first part describes the atmosphere of simplicity and contentment that prevails among the shepherds. The myth of such a state was firmly fixed in the minds of Renaissance readers of pastoral verse, which from Theocritus forward had contrasted the rural and the urban way of life, to the disadvantage of the latter. But even among Arcadian surroundings there exists the possibility of wrong-doing. The lay of Bregog and Mulla which Colin sings is an example of how, even amidst scenes of simple nature, a single mis-deed may breach the original order, break the great chain of being, and disturb the tranquillity imposed upon the world by the power of love. Within the seeming peace of rural habitation, moreover, there is the possibility of crudeness, even of savagery and violence. All is not benign nature, as Colin makes abundantly clear in the passage where he speaks of "wayling", "bloodie issues", "griesly famine", "nightly bodrags", and "rauenous wolues".

The second section depicts the court as the apogee of civilization —the culmination of social progress. It is the seat of the Prince ruling by divine right. It is the Parnassus of elegance and learning. It is the lodestar for men who wish to advance honorable ambitions by honorable means. It is the cornucopia, from which flows wealth and power in tangible forms—titles, grants, patents, pensions, privileges—in short, all manner of material rewards.

The third section portrays the seamy side of court life. The possibilities of material advancement attract the unscrupulous equally with the honorable. Rivalry sets in motion an unseemly struggle for aggrandizement by men whose dispositions are such that they will stop at nothing to gain their nefarious ends. In this mad scramble by schemers and rascals, the honest man who seeks to rise by merit has no chance at all. Among the former, ill-gotten gains lead to idleness, and idleness, to depraved love and other vices.

The fourth section alters the locus of men's choice: it removes it from meadow and court and places it in the realm of thoughtful action—in the province of love as the original creative force of the world—love, the everlasting counter force against the vicissitudes of place and chance.

The final section glorifies the love of one man for one woman.

Now if one regards these five respective units in the nature of "plot" components, opposed one to another, he can postulate that neither the pastoral ideal, with its suggestion of contentment through the contemplative, unambitious life, nor the courtly ideal, with its suggestion of self-realization through the active life, is wholly satisfying. Both possess distinct advantages and drawbacks. The benefits of one, moreover, cannot be gained without sacrificing the benefits of the other.

But the fourth unit—love as a universal force—places the focus of desire on a higher plane than either of the preceding two alternatives. It therefore resolves the conflict between the pastoral ideal of leisure and contentment on the one hand and the courtly ideal of culture and activity on the other. It does this by reconciling the best parts of the two into a single sublimated ideal of love. Love in its absolute form stands forth as a kind of king—"Lord of all the world by right" (l. 883)—who has his Heavenly Court not at Greenwich, Whitehall, Oatlands, Nonsuch; who has his Garden not in Arcadia or at Kilcolman; but who has both Court and Garden everywhere and forever.

The ideal of love into which Spenser has reconciled the two positive ideals of pastoralism and courtly grace are, in the final section, brought directly back into the normal human atmosphere of the poem by giving to this abstraction a habitation in the world and an incarnation in a lady named Rosalind.

Such is the universal applicability of the poem—and one important reason for its lasting appeal—that it gives eloquent expression the *vox humana* of one individual to a fundamental problem by no means restricted to the Renaissance: contentment and self-sufficiency as symbolized by the pastoral life over against restless striving for fame, wealth, and power as symbolized by the courtly life and epitomized in the Marlovian phrase, "aspyring minde".

As between the pastoral and the courtly ideal, the poem suggests that there is a third ideal which both reconciles and transcends both—that of love. To find this ideal for himself man must make many "agonizing reappraisals" and harsh choices; to achieve it, he must make difficult sacrifices. If he would live at peace with his conscience and his God, he can do no other.

Construing the five sections seriatim as plot components in this way enables one to perceive, for the first time, the rationale of their order. The sequence of these sections is determined by the need to pose the problem and to suggest a solution. The first three sections thus establish analogies and contrasts vis-à-vis the pastoral and courtly ideals. The last two sections resolve the dilemmas posed by these comparisons.

All five parts combine to illuminate a problem philosophical in nature but neither highly abstract nor impractically theoretical: how best to live in the world. Spenser shows the very human and highly personal nature of this problem by having one believable and recognizable personage "experience" it in its various aspects. He employs Colin Clout, a sympathetic imaginary character, who bears some features of resemblance to his creator, to present in first person discourse a posture of imagined affairs. These imagined affairs are analogous, not only to the real affairs of his creator, but to those of his creator's learned compeers as well.

Although the posture of imagined affairs set forth in the "experience" of Colin Clout is applicable as allegory to all mankind, it has special interest for members of the aristocracy and for those anxious to establish themselves or to rise in court society. Spenser himself belonged to this numerous group, which included as typical members other poets like Fraunce and Daniel, scholars like Florio and Harvey, and courtiers like Raleigh and Sidney. The personages in the poem are shepherds only by a conventional fiction; they represent, in rather thin disguise, people of standing in the realm, including her who held pride of place in the aristocratic hierarchy.

It is especially to this class, united in their adherence to aristocratic ideals and in their respect for learning and the arts, that Spenser addresses himself in *Colin Clout*. Adaptation to accord with the presumed desires of these learned compeers may well have suggested the theme. The same accommodation to this ideal audience envisaged for the poem helps account for the special characteristics of the figures, the diction, the versification, the imagery, and the tone and feeling. It helps explain the relation of these elements to something outside themselves.

Spenser could count on members of this elite set to appreciate to the full his virtuosity in handling these elements of style and tone. And by means of this same virtuosity he could also separate himself as far as possible from the "Poet-apes".[31] Commitment of his court poem to print placed him in inevitable association wih these poetasters. In this connection it may be recalled that E. K., the editor of Spenser's earlier pastoral printed in 1579, had deliberately invited comparison between the new poet and the numerous tribe of mere versifiers, whom he excoriates picturesquely as "the rakehellye route of our ragged rymers ... which without learning boste, without iudgement iangle, without reason rage and fome".[32] Spenser's incorporation in the poem of effects especially chosen to merit the approval of the favored audience need not be censured as proof of timeserving on his part. The court group actually possessed a highly cultivated taste in letters. Indeed, if Spenser was to remain true to his conception of the poet's high calling, he needed to exert his utmost poetic powers to please that audience. In the "Letter of the Authors" he embraces with enthusiasm the standard conception of the poet's mission—to serve as a moral preceptor, teaching through aesthetic means. On this principle, the audience could profit from the poet's vision of truth only through being moved by the poem. They could be moved by it only as a consequence of their delight in it. Without unqualified acceptance by this discriminating audience of the recherché effects which the poem exhibits, its cause would be unfulfilled. Accordingly, the elaboration of *Colin Clout* represents on Spenser's part a consciously employed adaptation of means to end.

Lesser poets than Spenser who attempt to write court poems of display fail to win favor in the higher circles of polite society because they lack the skill to conceal their art,[33] or they lack the

31. Sidney, *Apologie,* in *Eliz. Critical Essays,* I, 205.

32. Dedicatory Epistle to S.C., *Works,* VII, 9.

33. The familiar classical principle of art concealing art is eloquently expressed in Quintilian, *Institutio Oratoria,* I.xi.3, I, 184: "The height of art is to conceal art". (Quintilian's own words are: "Nam si qua in his ars est dicentium, ea prima est, ne ars esse videatur".) The principle finds strong support in Renaissance poetic theory. Cf., e.g., Sidney, *Apologie,* in *Eliz. Critical Essays,* I, 203: "I haue found in diuers smally learned Courtiers a more sounde stile then in some professors of learning: of which I can gesse no other cause, but that the Courtier, following that which by practise hee findeth fittest to nature, therein (though he know it not) doth according to Art, though not by Art: where the other, vsing Art to shew Art, and not to hide Art (as in these cases he should doe), flyeth from nature, and indeede abuseth Art"; and Puttenham, p. 302: "we doe allow our

taste to know when to stop.[34] In the former case, the result of the poetaster's labor may be no more than "Heapes of huge words vphoorded hideously,/With horrid sound though hauing little sence";[35] in the latter, the fruit of the versifier's efforts is all too often "rymes of shameles ribaudrie/Without regard, or due Decorum kept".[36]

The principle of "Decorum" alluded to in the above quotation from Spenser's *The Teares of the Muses* deserves special notice at this juncture. It is the nexus, as it were, between the audience at which Spenser aims and the elaboration of poetic effects discoverable in the poem. Accordingly, it can also be thought of, to change the figure, as a kind of magnet which polarizes these elements along certain lines of force to give them unity.

Spenser's observance of decorum is what chiefly invests his poem with a peculiar distinction and gives it, in its totality, a harmonious effect. Insistence on this principle, defined by Puttenham as the "good grace of euery thing in his kinde",[37] is an invariable tenet of Renaissance criticism. Puttenham conceives the principle in a somewhat wider sense than that accorded to it by classical authors from whom it is derived. Perhaps because of the close association of decorum with the social distinctions which pervade Tudor life and letters, Puttenham as a courtly writer[38] places greater stress on the principle of propriety than do some of the other critics. But his views are especially germane since they very likely approximate those of Spenser, whose associations and sympathies were, by deliberate choice, with the aristocratic class.

Puttenham devotes the twenty-third chapter of *The Arte of English Poesie* entirely to decorum, which he advisedly calls "the line & Leuell for al good makers to do their busines by".[39] In this chapter he places particular stress on the high degree of taste and

---

Courtly Poet to be a dissembler only in the subtilties of his arte: that is, when he is most artificall, so to disguise and cloake it as it may not appeare, nor seeme to proceede from him by any studie or trade of rules, but to be his naturall".

34. Excess of any kind violates poetic decorum, which prescribes, among other things, the principle of "ne quid nimis" (Puttenham, p. 155).

35. *T.M.*, ll. 553-4, *Works,* VIII, 78.

36. *Ibid.*, ll. 213-4, p. 69.

37. Page 262.

38. Puttenham, pp. xxiv-xxv. Puttenham, like Spenser, dedicated his *opus magnum* to Queen Elizabeth (n. opposite p. 1).

39. *Ibid.*, p. 261.

experience requisite to judging adequately a writer's success in maintaining decorum :

> and verely it seemes to go all by discretion, not perchaunce of euery one, but by a learned and experienced discretion, for otherwise seemes the *decorum* to a weake and ignorant iudgement, then it doth to one of better knowledge and experience : which sheweth that it resteth in the discerning part of the minde, so as he who can make the best and most differences of things by reasonable and wittie distinction is to be the fittest iudge or sentencer of [*decencie*].[40]

Now the "discretion" of which Puttenham speaks was peculiarly within the province of Spenser's courtly audience to exercise when it came to this all-important matter of decorum. The leading aspects of a poem to which decorum or "decencie" apply are set forth by Puttenham in the following pronouncement :

> But by reason of the sundry circumstances, that mans affaires are as it were wrapt in, this [*decencie*] comes to be very much alterable and subiect to varietie, in so much as our speach asketh one maner of *decencie*, in respect of the person who speakes : another of his to whom it is spoken : another of whom we speake : another of what we speake, and in what place and time and to what purpose.[41]

Puttenham regards decorum as the application of the poet's sensitivity in the intellectual, emotional, and aesthetic areas to the demands of his subject when that subject is adequately conceived and when it is presented under varying artistic conditions. Decorum, in Puttenham's view, assumes the subordination of form to matter. Puttenham's concept of decorum as a flexible[42] and all-encompassing literary principle accords with its general acceptation in Spenser's day.[43] This construction of the principle goes far

40. *Ibid.*, p. 263.
41. *Ibid.*
42. *Ibid.*, lvi.
43. Cf. Roger Ascham, *The Scholemaster* (1570), in *Eliz. Critical Essays*, I, 23: "And here, who soeuer hath bene diligent to read aduisedlie ouer *Terence, Seneca, Virgil, Horace* . . . and shall diligently marke the difference they vse, in proprietie of woordes, in forme of sentence, in handlying of their matter, he shall easelie perceiue what is fitte and *decorum* in euerie

toward suggesting the reasons for the variations in style and mood found in the poem. Spenser constantly adjusts both to suit the changing relationships among the various bases for decorum familiar to educated readers.

From time to time the preceding chapters have invited attention to ways in which Spenser observes decorum in *Colin Clout.* In many cases, however, both considerations of economy and the more pressing demands of the immediate topic have precluded signalizing particular devices and techniques as examples of decorous observance on the author's part. In any event, to pass in review, at this closing juncture, some notable instances of Spenser's imaginative response to the regulating principle of decorum will demonstrate the way in which he harmonizes by reference to this "line and leuell" rhetorical figures, diction, versification, tone, and feeling.

In the chapter of his *Arte* entitled "Of Figures and Figuratiue speaches", Puttenham takes great pains to caution against violation of decorum in the use of figures which, according to him, could result from "any foule indecencie or disproportion of sound, situation, or sence".[44] Thus the poet was considered to be under obligation to choose figures with due regard for "the cause and purpose he hath in hand".[45] This Spenser indeed does throughout. Examples come readily to mind. The sea-pastoral figure *allegoria* (ll. 240-63), for instance, represents a happy choice on the poet's part. It is particularly suited to honoring tastefully the Queen and one of her favorite lieutenants. Through a topographic myth, *topographia* (ll. 100-55), Spenser has Colin recount a charming tale with a delicately concealed but significant moral.

---

one"; and Sidney, *Apologie* (1595), *ibid.,* p. 160: "the Senate of Poets hath chosen verse as their fittest rayment, meaning, as in matter they passed all in all, so in maner to goe beyond them: not speaking . . . words as they chanceably fall from the mouth but peyzing each sillable of each worde by iust proportion according to the dignitie of the subiect". Modern scholars also comment on this pervasive function of decorum as conceived by Renaissance poets. Cf. Renwick, *Essay,* p. 75: "Decorum controlled the arrangement of phrase, the use and the choice of images and figures; above all, it controlled the first element in style, the choice of words"; and Tuve, *Elizabethan and Metaphysical Imagery,* p. 192: "Propriety or decorum was the basic criterion in terms of which all the others were understood".

44. Page 155.

45. *Ibid.*

When Spenser wishes to elevate the style in "speciall regard to all circumstances of the person",[46] he uses ornate figures of high connotation. Illustrative of such figures is the series of similes in Colin's speech (ll. 590-615) lauding the words, deeds, looks, and thoughts of Queen-Cynthia. These similes, it will be recalled, are very close in phrasing to similes occurring in the Song of Solomon. Colin, in his role of humble shepherd who pays tribute to one far above himself in rank, appropriately prefaces this extravagant panegyric with *meiosis* (ll. 590-91), a figure of diminution. When Spenser wishes to impart a quality of great excitement and stimulation to a passage, he selects figures especially efficacious to this end. Colin's speech (ll. 464-79) in which he expresses passionate devotion to Rosalind is a structured sequence of emotion-arousing schemes: *exclamatio* or exclamation, *expolitio* or amplification by variation of phrase, *synathroismus* or "the Heaping figure", and *acclamatio* or climatic summary. These major schemes of thought and amplification are interlaced with figures of harmonic repetition, *anaphora* and *paroemion,* and capped by *antimetabole* and *antistrophe,* word play employing verbal opposition and repetition.

Decorum in the use of figures is achieved not only by their being perfectly adapted to their function in a given situation. It is achieved also by reason of the satisfaction inherent in the patterning itself, provided the execution is sufficiently artistic. In this connection it is helpful to recall that one of the Renaissance synonyms for decorum is "comelynesse".[47] Thus the mosaic of figures in Colin's grandiloquent avowal of vassalage to Rosalind just mentioned not only induces the kind of stimulation fitting to the circumstances, but it also affords delight to the reader alerted to recognize the particular patterns involved. The educated Elizabethan was, of course, thoroughly accustomed to listen and look for rhetorical patterning. Identifying the precise figures employed in a given passage of poetry was for him an act of high intellectual pleasure.

With respect to diction, Spenser employs enough archaic locutions to give a rustic coloring to the language, but not so much as to make the language seem outlandish. When necessary, he adapts some words and borrows others from Romance vernaculars, but he takes care to make these innovations follow established linguistic

46. *Ibid.*
47. *Ibid.,* p. 262.

patterns. Adaptation of vocabulary to situation and subject is characteristic. To represent sadness, he chooses monosyllabic words with long vowels, as in the all-nature-mourns speech of Hobbinol (ll. 16-35); to dignify the passages on the poets and ladies at court (ll. 380-451; 485-577), he employs abstract words and phrases from the courtly vocabulary; and to inveigh against base courtiers (ll. 680-730, 749-70, 775-94), he finds some concrete words of vulgar currency.

The choice of the heroic stanza for the versification, too, is right. The stanza form is not too elaborate to go with the pastoral motif or with the predominantly middle style of the poem. The fairly long verses and alternate rhymes lend themselves to a stately movement in keeping with the important subject and fundamentally serious tone. Then, also, the five-stress measure facilitates varying the caesura to simulate natural speech rhythms. The iambic meter, of course, is likewise ideal for a poem almost entirely dialogue. At the same time, the quatrain pattern facilitates larger groupings to form strophic speech units.

The outward aspects of style just discussed—formal figures, vocabulary, and versification—conform to the demands of decorous usage; so also does the inward aspect of style—imagery. Spenser's imagery—the mediation of sensuous, emotional, and intellectual experience through the re-creative aura of words, phrases, and larger rhetorical structures—is particularly appropriate in *Colin Clout*. The expectations of his discriminating audience—expectations reflected in received poetic theory—placed certain demands upon him. The success with which Spenser meets these demands constitutes the measure of his "propriety" in the work. He was expected, for example, to maintain an overall balance between the experience and the representation of it. The representation had to be "imitative", not direct or "realistic". It had to have more than an individual interest or application : it also needed to possess a universal relevance. It had to command intellectual assent, but it could not afford to overlook one of the readiest paths to that goal—appeal to the physical senses. It had, in other words, by a series of "fictions" to add up to a significant truth; yet these "fictions" had to stay within the realm of the recognizable.

All imaging in *Colin Clout* serves as a means to afford the peculiar pleasure which arises from the maintenance of this delicate and deliberate interplay of fact and fancy. For example, the visual description of the ship (ll. 212-23) is partly consistent with objective reality. Yet the fact that the "picture" is embodied in one of the conventional "colors of rhetoric"—in this case, *prosopopoeia*—has the effect of muting the sensory stimulation. In other cases, the image only partly succeeds in conjuring up before the reader the actual world of sight or sound because the passage containing the image echoes a classical prototype.

The pervasive image of the poem—the pastoral allegory—is, of course, the principal device for veiling reality. By means of it, Colin is not Spenser but a "shepheard" (l. 14). Queen-Cynthia's demesne is not England, Wales, and her overseas possessions, but "hills and pastures" (l. 238). The commander of the southwestern coastal defense is not Sir Walter Raleigh, Vice Admiral of Devon and Cornwall, but the "shepheard of the Ocean" (l. 66). In the context of the pastoral, Raleigh would doubtless take pride and pleasure in this appellation, although in real life, where a different order of decorum prevailed, he could (and did) express his utter distaste for the actual vocation of keeping sheep.[48]

The pastoral image gives aesthetic distance and for that reason provides a vantage point from which tasteful praise may be lavished upon the Queen herself, as well as upon some of the highest ranking ladies in the realm. The ladies themselves appear under pastoral pseudonyms; they are adumbrated as "Nymphs" (l. 459) of Cynthia's retinue. Covert allusions have enabled scholars to identify all but two of the twelve with reasonable certainty, but the praise accorded to the ladies is only incidentally concerned with their individual merits; rather it is directed mainly to bringing them into symbolic relationship with abstract virtues in a transferral of praise from personal to etherealized qualities, which is characteristic of Neo-Platonic thought.

Especially when employed in figures of comparison, value terms which Spenser's French and Italian predecessors had assimilated to pastoral poetry furnish a controlling context for generalized blame as well as for praise. Colin, inveighing against the evils of court society, in effect reverses the Neo-Platonic value symbols employed to glorify the admirable side of court life. Such a reversal

48. Letter to Robert Dudley, Earl of Leicester, 25 August 1581, in Edward Edwards, *Life of Sir Walter Ralegh,* II, 17: "I have spent some time here under the Deputy [Lord Grey of Wilton], in such poore place and charge, as, were it not that I knew him to be on [sic] of yours, I would disdayn it as miche as to keap sheepe".

of terms, along with much coarse-grained language which is highly pejorative, acts to "diminish" the subject. It lowers the style to accord with the dictates of decorum, which call for the base style in satire.

The pastoral allegory, the primary image of the poem, with its contextual richness and resultant built-in tensions, permits the poet to pose, and also to suggest a solution for, a universally engrossing problem. The conceptual import, arising from the delicately maintained balancing of fact and fiction, is in itself a product of the poet's adherence to the demands of decorum. This "meaning" gracefully veiled throughout beneath the interplay of reality and fancy is not neatly summed up at the poem's conclusion. For the poet to have done this would have been for him to violate the "maner of decencie, in respect of the person . . . to whom it is spoken" by offending the intended reader's intelligence. Indeed, the "meaning" cannot successfully be stated even in paraphrase since it is organic to the poem. Perhaps its character can only be shadowed figuratively as a kind of point where parallel lines of fact and fiction meet.

The preceding section highlights some of the ways Spenser keeps decorum with respect to stylistic elements in the poem. The emotional drive of *Colin Clout* necessarily arises out of these elements. In one sense, then, the summary just given of the manner in which the style is rendered consistent by being subordinated to commonly accepted criteria of decorum can be considered to include—and does, in fact, include—attitudinal aspects. In another sense, however, the poem's orectic climate is a kind of entity in itself which adds up to more than the sum of its contributing parts. Thus viewed, the attitudinal plexus may be regarded as a prime integrating factor. Specifically, tone and feeling, operating within a mechanism of voice and address, play a vital role in determining how the whole poem should be "taken". That Renaissance poetic theory considers these phenomena as coming within the province of decorum is manifest from Puttenham's definition quoted earlier in the chapter. The part germane to the present matter states: "this [decencie] comes to be very much alterable and subiect to varietie, in so much as our speach asketh one maner of *decencie,* in respect of the person who speakes: another of his to whom it is spoken: another of whom we speake: another of what we speake, and in what place and time and to what purpose".

In essence, there are two "voices" in the poem: that of the "outside" narrator, and that of the ten interlocutors, collectively considered. Though Colin is one of the ten members of the immediate gathering, it is probably more constructively accurate to consider his a third voice in view of the difference in tone, scale, and character between his discourse and the utterances of the others. To correspond with the two basic voices, there are actually two "audiences"; one "interior", that of the interlocutors; the other "exterior", that of the courtly reading group.[49]

The interior audience of shepherds is necessary for a number of excellent reasons: to objectify the pastoral motif, to provide an atmosphere of warmth and acceptance, to give life and movement, and to make natural emotional presentations. But its presence gives rise to a difficult problem of decorum. The third person narrator addresses the exterior audience only. His opening and closing utterances provide a pleasant introduction and conclusion for the main action. His verses, aimed at a single, relatively homogeneous audience, would present to the poet no particular problem of decorum with respect to tone and feeling. Such would emphatically not be the case for lines assigned to the interlocutors. Their speeches have to be "right" for *both* the interior audience of shepherds and the exterior audience of elegant readers. How does Spenser solve this apparent dilemma?

He solves it in a number of ways. First, he permits an air of naïveté to enter into the remarks of some of the interlocutors, including, in one instance, Colin himself, who evinces an inland shepherd's awe at his first sight of the ocean (ll. 196-9). Corydon echoes this wonderment that the sea is "so fearfull" (l. 200). Cuddy expresses surprise that there is any land other than the one he stands upon (ll. 290-91). In a later passage (ll. 304-7) he ingenuously asks if heavenly graces also exist in that foreign land. Such comments as these, appropriate for a shepherd, naturally give rise to humor at the level of the exterior audience. Irony of this kind is particularly effective in connection with Cuddy's "artless" question about heavenly graces at court.

The second way in which Spenser maintains the dual level without "disproportion of ... situation, or sence"[50] to either audi-

49. Puttenham, p. 155, lists the typical members of this group as consisting of "princely dames, yong ladies, gentlewomen and courtiers".
50. *Ibid.*

ence is by keeping a minimal difference between the perception of the immediate audience and that of the removed audience. Thus, most of the shepherds evince no trace of the naïve tendency. In fact, the remarks of some of them, notably Thestylis, are rather shrewd. Yet none of the utterances noticeably departs from character.

Third, when Colin's speeches become too lofty in mood to come from the lips of a mere shepherd, one of the interlocutors himself calls attention to its unseemliness (ll. 616-19, 823-34). In these cases Colin concedes the point and explains the breech of propriety on the ground that he was "carried away" by his subject.

And, finally, Spenser solves the knotty problem of decorum inherent in the dual system of address by skillfully simulating, throughout the entire dialogue, the normal give-and-take of friendly conversation. Hobbinol expresses deep concern and affection for Colin in his welcoming speech:

> *Colin* my liefe, my life, how great a losse
> Had all the shepheards nation by thy lacke? (ll. 16-17)

Thestylis colloquially exclaims at the end of Colin's song of the Bregog and Mulla, "Now by my life this was a mery lay" (l. 157). When Colin completes his praise of the poets at court, Lucida comments with mock asperity, "Shepheard, enough of shepheards thou hast told" (l. 457). Lucida "joshes" Colin because Rosalind has been "to that swain too cruell hard" (l. 909). These piquant sentiments go well with the bucolic *conversazione*. The bantering and the by-play, though relatively infrequent, tend to obscure on the surface at least and for part of the time the predominantly serious orientation of Colin's entire discourse, with its range of emotional nuances. Gravity and emotional vibrancy suit Colin's discourse, the core of the poem, because of the character he is given and because of the doctrinal content of the disquisition. The discourse is concerned with weighty and significant matters—matters actually too complex for the understanding of the fictitious (interior) audience of shepherds, but in perfect accord with the tastes and intellectual capacity of the real (exterior) audience of educated Elizabethans.

All in all, it is Spenser's sensitive response to the regulating principle of decorum which gives consistency to the poem. It is also mastery of this flexible control that endears him so highly to "the few that onely lend their eare", that fit audience of which Daniel speaks in a poem reciprocating Spenser's compliment in *Colin Clout*.[51]

In summary, Spenser as a learned poet and the author of a treatise on poetic theory may be presumed to have been thoroughly familiar with the artistic requirement for unity in a literary work. Famous classical authorities like Plato, Aristotle, and Horace, with whose dicta on the subject of unity Spenser was undoubtedly conversant, stress this requirement. Certain critics of our own era, nevertheless, have censured *Colin Clout* on the ground that it lacks unity. Their allegations of disunity may arise from the disinclination to read the poem in the light of its original literary milieu. Legouis, for example, in calling the poem inconsistent errs partly because he neglects to give weight to the standard Renaissance concept of poetry as imitative discourse, concerned with presenting not truths, but rather, as Ben Jonson has it, "things (like truths) well fain'd".[52]

As a matter of fact, *Colin Clout* conforms very well to Aristotle's prescription that a work of art be a one and a whole. The poem presents a single action occurring in one place and within the time span of a single day. This action, which remains the same throughout, is the dialogue between Colin and his fellow shepherds. The dialogue itself is set within a frame narrated by a third person. The main speaker in the dialogue is Colin himself, who recites in first person discourse a single sequence of connected happenings and reflections arising directly from these happenings. Colin's discourse is unified in part by its being confined to topics already acclimatized to pastoral poetry by Spenser's predecessors in this genre. In greater part, Colin's discourse is unified by having its topics polarized around himself, a fictive character, in his respective roles of scholar, poet, amorist, moral philosopher, and devout Christian. In greatest measure, Colin's discourse, which constitutes the heart of the poem, is unified by having its topics—Colin's adventures and thoughts—crystallized around the theme of love, with that term employed in its common courtly acceptation during Spenser's era.

51. *Musophilus* (1599), l. 555, *The Complete Works in Verse and Prose of Samuel Daniel,* ed. Alexander B. Grosart (n.p., 1885), I, 243. In ll. 440-3, Daniel singles out Sidney and Spenser as the most famous of poets.

52. Second Prologue to *Epicoene, or The Silent Woman* in *Ben Jonson,* V, 164.

In this acceptation of the term, all the material in the poem can be subsumed without difficulty into five divisions of the subject. When these five divisions or schematic sections are surveyed in relation to one another, they assume a clear-cut pattern. The first three sections compare the advantages and disadvantages of the pastoral and the courtly ideals. This comparison poses the problem. The last two sections set forth the alternative ideal of love, both in its abstract and personal manifestations. This latter presentation suggests a solution to the problem. All five sections concern themselves with the intensely practical and always relevant matter of the *summum bonum* in human life.

The lasting human values which the poem explores confer upon it a truly universal quality. For a select circle of courtly Tudor readers and listeners, appreciation of this universality was undoubtedly enhanced by the overall aristocratic cast of the poem. It was, indeed, for the instruction and delight of this group that Spenser originally penned it. The elaboration of all the elements—subject, style, and tone—gives the poem a comprehensive consistency, causing the whole to bear the stamp of formal artistry. Upon this quality of elegant finish, courtly readers of the time placed great importance. In addition, the characters, settings, and events alluded to mask, with varying degrees of concealment, actual people, places and happenings which held special significance for members of Queen Elizabeth's court society. Finally, decorous observance on Spenser's part lends harmony to rhetorical patterning, diction, imagery, tone, and feeling. The fastidious audience, judging from Puttenham's comments, took particular pride in its ability to evaluate a poet's skill in keeping decorum. The way in which a poet observed decorum was, in fact, regarded as the chief means by which a true maker could be distinguished from a mere versifier. Because the classical concept of decorum reflected in its origins a long-standing system of hierarchical values and because the principle of decorum served as an indispensable artistic gauge, Spenser's sensitive response in the poem to this principle constitutes, in terms of the special coterie for whom he intended it, a particular triumph.

In conclusion, then, *Colin Clout* stands forth as a polite poem, composed by a courtly maker for a select group, its cause being to instill a "vertue-breeding delightfulnes'[53] in the minds, hearts, and

53. Sidney, *Apologie,* in *Eliz. Critical Essays,* I, 205.

sensibilities of a courtly reading circle, distinguished by learning, sophistication, and elegance. The relatively circumscribed audience which Spenser seems to have conceived for his "simple pastorall" has grown, in the nearly four centuries since its publication, to one of world-wide dimensions. This circumstance makes fitting a dictum enunciated by Puttenham in the twenty-third chapter of the *Arte* with explicit reference to the poet's keeping of decorum: "The election is the writers, the iudgeme[*n*]t is the worlds, as theirs to whom the reading apperteineth". Spenser needs no apology for his election. But perhaps the passage of centuries, which have witnessed so many silent shifts in the tides of literary fashion, now justifies a little buttressing for the world's judgment!

BIBLIOGRAPHY*

Albright, Evelyn M. "Spenser's Cosmic Philosophy and His Religion", PMLA, XLIV (Sept. 1929), 715-59.

Andreas, Capellanus. *The Art of Courtly* Love, ed. and trans. John J. Parry. New York, 1941.

Aristotle. *The Works of Aristotle,* ed. W. D. Ross. 12 vols. Oxford, 1908-52.

Ascham, Roger. *The Scholemaster* (1570), in *Elizabethan Critical Essays,* ed. Smith, I, 1-45.

Babb, Lawrence. "On the Nature of Elizabethan Psychological Literature", in *Joseph Quincy Adams Memorial Studies,* ed. James G. MacManaway, Giles E. Dawson, Edwin Welloughby. Washington, D.C. Pp. 509-22.

Baldwin, T. W. *William Shakespeare's Small Latine and Lesse Greeke.* 2 vols. Urbana, 1944.

Baroway, Israel. "The Imagery of Spenser and the 'Song of Songs' ", JEGP, XXXIII (Jan. 1934), 23-45.

Blundeville, Thomas. *The Arte of Logicke.* London, 1617.

Bolgar, R. R. *The Classical Heritage and Its Beneficiaries.* Cambridge, Eng., 1954.

Botting, Roland B. "A New Spenserian Rhyme Scheme?" JEGP, XXXVI (July 1937), 384-6.

Bradbrook, Muriel C. *The School of Night: A Study in the Literary Relationships of Sir Walter Raleigh.* Cambridge, Eng., 1936.

Bradner, Leicester. *Edmund Spenser and the Faerie Queene.* Chicago, 1948.

Brooke, C. F. T. "The Renaissance", in *A Literary History of England,* ed. Albert C. Baugh. New York, 1948. Pp. 315-696.

Browne, Wynard. "Sir Walter Raleigh", in *The Great Tudors,* ed. Katharine Garvin. London, 1953. Pp. 597-610.

*The bibliography includes only those works which are referred to in this book. Abbreviations of periodicals follow the list published in the annual bibliography issue of *Publications of the Modern Language Association of America.*

Buchan, Alexander H. "Ralegh's *Cynthia*—Facts or Legend", MLQ, I (Dec. 1940), 461-74.

Carpenter, Frederick I. *A Reference Guide to Edmund Spenser.* Chicago, 1923.

Casady, Edwin. "The Neo-Platonic Ladder in Spenser's *Amoretti*, PQ, XX (July 1941), 284-95.

Cassirer, Ernst. *The Platonic Renaissance in England,* trans. James P. Pettegrove. Austin, 1953.

Castiglione, Baldesarre. *Il Libro del cortegiano de Conte Baldesar Castiglione.* Venice, 1528.

—— *The Book of the Courtier,* trans. Leonard E. Opdycke. New York, 1903.

—— *The Book of the Courtier,* trans. Sir Thomas Hoby, The Tudor Translations, ed. W. E. Henley. Vol. XXIII. London, 1900.

Church, Richard W. *Spenser.* English Men of Letters. London, 1886.

Cicero, Marcus Tullius. *De Oratore,* trans. H. Rackham. Loeb Classical Library. 2 vols. Cambridge, Mass., 1942.

—— *Orator,* trans. H. M. Hubbell. The Loeb Classical Library. Cambridge, Mass., 1939.

Clark, Donald L. *John Milton at St. Paul's School: A Study of Ancient Rhetoric in English Renaissance Education.* New York, 1948.

Clay, William K., ed. *Private Prayers Put Forth by Authority During the Reign of Queen Elizabeth.* Cambridge, Eng., 1851.

Coeffeteau, Nicholas. *A Table of Humane Passions,* trans. Edward Grimestone. London, 1621.

Coleridge, Samuel T. *Coleridge's Shakespearean Criticism,* ed. Thomas M. Rayser. 2 vols. Cambridge, Mass., 1930.

Congleton, J. E. *Theories of Pastoral Poetry in England, 1684-1798.* Gainesville, Fla., 1952.

Cook, Albert, ed. *The Art of Poetry: The Poetical Treatises of Horace, Vida, and Boileau.* Boston, 1892.

Cornwallis, William. *Discourses upon Seneca the Tragedian,* ed. Robert H. Bowers. Gainesville, Fla., 1952.

Crane, William G. *Wit and Rhetoric in the Renaissance: The Formal Basis of Elizabethan Prose Style.* Columbia University Studies in English and Comparative Literature, No. 129. New York, 1937.

Daniel, Samuel. *Musophilus* (1599). In *The Complete Works in Verse and Prose of Samuel Daniel,* ed. Alexander B. Grosart. 5 vols. Privately printed, 1885-96. I, 221-56.

Edwards, Edward. *The Life of Sir Walter Ralegh.* 2 vols. London, 1868.

Edwards, Philip. *Sir Walter Ralegh.* Men and Books Series. London, 1953.

Elcock, W. D. "English Indifference to Du Bellay's 'Regrets' ", MLR, XLVI (April 1951), 175-84.

Ellrodt, Robert. *Neoplatonism in the Poetry of Spenser*. Geneva, 1960.

Erasmus, Desiderius. *The Apophthegmes of Erasmus,* trans. Nicolas Udall, from the edition of 1564, ed. Robert Roberts. Boston, 1877.

Fogle, Richard H. *The Imagery of Keats and Shelley: A Comparative Study.* Chapel Hill, N.C., 1949.

Forest, Louise C. T. "A Caveat for Critics Against Invoking Elizabethan Psychology", PMLA, LXI (Sept. 1946), 651-72.

Fowler, Earl B. *Spenser and the System of Courtly Love.* Louisville, 1934.

Fraunce, Abraham. *The Arcadian Rhetorike* (1588), ed. Ethel Seaton. Luttrell Society Reprints, No. 9. Oxford, 1950.

—— *The Lawiers Logike.* London, 1588.

Galway, Margaret. "Spenser's Rosalind", TLS, 19 July 1947, p. 372.

Gascoigne, George. *Certayne Notes of Instruction* (1575), in *Elizabethan Critical Essays,* ed. Smith. I, 46-57.

Gill, Alexander. *Logonomia.* Rev. ed. London, 1621.

Gordon, George. "Shakespeare's English", S.P.E. Tract No. 29 (1928), pp. 255-76.

Gosse, Edmund. "Sir Walter Ralegh's *Cynthia*", Athenaeum, 9 Jan. 1886, pp. 66-7.

Gottfried, Rudolph B. "Spenser and the Italian Myth of Locality", SP, XXXIV (April 1937), 107-25.

Gray, Thomas. *Correspondence of Thomas Gray,* ed. Paget Toynbee and Leonard Whibley. 3 vols. Oxford, 1935.

—— *An Elegy Written in a Country Church Yard,* ed. Francis G. Stokes. Oxford, 1929.

Great Britain, Public Record Office. *Calendar of the Carew Manuscripts,* ed. J. S. Brewer and William Brewer. Vol. III : 1589-1600. London, 1869.

—— *Calendar of State Papers, Relating to Ireland of the Reign of Elizabeth,* ed. Hans C. Hamilton. Vol. IV: 1588-1592. London, 1885.

Greenlaw, Edwin A. "Spenser and British Imperialism", MP, IX (Jan. 1912), 347-70.

—— "Spenser and the Earl of Leicester", PMLA, XXV (Sept. 1910), 535-61.

Greg, W. W. *Pastoral Poetry and Pastoral Drama: A Literary Inquiry with Special Reference to the Pre-Restoration Stage in England.* London, 1906.

Groom, Bernard. "The Formation and Use of Compound Epithets in English Poetry from 1579", S.P.E. Tract No. XLIX (1937), pp. 295-322.

—— "Some Kinds of Poetic Diction", E&S, XV (1929), pp. 157-60.

Grosart, Alexander B., ed. *Miscellanies of the Fuller Worthies' Library.* 4 vols. Privately printed, 1871-1876.

Guiney, Louise I. "Sir Walter Raleigh of Youghal in the County of Cork", Atlantic Monthly, LXVI (Dec. 1890), 779-86.

Harington, John. *The Letters and Epigrams of Sir John Harington,* ed. Norman E. McClure. Philadelphia, 1930.

Hayman, Samuel. "Ecclesiastical Antiquities of Youghal", No. III, Journal of the Kilkenny Archaeological Society, N.S., I (1856-1857), 25-6.

Hebel, J. W., and Hoyt H. Hudson, eds. *Poetry of the English Renaissance, 1509-1660.* New York, 1947.

Heffner, Ray. "Spenser's Acquisition of Kilcolman", MLN, XLVI (Dec. 1931), 493-8.

Heninger, S. K., Jr. "The Renaissance Perversion of Pastoral", JHI, XXII (April-June 1961), 254-61.

Henley, Pauline. *Spenser in Ireland.* Cork, 1928.

Hennessy, John P. "Sir Walter Ralegh in Ireland", Nineteenth Century, X (Nov. 1881), 660-82.

Howell, Wilbur S. *Logic and Rhetoric in England, 1500-1700.* Princeton, 1956.

Hoskins, John. *Directions for Speech and Style,* ed. Hoyt H. Hudson. Princeton Studies in English, No. 12. Princeton, 1935.

Hughes, Merrit Y. "Spenser and the Greek Pastoral Triad", SP, XX (April 1923), 184-215.

Ibn Hazm. *The Dove's Neck-ring,* trans. A. R. Nykl. Paris, 1931.

Jack, Adolphus A. *A Commentary on the Poetry of Chaucer and Spenser*. Glasgow, 1920.

James VI, King of Scots. *Ane Schort Treatise* (1584), in *Elizabethan Critical Essays,* ed. Smith. I, 208-25.

Jenkins, Raymond. "Rosalind in *Colin Clouts Come Home Againe*", MLN, LXVII (Jan. 1952), 1-5.

Jonson, Ben. *Ben Jonson,* ed. C. H. Herford and Percy and Evelyn Simpson. 11 vols. Oxford, 1925-52.

Jortin, John. *Remarks on Spenser's Poems.* London, 1734.

Judson, Alexander C. *The Life of Edmund Spenser.* Baltimore, 1945.

Kermode, Frank, ed. *English Pastoral Poetry: From the Beginning to Marvell.* Life, Literature, and Thought Library. New York, 1952.

Koller, Kathrine. "Abraham Fraunce and Edmund Spenser", ELH, VII (June 1940), 108-20.

—— "Spenser and Ralegh", ELH, I (April 1934), 37-60.

—— "Studies in Spenser's *Colin Clouts Come Home Again*". Unpublished Doctoral Dissertation. The Johns Hopkins University. Baltimore, 1932.

La Chambre, Marin Cureau de. *The Character of the Passions,* trans. anon. London, 1650.

Landrum, Grace W. "Spenser's Use of the Bible and His Alleged Puritanism", PMLA, XLI (Sept. 1926), 517-44.

La Primaudaye, Pierre de. *The French Academy,* trans. Thomas Bowes *et al.* London, 1618.

Legouis, Émile. *Edmond Spenser.* Rev. ed. Les Grandes Écrivains Étrangers. Paris, 1956.

—— *Spenser.* London, 1926.

Lewis, C. S. *English Literature in the Sixteenth Century, Excluding Drama.* Oxford, 1954.

Lotspeich, Henry G. *Classical Mythology in the Poetry of Edmund Spenser.* Princeton Studies in English, No. 9. Princeton, 1932.

Lyly, John. *The Complete Works of John Lyly,* ed. R. Warwick Bond. 3 vols. Oxford, 1902.

McElderry, Bruce R., Jr. "Archaism and Innovation in Spenser's Poetic Diction", PMLA, XLVII (March 1932), 144-70.

McLane, Paul E. "Spenser's Cuddie : Edward Dyer", JEGP, LIV (April 1955), 230-40.

—— *Spenser's Shepheardes Calender: A Study in Elizabethan Allegory*. Notre Dame, 1961.

McNeir, Waldo F. "Spenser's 'Pleasing Alcon' ", Études Anglaises, IX (April-June 1956), 136-40.

Maher, Michael. *Psychology: Empirical and Rational*. 9th ed. Stonyhurst Philosophical Series. London, 1933.

Meyer, Sam. "Spenser's *Colin Clout* : The Poem and the Book", PBSA, LVI (fourth quarter, 1962), 397-413.

Mohl, Ruth. *Studies in Spenser, Milton, and the Theory of Monarchy*. New York, 1949.

Mounts, Charles E. "Spenser and the Countess of Leicester", ELH, XIX (Sept. 1952), 191-202.

—— "Two Rosalinds in 'Colin Clouts Come Home Againe' ", Notes and Queries, N.S., II (July 1955), 283-4.

Myrick, Kenneth O. *Sir Philip Sidney as a Literary Craftsman*. Harvard Studies in English, Vol. 14. Cambridge, Mass., 1935.

M.R.S.A. "Sir Walter Raleigh at Youghal", Journal of the Cork Historical and Archaeological Society, I (1892), 129-30.

Nelson, William. *The Poetry of Edmund Spenser: A Study*. New York, 1963.

Oakeshott, Walter. *The Queen and the Poet*. London, 1960.

Ogden, C. K. *The Meaning of Psychology*. New York, 1926.

Olson, Elder. "William Empson, Contemporary Criticism, and Poetic Diction", in *Critics and Criticism: Ancient and Modern*, ed. R. S. Crane. Chicago, 1952. Pp. 45-82.

Ong, Walter J. *Ramus: Method and the Decay of Dialogue: From the Art of Discourse to the Art of Reason*. Cambridge, Mass., 1958.

Ovid (Publius Ovidius Naso). *The Three First Bookes of Ovid de Tristibus*, trans. Thomas Churchyarde. London, 1580.

Padelford, Frederick M. "Aspects of Spenser's Vocabulary", PQ, XX (July 1941), 279-83.

Padelford, Frederick M., and William C. Maxwell. "The Compound Words in Spenser's Poetry", JEGP, XXV (Oct. 1926), 498-516.

Palgrave, Francis T. "Essay on the Minor Poems of Spenser", in *The Complete Works in Verse and Prose of Edmund Spenser,* ed. Alexander B. Grosart. 10 vols. Privately printed, 1882-84. IV, ix-cvii.

Parker, Roscoe E. "Spenser's Language and the Pastoral Tradition", *Language,* I (Sept. 1925), 80-87.

Peacham, Henry. *The Garden of Eloquence.* London, 1577.

Petrarca, Francesco. *The Sonnets of Petrarch,* trans. Joseph Auslander. London, 1932.

Plato. *The Dialogues of Plato,* trans. B. Jowett, 4th ed. 4 vols. Oxford, 1953.

Poe, Edgar A. "The Philosophy of Composition", *The Works of Edgar Allan Poe,* ed. John H. Ingram. Edinburgh, 1875. III, 266-78.

Pollard, A. W., and G. R. Redgrave, comps. *A Short-Title Catalogue of Books Printed in England, Scotland, and Ireland, and of English Books Printed Abroad, 1475-1640.* London, 1926.

Pope, Emma F. "Renaissance Criticism and the Diction of the *Faerie Queene*", PMLA, XLI (Sept. 1926), 575-619.

Puttenham, George. *The Arte of English Poesie,* ed. Glayds D. Willcock and Alice Walker. Cambridge, Eng., 1936.

Quintilian (M. Fabius Quintilianus). *The Institutio Oratoria of Quintilian,* trans. H. E. Butler. Loeb Classical Library. 4 vols. London, 1920-22.

Raleigh, Walter. *The Poems of Sir Walter Ralegh,* ed. Agnes M. Latham. London, 1929.

Ramage, David, comp. *A Finding-List of English Books to 1640 in Libraries of the British Isles.* Durham, Eng., 1958.

Rainolds, John. *Oratio in Laudem Artis Poeticae,* ed. William Ringler; trans. Walter Allen, Jr. Princeton University Studies in English, No. 20. Princeton, 1940.

Renwick, W. L. "Edmund Spenser", in *The Great Tudors,* ed. Katharine Garvin. London, 1935. Pp. 523-36.

—— *Edmund Spenser: An Essay on Renaissance Poetry.* London, 1925.

—— Review of *Edmond Spenser,* Les Grands Écrivains Étrangers, rev. ed. (Paris, 1956) by Émile Legouis, Études Anglaises, XII (Jan.-March 1959), 242-3.

Rhetorica ad Herennium, trans. Harry Caplan. Loeb Classical Library. Cambridge, Mass., 1944.
Richards, I. A. *The Philosophy of Rhetoric.* New York, 1936.
—— *Principles of Literary Criticism,* 5th ed. New York, 1934.
—— *Practical Criticism: A Study of Literary Judgment.* London, 1929.
Rix, Herbert D. *Rhetoric in Spenser's Poetry.* Pennsylvania State College Studies, No. 7. State College, Pa., 1940.
Rollins, Hyder E., ed. *England's Helicon.* 2 vols. Cambridge, Mass., 1935.
Rosenberg, Eleanor. *Leicester: Patron of Letters.* New York, 1955.
Ross Williamson, Hugh. *Sir Walter Raleigh.* London, 1951.
Rubel, Veré L. *Poetic Diction in the English Renaissance from Skelton through Spenser.* Modern Language Association of America Revolving Fund Series, No. XII. New York, 1941.

Sargent, Ralph M. *At the Court of Queen Elizabeth: The Life and Lyrics of Sir Edward Dyer.* London, 1935.
Shipley, Joseph T. *Dictionary of World Literature.* Rev. ed. New York, 1953.
Sidney, Sir Philip. *An Apologie for Poetrie* (1595), in *Elizabethan Critical Essays*, ed. Smith, I, 148-207.
Smith, Charles G. "Spenser's Theory of Friendship", PMLA, XLIX (June 1934), 490-500.
Smith, G. Gregory, ed. *Elizabethan Critical Essays.* 2 vols. Oxford, 1904.
Smith, Hallett. *Elizabethan Poetry: A Study in Conventions, Meaning, and Expression.* Cambridge, Mass., 1952.
Spenser, Edmund. *Complaints,* ed. W. L. Renwick. An Elizabethan Gallery, No. 1. London, 1928.
—— *The Complete Poetical Works of Edmund Spenser,* ed. R. E. Neil Dodge. Cambridge ed. Cambridge, Mass., 1908.
—— *Daphnaïda and Other Poems,* ed. W. L. Renwick. An Elizabethan Gallery, No. 4. London, 1929.
—— *The Poetical Works of Edmund Spenser,* ed. J. C. Smith and Ernest de Sélincourt. Oxford ed. London, 1912.
—— *Shepheards Calender,* ed. C. H. Herford. London, 1895.
—— *The Shepherd's Calendar,* ed. W. L. Renwick. An Elizabethan Gallery, No. 5. London, 1930.
—— *The Works of Edmund Spenser,* ed. Henry J. Todd. 8 vols. London, 1805.

—— *The Works of Edmund Spenser,* ed. John Payne Collier. 5 vols. London, 1862.

—— Spenser, Edmund. *The Works of Edmund Spenser: A Variorum Edition,* ed. Edwin Greenlaw *et al.* 10 vols. in 11. Baltimore, 1932-57.

Spingarn, J. E. *A History of Literary Criticism in the Renaissance.* Rev. ed. Columbia Studies in Comparative Literature. New York, 1908.

Spurgeon, Caroline F. E. *Leading Motives in the Imagery of Shakespeare's Tragedies.* Shakespeare Association Pamphlet, No. 15. Oxford, 1930.

—— *Shakespeare's Imagery and What It Tells Us.* Cambridge, Eng., 1935.

Stanyhurst, Richard. *Dedication to Thee First Foure Bookes of Virgil his Aeneis* (1582), in *Elizabethan Critical Essays,* ed. Smith. I, 135-41.

Stebbing, William. *Sir Walter Ralegh: A Biography.* Oxford, 1899.

Stovall, Floyd. "Feminine Rimes in the *Faerie Queene*", JEGP, XXVI (Jan. 1927), 91-5.

Strathmann, Ernest A. "Lady Carey and Spenser", ELH, II (April 1935), 33-57.

Susenbrotus, Joannes. *Epitome Troporum ac Schematum.* Zurich, 1563.

Thompson, Edward. *Sir Walter Ralegh: Last of the Elizabethans.* London, 1935.

Tilley, Morris P. *A Dictionary of the Proverbs in England in the Sixteenth and Seventeenth Centuries.* Ann Arbor, 1940.

Tuve, Rosemond. *Elizabethan and Metaphysical Imagery: Renaissance Poetic and Twentieth-Century Critics.* Chicago, 1947.

—— *A Reading of George Herbert.* Chicago, 1952.

Wallace, Willard M. *Sir Walter Raleigh.* Princeton, 1959.

Watkins, W. B. C. *Shakespeare and Spenser.* Princeton, 1950.

Webbe, William. *A Discourse of Englishe Poetrie* (1586), in *Elizabethan Critical Essays,* ed. Smith. I, 230-302.

Weinberg, Bernard. *A History of Literary Criticism in the Italian Renaissance.* 2 vols. Chicago, 1961.

Wemyss, Thomas. *A Key to the Symbolical Language of Scripture.* Edinburgh, 1840.

Williamson, George. *The Senecan Amble.* Chicago, 1951.

Wilson, Elkin C. *England's Eliza.* Harvard Studies in English, Vol. XX. Cambridge, Mass., 1939.

Wilson, F. P. "Spenser and Ireland", RES, II (Oct. 1926), 456-7.

Wilson, Thomas. *The Rule of Reason.* London, 1551; 1567.

—— *Wilson's Arte of Rhetorique, 1560,* ed. George H. Mair. Oxford, 1909.

Wrenn, C. L. "On Re-reading Spenser's *Shepheardes Calender*", E&S, XXIX (1943), 30-49.

Wright, Thomas. *The Passions of the Minde in Generall.* London, 1604.

Wyld, Henry C. *Studies in English Rhymes from Surrey to Pope: A Chapter in the History of English.* London, 1923.

INDEX